MANAGING ORGANIZATION QUALITY

MANAGING ORGANIZATION QUALITY

H. WILLIAM VROMAN

and

VINCENT P. LUCHSINGER

IRWIN
BURR RIDGE, ILLINOIS
BOSTON, MASSACHUSETTS
SYDNEY, AUSTRALIA

Senior sponsoring editor: Kurt L. Strand
Editorial coordinator: Michele Dooley
Marketing manager: Kurt Messersmith
Project editor: Stephanie M. Britt
Production manager: Bob Lange
Designer: Laurie Entringer
Typeface: 10/12 New Century Schoolbook
Printer: R. R. Donnelley & Sons Company

Library of Congress Cataloging-in-Publication Data

Vroman, H. William.
   Managing organization quality / H. William Vroman and Vincent P.
Luchsinger.
      p.   cm.
   Includes index.
   ISBN 1–256–14993–3
   1. Total quality management.   2. Quality control.   I. Luchsinger,
Vincent P.   II. Title.
HD62.15.V76   1994
658.5′62—dc20   94–341

Printed in the United States of America

1 2 3 4 5 6 7 8 9 0 DO 1 0 9 8 7 6 5 4

THE AUTHORS

♦ *H. William Vroman* (Ph.D., University of Iowa) is a
visiting lecturer at Morgan State University and an associate at
the Lattanze Center for Executive Studies in Information
Systems at Loyola College in Maryland.

Bill's career started as an academic followed by a fifteen year
interlude as an owner of a business, an investor, and a business
developer. While a professor at the University of Baltimore in
the 1970s, he and some colleagues pioneered an early application
of PC technology for the advertising industry. After developing
and selling the advertising business, Bill spent a decade in the
front-line developing businesses to meet modern quality standards.

Teaching and writing has been a full-time effort the last three
years. In addition, he writes a regular column for the <u>Baltimore
Business Journal</u>. He has two books and numerous publications
including articles, cases, and manuals. He is active in the
Academy of Management, several regional associations, and
several civic organizations.

♦ *Vincent Luchsinger* (Ph.D., Texas Tech University) is a
Maryland Eminent Scholar and Professor of Management in the
Merrick School of Business at the University of Baltimore. He
previously taught and consulted in management in Texas,
overseas, and at the Army War College. A life-long student of
the improvement of individual and organizational behavior, he
was also licensed as an industrial psychologist in Texas. In his
career with the U.S. Air Force, before retiring as a Major
General, Vince also had insights into high-tech organizations.
He has several books and numerous publications.

His teaching and research interests have been in strategic
management, management of systems, technology, and quality,
international business and organization development. Combined
with past operational and administrative experience, Vince is
active in service in the university community, as well as civic
and professional communities. He is a past president of the
Southern Management Association, Southwest Academy of
Management and Rotary Club. He and his wife are active in
several businesses, in environmental activities and tree farming.

◆◆◆

ACKNOWLEDGEMENTS

Readers know that no work like this is accomplished without a large supporting cast. Gratitude is due to spouses and families for understanding the demanding nature of this task.

We feel fortunate to have R.D. Irwin publishing this book. Kurt Strand managed a remarkably supportive process. Michele Dooley, Kurt's assistant, is a positive and encouraging person. She added a great deal to the positive climate. Thanks to Laura Hurst-Spell, Libby Rubenstein, and Michele for the last scouring for mistakes in an effort to increase the quality of the product. Our interaction was briefer, but impressions were clear of others in the Irwin organization. Stephanie Britt in production, Laurie Entringer in design, and Kurt Messersmith in marketing all run tight and competent shops. Their field reps are second to none. We have great hopes.

The book was in a constant state of evolution during the last year because of reviews and discussions. The reviewers of the book reacted to the manuscripts in a timely way. We received detailed criticisms that certainly enhanced the book's substance. Peter Postorino spent hours at breakfasts as a foil for ideas on quality. He had been working on a multi-year quality project with Rank Xerox, the first winner of the European Quality Award. Discussions with colleagues at the University of Baltimore, Loyola College in Maryland, Morgan State University, and many practitioners and colleagues from around the country round out contributors to the process.

We want to thank our colleagues for outstanding reviews.

◆ Peter P. Postorino
   Peter P. Postorino &
   Associates
◆ Mary Lou Roberts
   University of
   Massachusetts-Boston
◆ Dooyoung Shin
   Mankato State University
◆ Melissa Hartman
   Kansas Newman College

◆ J. Donald Phillips
   Clayton State College

◆ Charles W. Blackwell
   Nova University

◆ Jose Eulogio Romero-Simpson
   University of Miami
◆ James J. Carroll
   Georgian Court College

◆◆◆

THE PREFACE

The customer has assumed unprecedented power during the latter 20th Century. This is a result of a torrent of trends like international competition, new insights into managing and designing organizations, and technological advances. Within these forces the customer is better informed and organized. Companies offering products and services find customer demands for higher quality are exacting and incessant. This set the stage for the modern quality revolution.

Quality, in the modern rendition, had come to be symbolized by the term total quality management. The initial focus was on the operations of manufacturing plants. Even as it broadened to include service and non-profit organizations this phase became very technical and technique oriented. The strength of these ideas spread to leading firms worldwide. Many firms made amazing breakthroughs in producing higher quality goods.

Managing Organization Quality captures a significant evolution in the quality revolution. Strategy, technology, and transformational change issues became paramount as the basic technical issues were solved. Ideas associated with these issues joined the technical strengths of total quality management to impact the organization. There are two organizing images that underlie this book. They are:

1) **Phase I and Phase II**: Phase I of the quality revolution captured the powerful theories of W. Edwards Deming, Joseph J. Juran and Philip Crosby and their prolific followers. There were many practitioners of total quality management who added many practice-driven insights. Phase II of the quality revolution raises the quality standard and changes the complexion of the effective organization design. Writers like David Garvin, David Nadler, and James Brian Quinn and information technologists like Michael Hammer, James Cash and Thomas Davenport are leading Phase II contributors.

♦ **Old design and new design**: These terms succinctly capture the gulf between firms that are designed for the marketplace of the future (new design) from those that were designed for competition in the 1970s (old design). The trends converging in the latter part of this century rendered the traditional bureaucracy uncompetitive. Instead, there is a rapidly evolving new-design that thrives in this environment.

The challenge of this book is:
♦ to make the quality prerequisites of the new-design organization clear.

♦ to address the challenge faced by managers in old design organization as they go through the rigors of transforming old ways of structuring, old attitudes, and old strategies into the profoundly different company that responds to the needs of the quality revolution.

This is an exciting time for a student of organizations to write about events. The ground rules for the new-design organization are still being written. Many old-design organizations are searching for help in contending with an increasingly competitive environment. Add to that the icons of past glory like IBM and GM that are still reeling from the changes in the marketplace. They just represent the tip of the iceberg of companies which are wrestling with what to do to become competitive.

It is impossible to say much about organization quality or change without saying information technology in the same breath. Response to customer needs, customer complaints, or customer orders is made more accurately, flexibly, and quickly with information technology. Layers of information technology are giving more control to front-line employees and teams and integrating customers and suppliers in the core technology. Reengineering processes in old-design organizations into new-design processes using information technology is a major movement today.

Computers have been around for 30 years. It is the advances of the last decade, however, that helping erode any semblance of the corporation of 30 years ago. Local area networks, electronic mail, and client/server computing enable new forms of controlling, coordinating and communicating. The possibilities are endless.

The book captures these points:

♦ It captures the strengths of the total quality management, Phase I, movement. Thus, measurement and control are dealt with in detail.

♦ It highlights the international dimension of the quality revolution.

♦ It gives broad treatment to service organizations, as well as manufacturing organizations.

♦ It captures the roles of marketing, finance, and production in the new design organization.

♦ It is written with many illustrative stories reflecting the authors' backgrounds and successes of the early winners of quality battles.

♦ Points to Ponder is a section following each chapter designed to stimulate discussion. Questions and a reading are provided to increase the focus on key elements of each chapter.

♦ The teachers manual supporting this book gives additional exercises, questions, experientials, and video tips for each chapter.

The book is very versatile. It can be used as a supplement to a course in management, marketing, finance, or production. In addition, with suggested readings and supplements, it can be used as a course text.

The authors had fun putting this book together. Both have wide experience as academics, as consultants, as an owner, as a top-ranked executive of an organization. Hopefully, these experiences will make the book insightful to its readers.

Writing a book on quality brings a terrific responsibility to live up to its tenets. Too many times, we were reminded how difficult it is to actually do what you say you are going to do. Any mistakes in this work on quality are the responsibility of the authors, even though they tried to make this a quality effort.

B.V.
V.L.
February, 1994

Contents

◆◆

CHAPTER 3-- ORGANIZING FOR QUALITY

◆◆

CHAPTER 4-- ESTABLISHING ORGANIZATION
INFRASTRUCTURE

♦♦♦

CHAPTER 5-- THE SERVICE INDUSTRY AND QUALITY

◆◆◆

CHAPTER 6-- PROCESS STABILIZATION, IMPROVEMENT AND INNOVATION

◆◆◆

CHAPTER 7-- DEVELOPING ORGANIZATION QUALITY

CHAPTER 8-- THE WORLD QUALITY REVOLUTION

CHAPTER 9-- QUALITY IN AN INTERNATIONAL CONTEXT

CHAPTER 10-- PREPARING FOR THE FUTURE

MANAGING ORGANIZATION QUALITY

CHAPTER 1
THE QUALITY REVOLUTION

◆◆◆

The objectives of this chapter are:

1. To set the context for the rest of the book.

2. To introduce some of the key issues facing the field.

◆◆◆

INTRODUCTION

This book is about quality. Quality is the general reason given for the success of the Japanese, and the failure of traditional United States organizations to compete effectively against them. The Japanese organization could produce products that met customer needs very well. The traditional U.S. organization couldn't meet those standards.

The saga of the quality revolution started in the 1970s in American markets and progressed through the 1980s with more intense competition and higher stakes. Total Quality Management (TQM) as a movement grew dramatically as the older American firms had more competitive problems. Most large firms, to one degree or another, used TQM to help them solve their competitive problems. Some firms used TQM as a "silver bullet" to solve all their problems. W. Edwards Deming, a major leader of TQM efforts, said some firms expect the quality effort to be like making "instant pudding."

Other firms used TQM to make startling transformations from the traditional organization to a strong competitor in the marketplace. The stories of these firms suggest an arduous time transforming nearly all aspects of the firm from the traditional organizational design to a newer organizational design.

The rest of the story is that a newer design organization evolved. The power of this new design was increased by innovations in information technology. During the 1990s, it became increasingly difficult to say quality without connecting it with computers and information technology. Technology dramatically increased the international reach of a firm. From competitors and markets to supply chains the increasingly small world made its impact. Travel and telecommunication advances made many aspects of the international world part of people's organizations and neighborhoods.

As in most movements, there are multiple phases. It appears the quality revolution has grown beyond the TQM of the 1980s into another phase of its evolution. The 1990s organization design builds on the TQM base, but assumes a powerful organization level approach. In the thrust of the 1980s, phase one of the quality revolution, was to build in quality to the product or service, while phase two's approach is to manage in quality to the organization.

The book captures the complexity of the new design organization. The challenges are twofold. One challenge is for new organizations to build a new design organization and then develop the intensity to sustain its success. The second challenge is for all the traditional organizations to undertake the arduous transformational changes necessary to compete. After the transformation, they have the problem of maintaining the intensity required to sustain the performance.

The reality is that few organizations make changes successfully. Even those organizations make the changes and get a run of success, the challenge is to sustain it. As Winston Churchill said, "Success is never final."

JOHN DELOREAN

About 20 years ago, John DeLorean, vice president of General Motors' (GM) Chevrolet division, shocked people when he resigned his position. DeLorean had been a favorite to become the CEO of the world's largest corporation. After writing a book lambasting GM arrogance, he produced a sports car, suitably called the DeLorean, in Ireland. Entrepreneurial optimism is wonderful, even against the glum background of start-ups in the auto industry.

The American automobile industry consolidated during the 1950s, putting many automobile manufacturers out of business. Kaiser-Frazer, Studebaker, Hudson, Tucker, and many others didn't make it. Ford nearly failed during the early 1950s and Chrysler had major problems during the 1970s. During this period General Motors developed a competitive organization that completely dominated the industry. General Motors became the production, technology, and marketing leader. During the start-up's advantage, advertise heavily, foreclose access to critical components in the supply chain, hire away key people, and crush them in the marketplace with their distribution system.

The American market belonged to the Big Three (GM, Ford, and Chrysler), but mostly to GM, with nearly a 50% share, in the 1970s.

> The twist *on this story is that DeLorean soon found his sources of capital dry up, even as he was shipping cars. In desperation he thought he could smuggle some drugs to meet the payroll. The opportunity came from an FBI sting operation, which was interested in getting a "big name." His naive behavior got him time in prison.*

ALFRED SLOAN

Alfred Sloan was the leader of GM in the 1920s and 1930s. He established an organization design that balanced production expertise and financial expertise in managing large scale enterprise.[1] His work updated the old bureaucratic model that fueled the industrial revolution. By the early 1950s, Charles Wilson, an ex-president of GM, would say, "What was good for GM, was good for America." The organization design implemented by Sloan was perfect for the age and was widely emulated by other large scale organizations.

Because of the voracious appetite for cars in America, GM grew rapidly after World War II. Symbolizing America's wealth, companies like GM wrote marketplace rules while the rest of the world was rebuilding. These rules emphasized finance, size, low cost production, and marketing power. Finance began to dominate GM's corporate decision making during the late 1950s. The Board of Directors' Finance Committee approved all significant strategic decisions. Financial influence proliferated throughout the organization. For example, executive assistants to line executives were young financiers with reporting responsibility to the company treasurer. It wasn't until the 1990s, in the midst of their fight for survival, that Bob Stempel, a production engineer, became CEO of General Motors.

This success, coupled with the power that the company had, made General Motors arrogant. This story, however, was repeated in nearly every industry in America. Postwar America was a heady time for business. "From sea to shining sea" symbolized a relatively closed system for American business. No foreign organizations came close to threatening American business. Business adapted to this system with a set of strategies that maintained the equilibrium of marketplaces. Those

---

[1] Alfred Sloan, *My Years With General Motors* (Garden City, N.Y.: Doubleday, 1963).

companies that dominated their industry could easily defend their market share. The nation's antitrust laws kept the largest firms from exploiting their economies of scale and marketing power. The Sloan-type bureaucracy was the appropriate design for this period of time.

> GM gave *Ralph Nader his start. A relatively unknown Nader published a book about GM's Corvair titled* Unsafe at Any Speed. *GM unintendedly made Nader a national celebrity. A plot to associate Nader with illicit activities to discredit him was uncovered.*

While General Motors was dominating the American marketplace and establishing the norms for the industry, the Japanese were developing a new organization design. Starting with a devastated economy after World War II, the Japanese had to export to survive. They had little capital and many people. Over the years they learned unique ways of exploiting their comparative advantage; a well trained workforce to produce high quality goods that would sell in the export market. Quality was introduced early in their development process. The resulting design was fundamentally different from the Sloan bureaucracy.

THE JAPANESE

During the 1970s, the Japanese introduced their automobiles in America and learned what the American consumer wanted. The rest of the story is that during the 1970s and 1980s, the Japanese became powerful marketers and producers of automobiles in America. Honda, which didn't even sell an automobile in the early 1970s, became America's third largest automotive manufacturer in 1990, ahead of Chrysler. The Japanese share of the American market increased from a minuscule amount in 1970 to over 30% in 1993. During 1993, GM's market share slipped below 30%. The Sloan bureaucracy was unable to respond to the new quality standards in the marketplace.

Japanese companies won in the marketplace because they had a unique design and effective strategies. They beat determined American organizations with superior resources. The advantages of the American companies had resulted in defeating many companies like DeLorean over the years. They were entrenched in their homeland, with longtime customers and brand names. The Japanese companies had none of these advantages, except an organization design that produced high-quality automobiles.

The experience of General Motors during the last 20 years is shared by many other organizations. The bureaucratic organization design that seemed so appropriate just a few years ago, recently resulted in agonizing market failure. GM and most other bureaucratic organizations tried to change. Some companies, like Xerox, Milliken, and Motorola, are examples of old design organizations that successfully transformed themselves to become quality leaders in their marketplaces. Like these companies, the companies nearly failed before they started down the formidable road to successful transformational change.

> GM spent massively to change the company. During the 1980s, they spent over $50 billion on plants and technology. They tried numerous experiments to find the recipe that would make GM competitive. GM's continued frustration is representative of many traditional organizations that seem to be never-ending change efforts. Some observations based on GMs experience are:
>   ♦ Old design organizations that grew to prominence after World War II are ineffective in the 1990s.
>   ♦ The Japanese organization set the initial standards for the new design organization. The new design organization in the 1990s is a product of the impact of many insights from organizations around the world. Its base, though, is from Japanese innovations.
>   The message from the Japanese competitive successes is that quality wins in the marketplace. Customers buy a product that meets their needs, regardless of where it was produced, if they are given the chance. Customers worldwide bought Japanese products because they lasted longer, had more features, and met more immediate needs than did domestic products.

SUCCESSFUL TWENTY-FIRST CENTURY COMPANIES

Winning in the marketplace is the essence of successful companies. Winning in the 21st-century marketplace is correlated with producing quality products.

DEFINING WINNING
Winning in the marketplace results from continually satisfying customer needs. This means the product or service purchased by customers satisfies their needs for function, time, and cost. The product or services that come closest to the requirements, as seen by the customer, are the highest quality.

Gimmicks, pricing, and marketing tricks are used to increase the sales of products and service with only moderate quality. A high-quality item needs marketing to ensure that the item gets considered at the time of purchase. Quality sells itself.

All marketplaces are win-lose situations. A company wins by having its product or service chosen by a customer over other products or services. Another company loses because its product or service is not purchased. If a company doesn't get a contract, some other company does. If a customer buys another company's product, this company's product sits on the shelf. This is the day to day, win-lose nature of business.

Over time, equally competitive firms attain shares of the marketplace by producing products and services that meet customers' needs. Coca Cola and PepsiCo are successful firms that win consistently in the marketplace. Between them they share about 70% of the marketplace. Smaller firms sometimes win in niches within larger marketplaces. For example, Dr. Pepper, 7Up, and Snapple are niche products in this marketplace dominated by Coke and Pepsi.

Competition by good organizations is persistent and purposeful. Competent and confident organizations aim at every marketplace opportunity consistent with their strategy.

Less successful firms share some characteristics. Either they don't prepare intensely, don't present the right product, inadequately explain a service, have a noncompetitive product or service, make low level presentations, don't understand the customer's needs, or have a bad reputation. They are always late to market, presentations are inadequately prepared, and quality is a secondary consideration to cost, revenue, and market share. These companies don't do well. These characteristics result from underlying rationales that become part of the fabric of organizations. The culture seals in these underlying attitudes and behaviors. Future behaviors and strategies have minimal success, because of the underlying drag of the culture. Continual losing becomes a likely outcome for these firms.

> There are an array of firms in the marketplace. Those intending to be quality leaders often end up among the winners. But not all firms have the management intensity to achieve this level of competition. Firms that win in the marketplace have the discipline to change as the marketplace changes. Firms with a tradition of not winning consistently are less likely to have the resources and the will to make a fundamental change or to sustain a run of success.

Sustaining the winning is the real test of management. A run of successes sometimes masks the underlying malaise in organizations. Two or three successful contracts in a row, or a few years of increasing revenues and earnings, are possible in a favorable environment. In some cases, an organization is part of a fast-growing marketplace where all organizations participate in the beginning and get a run of success.

Organizations with widely divergent organization practices can realize a run of success under favorable circumstances. The organization that has an organization design reflecting the demands of the changing marketplace wins over time. This firm is likely to sustain its success. Firms that don't build strong organizations are likely to fail after their run of success. Most firms are so preoccupied with the present marketplace that they fail to prepare for future demands.

A careful study of organizations suggests that even survivors waver at some point in their history. The companies designed for flexibility survive for a long time. Citicorp, a $223 billion asset bank, has been successful for over 150 years. IBM ($70 billion in sales) and GM ($150 billion in sales) have sustained success from 50 to 70 years. No company's survival is assured, but a company with a long history of adaptation is likely to have the culture that will support significant change.

Some technology companies, like Oracle (database software), Lotus (software applications), Compaq (computer hardware manufacturer), and Microsoft (software applications), survived the consolidations within their respective industries. They are all billion dollar companies and about a decade old. They succeeded while others, like Vector Graphic and Ashton-Tate, had runs of success of three to five years. The former companies developed substantial organizations that could sustain success. The latter companies had a run of success, but weren't able to sustain it.

Firms able to sustain success develop organizations that constantly adjust to customers' changing needs and competitive strategies.

STUDENTS OF ORGANIZATIONS

Successful organizations constantly fine tune the details of their organization design. They are constantly studying the organization itself, knowing that its effectiveness in the marketplace depends on how strong the elements of the organization are and how well they work together. Topics include determining the intensity of training of employees, how to increase participation in the planning process, how to improve the rewards allocated to quality efforts, the strength of delivery processes, and how to increase the use of information technology as a strategic advantage.

There is nothing more practical than a good theory. Kurt Lewin

These kinds of efforts affect the design of the organization. Design is as important when referring to a whole organization as it is in any other reference. A Research and Development (R&D) team translates customer needs into the specifics of a product design, for example. This is parallel to a management team that translates the needs of a future environment into the specifics of an organization design that determines components like the nature of the R&D process, the kind of production process, likely marketing competencies that will be required, and the applications requiring information technology. These, among many other design elements, will support organization effectiveness.

The complexity of organizations can be equal to the difficulties in any marketplace. The challenge is selecting the appropriate design from among many possibilities. The defensible alternative ways of allocating resources are numerous. However, the successful ways of allocating resources so the firm sustains success are limited. The more time employees spend ensuring that the underlying systems, processes, structures, and employees are strong and integrated properly, the more likely it is that they will be successful.

Organization design is more than a management responsibility. Employee teams discussing the processes, subprocesses, and activities play a key role in the ultimate design. Front line employees are players in the modern organization. The culture makes it legitimate for them to be students to sustain the organization's continual improvement.

Underlying this focus on organizations is the notion of the learning organization. At the broadest level, the learning organization constantly adjusts to the changing marketplace. This adjustment comes because of an intense value on training and coaching employees that builds up intelligence at all the boundaries of the organization. This intelligence absorbs events for translation into actual adjustments. The culture supports and rewards the time and effort allocated to organization fine tuning.

The learning culture enhances change too. People are used to thinking in terms of changing or refining various organization components. Thus, when the organization is faced with a fast-paced environment, it has the cultural support for quickly and massively changing an underlying system, process, or structure.

Effective organization design results from the systems, processes, and structures of the organization that assemble and focus resources on meeting customer quality requirements more effectively than does even the best competitor.

The trap for most managements is that their world is often constrained to the present tactical environment. The day-to-day pressures of the marketplace, or quarter-to-quarter demands of the financial environment, often drive out learning opportunities. Managers stop being students and start living off their past intellectual capital. Time to put activities in perspective becomes nonexistent in the fast-paced environment. The result is that managers treat the data in a simplistic way. A management that doesn't learn eventually reduces the action to simple cause and effect relations. There is nothing simple in an organization- just nuances upon nuances.

Managers and employees of learning organizations enjoy organization. There are formal and informal sessions on the subtleties of everything from developing cultures to the complexities of product cycle excellence. The underlying learning process supports more complex problem solving and decision making. Ultimately, an elaborate underlying logic used by managers all over the organization diminishes the number of negative unexpected outcomes.

Being part of these presentations and discussions is tedious to those managers who are locked in the daily time trap. It is the rare organization that builds in safeguards to the learning process. Two examples come from McCormick Spice and CentraBank:

♦ McCormick and Co. is a billion-dollar producer of spices. They dominate the market. Over the years, they developed a system they call Multiple Management that plays a key role in their culture. Multiple Management is a complex web of teams of middle managers that constantly seek out problems to solve. The system has its own charter and independence. Members get paid extra and have extra vacation time. Membership results in an opportunity to learn ways to approach complex problems through training opportunities and discussions with others in a safe environment.

♦ Baltimore's CentraBank executives met for three hours every Thursday in a Strategic Planning Group (SPG) to talk about trends, strategies, and changes. No tactical (current) problems were addressed in this meeting. Books, lectures, and exploring nuances of change efforts dominated the discussion. This group met for years, generating innovative ways of serving the public. From a humble start as a merger between a savings bank and a thrift, CentraBank evolved into a commercial bank and eventually merged with a major regional bank.

Learning results in past problems occurring fewer times, more future situations being anticipated, and day-to-day activities conducted more confidently. The depth of understanding of these events naturally accumulates in cultural success stories, position papers/memos/notes, and a substantial planning process. The learning process underlies the honesty and significance of communications, the timeliness of decision making, complete problem solving, and the confidence behind organization planning.

> ***Organizations survive*** *and thrive because the management teams are students of organization. Students of organization read, talk, and take the time to problem solve issues relating to underlying systems, processes, structures, and culture. Addressing the organization design results in fewer unintended problems. A term for these organizations are learning organizations. Ultimately, a learning organization is a devastating competitor.*

SUCCESSFUL ORGANIZATIONS PROACT

The underlying message of this book is that the systems, processes, structures, and people of successful organizations represent formidable competitors in the marketplace. Changes are absorbed by organization intelligence in the form of people and computers. The changes, then, are continual and timely. This means that the successful organization proacts to its market environment. Contrast this with the organization that constantly reacts to market happenings. The intelligence of such companies is not in the front line, and consequently, their changes are always late or stimulated by competitor changes. These firms react, not proact.

Copying a strategy, process, product, or technique is commonly practiced by organizations. Trademarks, patents, and other legal constraints stop some of the grosser efforts. If a company looks like it is going to be a success, then the search is on for why that company is doing better. Once some innovation is singled out as being important to the customer or giving a competitor an advantage, all competitors try to copy it.

Without a substantial organization, most organizations that rely on copying as a major strategy lose. They steal ideas, but often don't have the infrastructure to deliver equal quality for long. These companies are not learning organizations, because learning organizations don't copy, they initiate. They initiate because they are constantly looking for ways to do their job of organizing better. W. Edwards Deming refers to the firms that rely on copying and expect instant change in their organization:

♦ Company A produced a product that had some gizmos on it that people liked. Sales of the product soared. Company B saw their sales decline. They reverse engineered the competitor's product. They copied all the gizmos and had an updated product out on the marketplace in months. Sales picked up a little, but they noticed that Company A's product had refined how their gizmos interacted on the product, and had lowered the price a little because of the experience curve. Company B reverse engineered this new product and within weeks had a product with similar characteristics. They upped the marketing budget and saturated the marketplace in order to overcome A's lead. They were only able to reverse the sales decline for a little while, because company A raised the competitive pressure a little more with additional features and supportive advertising.

Company B noticed Company A was an enthusiastic exponent of total quality management. This effort gave Company A a competitive advantage according to Company B, so Company B looked for a consultant that would quickly get them up to speed on TQM. Ony then, would Company B be as competitive as Company A.

Company B is in the position that many companies find themselves in. They are always reacting to another company's initiatives. They chronically lag behind changes in the marketplace. They find they can never get ahead of the market leader's efforts. However, they keep fooling themselves, because they survive, and their belief in "instant pudding" is very strong.

What is not obvious is that A's success is based on a successful organization design. This includes the integration of planning, suggestion, reward, benchmarking, and many other systems. The design of the winning organization is not obvious to competitors. The obvious elements like product features and marketing campaigns can be copied; the organization design features and intangibles like culture and will to succeed can't be copied.

Imagine how impossible it would be to catch up to a company that implements thousands of improvement ideas from employees who are involved in every stage of delivery of a service or production of a product. This constant improvement makes Company A a moving target for Company B and other competitors. They copy what they see in the market, and the systems have already been refined.

Company A's success is based on a sound organization. Internal systems are set up to involve everyone in the continual search for improvement. Company B is doomed to constantly falling back in the marketplace race because the organization's structure and systems stay essentially the same, and they constantly react, blind to the systems and culture that drive Company A's continual changes.

> *Sun Tzu* captured the strength of internal will and resolve thousands
> of years ago. He said, "All men can see the tactics whereby I con-
> quer, but what none can see is the strategy out of which great victory
> is evolved."

THE TWENTIETH CENTURY REVOLUTION

The changes going on in the latter 20th century will explode into the
21st century. It's apparent that most institutions built in the past are
having trouble. At the society level, the dismantling of the Soviet empire,
the capitalist reinvigoration of India and China, and privatizing in Great
Britain, Argentina, and Mexico indicate a secular trend of some significance. At the organization level, the transformation of organizations has
been underway for a decade and is amplifying. At the federal level there
is a major initiative to reinvent government based on the power of
information technology. The underlying goal is to make government more
responsive. Reengineering company processes based on the capabilities of
information technology is a major component of the quality revolution in
the 1990s.

Is this period one of the major historical watershed eras? Does the
latter 20th century have the significance of the Industrial Revolution?
Whether or not it achieves this status is left to the debate of others.[2]
What isn't left open to debate is that most organizations are under
extraordinary pressure to change quickly to adapt to the new market
environment.

The forces creating this destabilization appear to set the stage for
rapid change as a permanent state of nature. If the environment
continues to change at a higher rate than in the past, the organizations
that survive will have to be characterized by adaptability and flexibility.
This is the opposite of the certainty that characterized the old design
bureaucracy.

Organizations can expect customer demands for more custom products
and services. The organization design has to support rapid product or
service development cycles; more demands for custom products or services,
that requires shorter runs; and delivery at reasonable prices. Good
competitor organizations will have the ability to rapidly adapt to
competitive change.

---

[2] Robert Eccles, and Nitin Nohria, *Beyond the Hype*, (Boston: Harvard Business School,
1992).

These trends are worldwide. They aren't limited to one society or small group of nations. The background for the worldwide impact is the shrinking earth, based on elaborate advances in transportation and telecommunications. Satellite TV brings the laborers in the smallest states into the world community. Innovations in one part of the world reverberate around the rest of the world rapidly.

INFORMATION TECHNOLOGY

Computers began to have an impact about 30 years ago. The mainframe took over transaction processing in the old bureaucracy. The minicomputer came along in the 1970s and gave the first design options for decentralizing authority and distributing computing.

Personal computers (PC's) began the latest phase of computing in the late 1970s. During the first half of the 1980s, the vision of how the PC would impact the organization began to take shape. Initially, the PC empowered individuals by putting computing power on the desk. Besides increasing in power, the PCs were connected in local area networks and wide area networks. Increasing size and more powerful software are resulting in most organization functions being based on this PC platform.

The networked PC is eroding many of the communication, coordination, and control responsibilities of middle management in the old design bureaucracy. It makes possible many service and production innovations relevant to the quality revolution.

QUALITY REVOLUTION

This trend was stimulated by Japanese marketplace successes. The Japanese organization was designed around the principles of total quality control (TQC). For most managements, it was a significant emotional moment. The search for the antidote was frenetic. Most competitors adapted quality principles to their organizations. Consultants, books, awards, prizes, and benchmarking characterized the 1980s. Most leading firms, and firms trying to regain their competitiveness, tried to adapt to total quality management (TQM) principles.

The quality revolution mandated producing what the customer wants all the time; improving all processes to respond as quickly and accurately as possible to customer needs, changing every process, and adjusting all attitudes that don't lead to this goal. This emphasis came as a shock to most organizations, that usually discriminated against people with production experience; to organizations that optimized on such goals as cost, market share, or return to capital in place of customer satisfaction.

It also came as a shock to organizations that traditionally misused employees by simplifying jobs and depersonalizing roles. A rapid-response, high quality-output organization utilizes the intelligence and good will of those very employees to achieve high quality.

Systems for continued improvement increased day by day pressure on all employees. Detail, measurement, problem solving, and communication characterized the high-quality organization culture. Partnerships with customers and suppliers, along with benchmarking activities, created an organization boundary that was relatively open.

> *Most successful* societal revolutions result in a successful new-design fighting against a government encumbered by an archaic fighting mode. In America's revolution in 1776, for example, the colonials fought the red-coated British from behind trees. The British continued in their formal formations and never adapted to the slash and burn, guerilla tactics of the Colonials.

INTERNATIONALISM

CNN broadcast American missiles hitting Baghdad during the 1992 Allied war against Iraq in real time. People sat on sofas participating, real time. Managers and employees sit in their offices communicating through electronic mail (E-mail) to others in offices that could be next door, in Borneo, or Bonn. It doesn't make a difference. Communication by telephone lines or satellite decreases distances and makes national boundaries meaningless. Personal transportation at Mach 2 speeds makes physical movement very rapid as well.

Free Trade Agreements in Europe, North America, and Asia encourage the transmission of the highest competitive barriers across the world. The General Agreement on Trades and Tariffs (GATT) makes trade of goods and service across borders relatively easy. The supply chains of manufacturers of most products is international. Even though a product has a national origin in the U.S., or Europe, or Japan, it often is made with suppliers from many countries. Multimodal logistics makes fresh flowers from Holland and Colombia available the same day they are picked. Fresh fruit from Chile can be on U.S. fruit stands the evening after they are picked. Components can be shipped internationally for modification and back again for sale.

Firms of all sizes and in most industries are affected by the international world. There are several ways the impact of internationalism affects firms: (1) competitors might be an international firm, (2) suppliers might be indigenous to some other country, (3) customers might come from one or more countries, (4) financing might come from an international group, and (5) groups of foreign nationals might make up the employee pool.

COMBINED CHANGES

All three of the above trends have played off each other to accentuate the pressures for change. The international agreements make international trade easier. Telecommunications boosted the amount of the trade by increasing accuracy and ease of supporting documents. The quality revolution increased the reliability of companies worldwide. This increased the confidence manufacturers have to expand their worldwide supply chains. All three forces have their own dynamism, but the interactive effect makes the overall effect very powerful.

Most firms have some degree of understanding that times are different and change is required. The degree of awareness and the preparation for change vary widely among those firms. Some firms are sensitive to the changes but misinterpret the transformational change required. Others are mildly sensitive to the change, but unprepared to start. Only a few combine sensitivity to the changes with wide preparation for transformational change. A number of the firms will fail.

The early quality revolution was based on the principles of total quality control. The rapid changes in information technology and environment altered the revolution significantly, suggesting a different phase of the quality revolution.

NEW-DESIGN QUALITY ORGANIZATION

Organizations designed to best compete in the 1990s are called new design organizations. Organizations emerging from the bureaucratic era are called old design organizations. The new design architecture produces quality goods superior to those of the old design. Customers will eventually opt for quality goods over lesser quality. Old design organizations have a small window of opportunity to change before customers move to high quality competitors.

The new design organization uses information technology and human resources in a powerful organization architecture to meet increasingly stiff customer requirements. Adaptability and flexibility characterize the new organization design. This is the organization that meets the demands of the quality revolution.

TWO CATEGORIES OF ORGANIZATIONS

The two categories of organizations in the marketplace are:

1. Old design organizations: This is a large group of companies that are in various stages of change. Examples include General Motors, IBM, Governments, unions, education organizations, and many more.

2. New design organizations: This is a smaller group of companies that were recently founded, or that made the major changes necessary to become the leaders in their respective marketplaces. Xerox, Motorola, Ford, and Chrysler made massive changes to become quality leaders in their industries. Canon, Toyota, Sony, Honda, Saturn, most firms in the personal computer industry, and Federal Express are some examples of firms that were built with new design principles.

Table 1-1 shows what happens to a customer, employee, and manager in the old and the new organization. As you look at the columns maybe some experiences of these people in old, bureaucratic organization will come to mind.

TABLE 1-1
Contrast Between Old-Design and New-Design Organization

ACTORS	Old-design Organization	New-design Organization
Customer	Treated impersonally and subject to limited warranty on products and services.	Treated as a partner in the effort to design and produce high quality items that satisfy needs.
Employee	Hired into simplified jobs controlled by rules and regulations with close supervision.	Carefully hired, intensely trained for a position with expanded authority.
Manager	Drove the process through directing and controlling people lower in the hierarchy.	Involved in extensive problem-solving projects, training and coaching empowered front line employees.

There are many stories describing how difficult it was for people in the old organization; stories about discourtesy for customers, anomie for workers, and boredom for managers. The overuse of authority and punishment, and reactions by employees through unionizing and informal activities, are plentiful. Here are some more examples:

♦ Customer: Returning items to department stores was very difficult. Front-line employees seldom had authority. You were directed to a unit in the back of the store, that reluctantly dealt with your problem.

♦ Employees: You never bought cars produced on Monday or Friday in the old days. Workers, bored with their work, often took extra days off.

♦ Management: Managerial environments were "grey." This meant a simplified role in a conformist culture.

MANAGEMENT CHALLENGES

There are huge amounts of resources worldwide invested in old design companies. The challenge is to change them from old design to new design. Management has three arenas to master simultaneously.

♦ Tactical management: The firm has to sell products or services every day in the marketplace in order to survive. The sales intensity has to be maintained to provide the resources for change.

♦ Strategic management: The firm has to devote a massive amount of time developing long term competitive strategies that make the firm a quality leader in a future marketplace.

♦ Transition management: While developing tactical and strategic plans, the firm focuses on interventions to fundamentally change cultures, behaviors, competencies, and design. The ongoing demands of the dynamics of change require immense efforts in areas that challenge most managements' competencies.

There are only a few firms that have a continuous tradition of success. Those firms that have a history of moderate success have other barriers to get over. They must overcome the norms of mediocrity, in addition to all the demands required in a change. On the one hand, the required change has a chance of elevating them into the ranks of leaders, and might make them into a better organization. On the other hand, the tradition of rationalizing mediocre results is unlikely to support the massive changes necessary.

ISSUES ABOUT QUALITY

There should be no question in your mind about the importance of quality, nor about the arduous task of achieving world class levels of quality by your completion of the book. However, there are a number of points to be made now as to how some people exaggerate the effect of quality, about how some organizations have failed, and about the basic American business predisposition for fads.

THE QUALITY REVOLUTION

The term Total Quality Management (TQM) encompasses the strategies companies use to increase the quality of their output. It entails a massive effort to understand the details about the processes supporting the company's product: design, manufacturing, and delivery. The goal is to align all these efforts with the satisfaction of customer needs. Systems and structures associated with TQM increase the intensity of daily work.

Quality initiatives proliferated during the 1980s. For example, consulting organizations developed powerful services around TQM. In the United States, a national prize for quality, the Malcolm Baldrige National Quality Award, was put into law by Congress in 1987. Congress felt the award would encourage more organizations to concentrate on quality. Many companies implemented quality programs and made progress. Most of those that did implement quality were in some degree of trouble competitively.

Three "gurus" led the quality movement in the 1980s. W. Edwards Deming, Joseph Juran, and Philip Crosby led many practitioners who adapted their principles to organizations. Each guru jealously guarded his approach to quality.

The quality revolution was at a fever pitch in some companies and some industries. Many of those were in pitched battles with the Japanese and recognized the edge that the new design gave an organization. The quality field developed rapidly during this period with messianic zeal in some cases. Some extremism was plainly evident. It hinted at the first stages of fad. If an organization didn't follow one or another of the quality gurus they weren't likely to succeed.

Phase 1 of the Quality Movement can be described as a tightly developed set of techniques and procedures with highly motivated adherents. During the early 1990s, the excesses of Phase 1 claims were evident in the mounting failures. Attesting to the importance of the underlying quality movement, thoughtful consultants and some academics reassessed the movement in the 1990s.

The reassessment suggests that Phase 2 of the quality revolution is underway. Phase 2 still adheres to the essence of TQM, leavened with an organization perspective:

- ♦ The instrumental nature of information technology in the design of competitive organizations is recognized.
- ♦ It is difficult to suggest a quality initiative without including information technology in the equation.
- ♦ Further, the problems with organization change are addressed. Notions of managing-in quality, reengineering organization processes and transformational change are also part of Phase 2 as well.

☑ See Chapter 2 for more on managing in quality;
☑ Chapter 7 begins to examine change in the organization

Not everyone succeeds at quality efforts. In the early 1990s, there were several noted failures of quality efforts. The Wallace Company, for example, succeeded in winning the Baldrige National Quality Award in the Small Business Category. Just over a year later it went bankrupt, to the glee of the detractors of the quality movement. Other stories began to emerge about firms that had implemented programs and found they were expensive and unsuccessful.

THE WALLACE FAILURE

The Wallace Co. is a small distributor to the oil industry, based in Houston, Texas. People were shocked when they were put into receivership a short time after being awarded the Baldrige National Quality Award in 1991. The court-appointed administrator laid off workers and suggested that the quality efforts were too expensive. Others said that quality didn't make a company a better competitor.

There are lessons to be learned from the Wallace situation. The facts are that a Baldrige winner can go bankrupt. Further, a quality initiative can prove to be too expensive. Just as in every competition, there are winners and losers. The organizational effort to implement and to sustain quality is exceedingly complex, and people with the best of intentions lose organizations--even Baldrige winners.

The managers of Wallace made several mistakes. The first was that they lost sight of the changing market environment in the oil industry. Apparently, they thought they could evade the worsening recession and not lay off the workers that had brought Wallace the Baldrige award.

Management was spending an inordinate amount of time and money traveling around the country telling others how they won the award. Not only was this expensive, but it took management's "eye off the ball." One legacy of Wallace's problems is that now the Baldridge winner only appears in several regional conferences, instead of being constantly on the road.

IMPLEMENTATION FAILURES

There are so many variables involved in an organization change that it is difficult to fault a thoughtful management for failing, and it is difficult to untangle the reasons why it happened. Here are some observations on unsuccessful changes:

 ♦ Many firms don't recognize the fundamental transformational change required to achieve new design status. Instead, these firms implement change thinking it is more like an adjustment to the usual way of doing business. Consequently, they are not ready for the resistance and stress associated with transformational changes.
 ♦ Some firms just follow the latest ideas and try to implement them. The employees in these firms have generally been through many of these programs in the past. They feel it is the "program du jour" and play a game with management, but never try for fundamental change.
 ♦ Some firms don't recognize that quality initiatives are hard-nosed, competitive strategies. Quality is sometimes treated separately from the competitive, cost-based strategies of a firm. The firm that implements quality changes separately is subject to inevitable pressures to contain costs and "sniping" from those who don't want to change.

Critics love these examples, maintaining that the quality effort is a fad and isn't worthwhile. "It too shall pass" is a watchword of the dubious. A major premise of this book is that no matter how people rationalize the old way of managing, they'll soon change or watch the company fail.

FAILURE BY SUCCEEDING-- THE HUDIBERG PRINCIPLE

John Hudiberg was the president of Florida Power and Light (FP&L). FP&L won the Deming Prize awarded by Japan in 1989. The Deming prize, named after an American, W. Edwards Deming, rewards companies that meet exacting standards for quality. FP&L is the only foreign firm to win the prize to date.

Hudiberg visited Japan in the early 1980s and was amazed at the performance results of Japanese utilities. Using total quality control principles, they achieved amazing service and performance results.

Hudiberg's enthusiasm and evidence of the possibilities for high quality encouraged FP&L to implement a total quality management program.

During the 1980s, FP&L helped spearhead the development of the Baldrige movement, along with transforming their own organization. Because they were so close to the development of the Baldrige, they thought it would be more appropriate to try for the Deming Prize.

The standards for the Deming are exacting. Competing for the award includes using a member of the Japanese Union of Scientists and Engineers as a counselor. The counselor works with the company until it is so good that it is virtually assured of the award. The company is grilled by the Japanese consultant under stressful conditions until it is ready for the competition. Elaborate detail is required to pass these grillings. The systems, records, and details required kept the staff at FP&L working extra hours and many weekends for several years.

The results at FP&L were excellent. Performance reached levels not thought possible before the effort. They passed the strenuous two-week grilling by the Japanese Deming officials, and the Prize was awarded in 1989.

Shortly before the Deming Prize was awarded to FP&L, however, events took an unusual turn. First, in spite of the Deming success, Hudiberg was not given the job of chairman of the board when it became vacant. Instead, an outsider was hired for the position. Second, the new chairman began to dismantle some of the elaborate infrastructure built to prepare for the Deming competition even before the ceremony to receive the prize. Third, John Hudiberg took early retirement from the organization shortly after the award was received.

The new chairman of the board thought that the effort took too much out of the employees at FP&L. In addition, he thought that the approach championed by Hudiberg reflected the Japanese culture instead of the American culture. As a result, he concluded that the demands put on the FP&L workers in this infrastructure violated basic norms.

This example is used by some of the critics of quality as a black mark on the quality revolution. These critics maintain that American organizations reflect a different culture and should be organized differently; the quality principles adopted from the Japanese are, therefore, suspect.

Culture does make a difference in the organization design. How big a difference it makes is an open question. The fact that the American workforce is more diverse racially and ethnically is a contrast with the more homogeneous Japanese workforce. Another factor is the American management reputation for not being as diligent day by day as the Japanese. Instead, the Americans are moderately intense in everyday management and trust periodic innovations to put them ahead of competitors. Do Americans work as hard as the Japanese? If not, is this cultural, or just laziness?

There is some evidence that this cultural laziness is less important than the basic architecture of the organization. During the last 20 years, the Japanese have bought and built American plants. In many cases, they bought plants from American owners who couldn't compete with Japanese quality. Then, using the same plants and workers, the Japanese brought in their systems, tools, and management philosophy. They were able to achieve quality levels comparable to those in Japan. Thus, American workers can achieve high quality levels under a Japanese design. This suggests that the Japanese organization design is a world model.

Another factor might play a role in the FP&L case. The change effort itself requires a lot of energy from the labor force. During the period when people are developing systems and plumbing deeper levels of detail, the outlay of personal energy is uncommonly high. Once the systems are implemented, the intensity is high, but much less so than during the development period. FP&L was near the peak of both long term exhaustion and competitive stress, and these factors played a role in the new chairman's decisions.

There are some lessons to be learned from the their experience, however. The change period is extraordinarily stressful. Leadership has to remain intact throughout the effort. Leadership instability can cause momentum for the change to stop. The Hudiberg results show the personal risk in leading a change. If a "report card" on a manager's performance is drawn while the employees are under stress, the manager might not look very good. The Hudibergs of change put their faith in the end results for their rewards.

Another lesson is in managing organization energy. Individuals can exert themselves for only a limited amount of time before they need rest. Working with thousands of employees is a little different, but there are similarities. Systems can be generated to increase the intensity and the overall amount of energy a workforce offers the company. Care has to be taken to increase the pressure within the range of what the company's culture thinks is legitimate. Reaction is likely when the pressure is thought to be illegitimate. The competition for a prize like the Deming builds its own pressure. Together, the pressure can be terribly high. If the pressure peaks too soon, the organization is flat for the competition. Under any circumstances, the aftermath of the competition can be disastrous depending on the outcome and how the organization is managed.

If the contest isn't kept in perspective, there are nearly always reactions. A healthy perspective puts the competition for the prize in the context of a never-ending journey. The prize is just a stop on this journey.

There is no end point. The standards for the organization constantly improve, requiring constant improvement in employee efforts. Hudiberg didn't keep the effort in perspective.

If they are doing it, we can do it better. American companies traditionally use new ideas that came along to (1) reinvigorate their companies and (2) co-opt any advantages their competitors might adopt. When American and European companies wrote the rules for their respective marketplaces, it was a good approach. It was unlikely that any of these programs could fundamentally change the marketplace positions of the competitors. But, just in case it positively affected competitive success, others would immediately adopt it. The result is that no one had an advantage.

A basic program goes through phases. While leading companies adopt an idea, it isn't visible. Once the connection between marketplace performance and program is seen by competitors, the stampede starts. The innovation ripples through firms in different industries. The consulting and publishing infrastructure in the country provide the impetus to quickly raise the visibility and impact of ideas. Soon the positive effects of the innovation turn into exaggerated hype. The fad stage is the beginning of the end for the innovation as implementations fail to meet expectations.

For example, management by objectives (MBO) is a management technique that was first suggested in the 1930s. MBO is an elaborate participative system that ensures that objectives flow from the top to the bottom of the organization. Objectives are statements about what is to be accomplished and when it is to be done.

During the 1960s, MBO was elaborated and put into a program to help firms focus many levels of the hierarchy on the organization goal. This logic was helpful to many leading firms. The movement took off in the 1970s, when many organizations thought it was the "silver bullet" that would make them competitive in the marketplace. At the height of the trend, companies took the concept to the extreme, made outrageous claims, and couldn't implement it properly. Naturally, this powerful concept was discarded because of the over zealousness of its adherents.

Is quality on that list of fads or potential fads? There are people who believe that quality is a fad now. Others believe that some aspects of the quality movement are faddish. From our perspective, the quality revolution is real and progressing. The changes in the environment are moving faster than the people who would turn it into a fad.

COST IS IGNORED IN THE QUALITY ENVIRONMENT

There is a lot of controversy over the use of finance and accounting during the last phase of the bureaucratic era. The marketplace was stable.

Products and services were sold to masses of customers, who behaved reliably. Marketing and finance ruled in this environment, in which the ability to optimize financial return was prized. Many financial models were powerful. Accounting for resources and the cost orientation complemented the control orientation of the old design organization. Organization were compartmentalized into functions and homogeneous units, which complemented the accounting logic.

> **"Cost-accounting** is wrecking American business. If we're going to remain competitive, we've got to change (our costing systems)."
> T.E. Pryor, *Business Week*, 1988. quoted in John Shank & Vijay Govindarajan, *Strategic Cost Management* (New York: The Free Press, 1993), p. 1.

Chief financial officers (CFO's) and controllers found themselves in key positions to make critical decisions in these environments. As the age of the bureaucracy drew to a close during the 1970s and early 1980s, the financial decision tools resulted in major failures for the organizations. On the one hand, the financial tools reflected the right way to manage capital in the closed market environment (from "sea to shining sea"). On the other hand, when the Japanese entered the market and American consumers chose their quality goods over American products, the use of these techniques resulted in bad decisions.

American strategies emphasized short term return to capital. The rules were sophisticated, but easily interpreted by the Japanese. These rules made strategic moves by American corporations predictable. This predictability made big corporations vulnerable to the superior organization design of the Japanese. Japanese pricing, marketing, joint venture, manufacturing, and subcontracting strategies were designed to force the almost automatic financial decisions to sell entire divisions, or abandon marketplaces. The financial and strategic models used by American companies said to sell when the actual or potential returns didn't match alternate uses of that capital. Consequently, markets like the American small car markets and consumer electronics became dominated by the Japanese.

The term "21-18-15" is used by some management observers to describe American management. It stands for 21st-century information technology, 18th-century management, and 15th-century accounting. Management in the 1980's was not able to keep up with the rapid change in information technology and had some archaic views toward people and production. Accounting was used in ways that resulted in constraining the organization's flexibility.

During the 1980s, the quality movement had a running battle with the finance side of the organization. In part, the quality efforts were fighting a power battle for resources in the organization. As well, quality and the cost focus of the old design organization were at odds. In the quality movement, the organization does what is necessary to achieve high quality standards. With the cost focus, nothing is financed unless the efforts can be shown to have the appropriate cost/benefit ratio.

Louis Rukeyser,[3] the host of television's "Wall Street Week", captured the issue when he said, "American business appears to have made an astonishing discovery: Cost control alone will not be enough to enable us to lick the world. We'll actually have to have some products."

LOOKING AHEAD

Achieving quality leadership in the marketplace and then sustaining that leadership is the goal of successful organizations. The quality revolution was detailed and extended by the practice driven insights of leading organizations during the 1980s. Practitioners and consultants led an amazing revolution in how Americans designed and managed companies. These insights are chronicled in thousands of books published on various aspects of total quality management.

The sum of these insights make up Phase 1 of the quality revolution. As in every movement, the sophistication increases and the challenges multiply. The perspective has changed with this increase in sophistication and challenge. The Phase 1 view was technical, operations oriented, with limited organization utility. Phase 2 builds on the technical base and adds powerful organizational, behavioral, and managerial insights.

Total quality management principles emanated from the manufacturing sector, where it found its greatest. Many of the concepts are equally valuable in parts of the service sector, however. The service sector has grown to represent 80% of the American economy. Although many of the TQM principles and tools are applicable, new insights are required to enhance the quality of service efforts.

Phase 2 of the revolution is a broader, more inclusive look at the organization. It integrates many of the practice driven insights of Phase 1. But it accepts the reality of the major impact that information technology began to have on the design of organizations. The intense pressure on supply chains generated by increasing quality standards rippled to all countries of the world. Finally, competitive, cost, financial,

---

[3] *International Business* (May, 1993), p. 98.

and change requirements added an organization component to the quality revolution. The emphasis in phase 1 was to design in quality. Phase 2 added pressure to manage in quality to the phase 1 focus.

This book methodically explores issues, insights, and models associated with the quality organization. These include observations ranging from the core technology to the international world.

◆◆◆

POINTS TO PONDER

1. What does quality mean to you? Has your concept of quality changed over the past five years? If so, how and why?

2. Would quality mean anything different to a coach, a plant manager, a hospital administrator, or an owner of a travel service?
What do different perceptions of quality mean?

3. Surely, the concept of quality has been around for hundreds of years. Why are we now getting so involved in the "quality movement"?

4. What are some reasons people don't or won't take the quality movement seriously?

Please find a discussion question at the end of the reading.

◆◆◆

READING

Miniscribe and the Dog Pile

In 1985, Miniscribe was a troubled hard drive manufacturer after its prime customer, IBM, decided to make its own hard drives. Q. C. Wiles is a famous turn-around manager hired by the board to help rescue Miniscribe. The usual approach for the turnaround manager is to come in and get the organization in shape to sell. Q. C. Wiles decided he wanted to reap the benefits of the turnaround and manage the corporation. Instead of leaving in 1988, he stayed on. The roof fell in two years later.

Q. C. Wiles left amid lawsuits and the results of an internal study that concluded that massive fraud had been perpetrated by miscounting sales, manipulating reserves, and fabricating figures. Looking between the lines of the story yields some interesting insights into organization.

Q. C. Wiles had a "swat team" approach to management. It had an unintended outcome as top engineers were driven away by this mentality. One engineer who had just come to Miniscribe quit after one meeting, because of Wiles' approach. The entire culture was oppressed by this leader style. He was known as "VC," ostensibly standing for venture capitalist, but really meaning Viet Cong to the employees.

Another malady at Miniscribe was the obsession with "hitting the number." "The number" was the quarterly sales number, which, of course, was necessary to keep Wall Street recommending Miniscribe's stock. At its worst, managers were told to "force the numbers" to meet the grossly inflated sales projections.

Bad hard drives were dumped into a "dog pile", and then reshipped as orders. Actual orders from dealers were doubled arbitrarily and then shipped so the extra sales could be registered that quarter. They built some warehouses in different sectors of the country so they could respond to customers more quickly. However, when they shipped to the warehouses, known as the "Big WH" internally, they chalked the shipments up to sales even though they wouldn't be billed to customers for some time.

"The old man wants it" was the operant excuse. Q. C. Wiles of course says that these abuses went on behind his back. He was not aware of them. Wiles style was autocratic and it was also abusive.

A number of key employees left as the culture changed. Many, but certainly not all, of those that stayed responded favorably to autocratic leadership. This created a "lockstep" management team that enforced the behaviors necessary to achieve "the numbers."

Miniscribe lost track of the goal of sustaining performance through good management, in the face of the "feeding frenzy" behaviors associated with meeting quarterly sales objectives. The short-term goals drove out the long term effort too easily. The attainment of short-term growth seemed so honorable that it justified all kinds of behavior.

5. Do the tendencies to emphasize "the numbers" and abusive leadership characterize poor-quality organizations?

◆◆◆

CHAPTER 2
THE ROAD
TO THE QUALITY REVOLUTION

♦♦

The objectives of this chapter are:
1. To build a context for the rest of the book.

2. To introduce key terminology and leaders of the modern quality scene.

Key words introduced in this chapter.

American Leaders:	Concepts:	Inspecting-in
Crosby	Costs of quality	quality
Deming	Inspection	Building-in quality
Feigenbaum	Job simplification	Old-design
Garvin	Malcolm Baldrige	New-design
Juran	Quality Award	
MacArthur	Quality assurance	
Shewhart	Reliability	
	engineering	
Japanese Leaders:	Statistical Quality	
Fujisawa	Control	
Ishikawa	Variation	
Taguchi	Zero defects	

♦♦

INTRODUCTION

The "quality journey" has a long history. As the conventional wisdom indicates, it's not the destination, but the journey that counts. Much the same applies to the quality chronicle. The concern for performance to high standards has existed for a long time, but not with the sophistication and urgency that exists today. Over the years, a stronger concern for customers has emerged. This customer orientation not only drives the development of quality process, but provides impetus for the developing customer service quality movement. This chapter will examine some of the milestones and major participants in the history of the quality revolution.

Tracking these milestones through the 20th century gives us insights into trends impacting organization design. As the pace of change increased during the 20th century, the world became more complex. In industry, for example, there has been a progression from the efficiency of Frederick Taylor, to the mass production of Henry Ford's time (1920s and 1930s), to the advanced technology of the 1980s and 1990s, and possibly a new industrial-social order going into the 21st century.

> *Most of the early history of quality refers to manufacturing quality. Manufacturing provided the base for the wealth of the present day economy. Understanding the subtlety of mass manufacturing high quality products took most of a century to learn. Many of the lessons of quality in manufacturing are now being applied to service organizations. Service organizations now dominate the economy.*

Over time, the emphasis in the quality movement shifted from a purely economic basis to a market-driven, value-added, culture-laden, and customer focused orientation. This means that the definition of quality has become much more complex. What started as primarily a product, or manufacturing, view of quality has been expanded to include customer service quality and value. A stronger understanding of the role of leadership has expanded the meaning of the management functions. Culture-enriched systems approaches and empowerment have modified the understanding of control.[1]

Going back to the pyramids of Egypt gives the first glimpse of quality organization. The pyramids are still objects of amazement. It's difficult to imagine the feat of engineering and architecture that resulted in these objects. Famous works of art from the Renaissance are also held in high esteem, and the work of craftsmen in medieval guilds indicate their observance of high quality.

Through the period of the 19th-century Industrial Revolution, mechanics, engineers, craftsmen, and manufacturers made products that achieved ever-higher levels of performance. The Industrial Revolution set the scene for today's quality revolution. Large-scale production possibilities led to the inventions of machines and processes and the questions of human resource management. The history of clock and watch making shows that craftsmen could and can make intricate timepieces of high

---

[1] K. Albrecht, "A Review of Quality History" *Quality Digest,* May 1993, p. 102.

quality. Many of these watches have survived many years, and are of increasing value to collectors.

One applicable milestone is the case of the Springfield Armory in Massachusetts in the mid 19th Century. This case was typical of the rise of American manufacturing prominence in the 19th century. The factory featured interchangeable parts for rifles. Dedicated machinery and jigs that operated in a prescribed method were the innovations. By using these means, workers produced highly consistent and interchangeable parts with little variance. The attention to variance as a predictor of quality is a major factor in later developments. This capability enabled Union munitions makers to produce reliable weapons in the Civil War.

Manufacturing spread with the growth of the industrial revolution throughout the world. Manufacturing was the basis for much of the wealth of the organized world. This wealth was the basis for rapid advances in the standard of living in Europe, Asia, and the Americas in the early 20th Century. Manufacturing capabilities also provided the capabilities for the devastating world wars in the 20th century.

♦ *"History is bunk."*
♦ *"Those that don't know history are condemned to repeat it".*
    People generally believe one or the other of these sayings. This chapter is relatively short for those "bunkers" among us, and helps set the scene for the rest of the book, for the "knowers" out there.

THE ERAS OF QUALITY IN AMERICA

INTRODUCTION

The history of contemporary quality is characterized by periods of rapid advancement in technique and insight. These periods are associated with individuals, who were widely acclaimed leaders. Deming, Juran, and Crosby are considered the American leaders of the quality movement. They each attracted many followers. Ishikawa and Taguchi are the Japanese leaders who have played instrumental roles in the formation of the modern quality organization.

The picture of the quality journey is characterized in this section as a continuous improvement, with periodic breakthroughs. The continuous improvement of ideas constitutes an era. With a breakthrough in thinking, a new era starts. This new level of sophistication is then improved over the years until the next breakthrough comes, and another era begins. David Garvin described those eras as:[2]

- ◆ Rise of inspection --> inspects-in quality
- ◆ Statistical Quality Control period --> use statistics to control
- ◆ Quality Assurance period --> builds in quality
- ◆ Strategic quality management period --> manages in quality

Each period focused on a particular element in the quality process. Inspecting-in quality was important because machines and design were too unreliable. Later machines became more reliable and consequently controlling, or building-in quality was possible. The quality assurance period was an elaboration of the statistical quality control period. The quality management period is a reflection of the understanding of the entire process from design-in through build-in, to inspect-in quality. Later, the other elements of fixing-in quality and educating-in quality will be added.

> *The **value chain** is a fundamental idea in this book. It refers to the relationship of suppliers to the manufacturer which has a relationship through a distribution channel to a store which sells to a customer. Suppliers are upstream and customers are downstream. The craftsman collected his or her own materials for a single customer. A simple value chain. General Motors has thousands of suppliers for millions of customers. This is a complex value or supply chain.*
>
> See Chapter 3 for more detail

Two forces underlie these eras.

(1) The nature of the production process: Craft work was accomplished by an individual, or a small group, for a customer. Each craft was stylized for that customer and often build in front of the customer. The craftsman did the design, his or her skill was the operations, and the inspection and rework (fixing) was done at that moment.

As machines entered the picture, the craftsman was pushed aside. Designers, manufacturing supervisors, and delivery people took his or her place. The craftsman hung on until manufacturing became reliable and the product reflected customers needs for quality and price. It was only

---

[2] D. Garvin, *Managing Quality* (New York: Free Press, 1988).

a matter of time until more sophisticated means of manufacturing and organizing for manufacturing dominated the manufacturing marketplace.

The early machines required inspection of the goods, because they were rather primitive and could only be controlled to a certain degree. As manufacturers devoted attention to this limitation, the problem was solved. Machines could be adjusted and changed and became flexible enough to control for quality. It was here that statisticians helped gather information for this attempt to build-in quality.

This approach was extended into a quality assurance era. At this point manufacturers built elaborate inspection units. The design of plants and shop floors capitalized on this quality assurance capability. The intent of the production unit was to meet the specification set down by the designer. Machines were adjusted to these specifications. Work in progress was inspected closely to see if it was close to those specifications. Finally, work that did not meet specifications was sent in for rework. The system held up through the 1970s.

Then the Japanese learned to exploit major differences in the quality of their products and the American products. They learned how to design-in quality and minimize the inspection and rework expense. This began the managing-in quality era. It broadened the effort to the entire enterprise. All elements of the operations and the hierarchy now had a role in sustaining the success of a high-quality organization.

(2) The increasing importance of the customer: In earlier times, the craftsman was the arbiter of whether he or she met a given standard of performance. Manufacturing brought more customers into the mass market. The need for more reliability and quality became increasingly important. The modern customer's sensitivity to stimuli like governmental regulations, international competition, and immediate communication is high. The increase in numbers and awareness combine to make the customer the arbiter of quality. Before, the quality was determined in the factory and the customer had to buy that or do without. The "tail wags the dog" now. Customers have the power because of a wide choice of products that meet their needs. Consequently, organizations spend a lot of time translating their understanding of the dynamics of the consumer into product or service ideas.

THE INSPECTING-IN PERIOD

The inspecting-in period existed for centuries. Production was centered on the craftsman's work. It stayed this way until the Industrial Revolution. As the Industrial Revolution swept across the world in the middle 1800s, the same inspection procedures characterized the new manufacturing plants. Inspection worked well for artisans and craftsmen because their products were limited in variety and number. Defects could be easily seen and corrected. Was the job accomplished well enough or not? The inspector was the keeper of quality. The inspector was the master, the supervisor, or some agent charged with the maintenance of standards.

Large quantities of product coming from assembly lines tested the limits of inspection of all output. When less than all the product were inspected, no one was certain that things were all right on the line. In these early organizations, there were problems with all aspects of the operations area from design and machines to employees. Quality depended on seeing the defect and fixing it. This clumsy system lasted until early in the 20th century. Quality increased slowly in the 19th century, mainly as a response to demands for armaments to wage war. Towards the end of 19th century, the growing size of organizations presented more complex problems.

Frederick Winslow Taylor was an engineer who addressed the problem of making the production itself more reliable. People had put large numbers of machines, tools, and people together without carefully thinking through the relationships. Taylor became an efficiency expert. Working with a largely immigrant, non-English-speaking workforce, Taylor developed an approach that increased productivity. He simplified jobs to minimize communication difficulties and assumptions about brightness. He studied jobs until the most efficient way of accomplishing each job became clear. The job entailed tasks like this: designing the right shovel for the material to be shoveled; teaching a worker how to shovel, or pick up a wheel barrow; or developing an incentive wage to increase quantity. These methods increased productivity and cut down on problems.

Many people thought Taylor's scientific management was applicable to any organization and at all levels. Followers applied the principles of scientific management to international relations and school systems. To some degree problems in institutions resulted from the experiment with scientific management. Inherent in the principles was the assumption that the worker was lazy and not too bright. Simplifying the job, studying it for the highest efficiency, and training the worker to do it one way became a core process. Obviously, the worker isn't lazy, nor ignorant. The assumptions that they were just compounded problems as workers reacted against such systems with elaborate informal systems.

Personnel and industrial relations use time and motion studies in organizations. This entails studying a position and measuring the speed of each step with an eye to making it more efficient.

THE STATISTICAL QUALITY CONTROL PERIOD

The milestone signaling the statistical quality control period was W.A. Shewhart's book, Economic Control of Quality of Manufactured Product in 1963. This book reflected on his work solving quality control problems at Western Electric (AT&T).

The Western Electric plant made telephone switchboards and telephones. The waste in the plant was significant. Quality was low and absenteeism and turnover were high. Visual inspection as a quality technique was limited. Sometimes all the items from an assembly line had to be inspected. The time and manpower required to do this was very high. Sometimes the visual inspection was done on a few items. The number of items inspected was based on inspiration. No one knew whether the products from that line were sufficiently defect-free. Maybe just the items checked were defect free. There was a constant pressure to inspect all (a census) of the items. When Shewhart began his work, the problems of defects and rework dominated the factory. Reducing problems and cutting back on inspectors became the goal.

> *Shewhart started his great career at the Western Electric plants of AT&T in the late 1920s. Later quality gurus W. A. Deming and J. J. Juran, also got their start with Western Electric. In addition, seminal research was being conducted on the behavior of employees at the Hawthorne Plant. The Hawthorne studies showed how important people were in getting higher productivity and quality.*

Process Variance: As a statistician, Shewhart recognized variance (a lack of constancy) in processes. Variance and process are key terms in the analysis of production systems. These concepts, supported by the insights of other statisticians, powered major improvements in manufacturing technology across the world over the next 50 years.

A process refers to a set of interconnected activities under active management. Building an automobile is a process. The order process from the customer sale through the production order is another example. A subprocess of the automobile assembly process includes assembling the engine. A subprocess of the order process includes checking the credit of the customer. Processes generally cut across an enterprise. For example, the order process cuts across many functional units. The order is taken by the marketing unit. It then goes through the finance and operations units before the production order is cut.

Variance is change. Consider a task to sharpen 20 pencils so that they would be identical. The measure of quality is the amount of pencil left after it is sharpened which leaves more length for future use. After the task a measurement was taken on each unsharpened pencil remaining. After the task, the lengths of the pencils were in a range from 7.33" to 7.83". The range was 0.5". This represents the variation in the rather simple process of sharpening a pencil. Assume the customer won't buy anything that gives less than 7.6" of unsharpened pencil. The result is a number of pencils are thrown out with lengths less than 7.6".

Every process has natural variation. In the example above, the sources of variation could be (1) some pencils have softer wood; (2) the sharpener blades become worn; (3) the employee sharpener becomes bored. These are sources of variation. If we were doing thousands of pencils each day, it would be a daunting task to measure each pencil to see if it met the quality standard.

> *Variation* became the core of what W. Edwards Deming would later call profound knowledge. Understanding this concept was prerequisite to managing competently. He said, "Executives meeting to discuss policy without benefit of profound knowledge are... off to the Milky Way."

This is where statistics comes in. It provides a scientific method for determining what size sample is required to approximate the universe of all sharpened pencils. In the pencil example, assume that the managers have dealt with the source of variation. They (1) bring in only harder woods, (2) replace the sharpeners every day, (3) give the employee three breaks a day. The average unsharpened pencil is 7.7" and the range is 7.61" to 7.79". This performance meets one of the customer's quality needs.

Using Shewhart's theories would suggest how many pencils would have to be sampled to determine the amount of variance in the entire production process. Now that the pencil factory understands the process, thousands of pencils per day are flowing out. How many pencils have to be measured to determine if the range is above 7.6"? Statistical calculations would determine a sample size of, say, 100 pencils gathered every hour. Measuring the pencils in this sample would tell us, with a high degree of confidence, whether the production process is out of control. If the range is 7.5" to 7.7" the process is out of control. The line will have to be shut down and sources of variation investigated until the problem is found. Alternately, all the pencils could be inspected and measured, throwing out the bad ones.

This logic is applied to making telephones, automobiles, foods, and most other manufactured goods. It is the basis for seeking out sources of variation and getting additional control over the process. Getting control over sources of variation is building-in quality. Building-in is one of five ways to integrate quality into the product. The five components include designing-in, building-in, inspecting-in, fixing-in, and educating-in quality. Statistical quality control increased the effectiveness of inspection on mass production lines. Looking for sources of variation in processes or subprocesses became logical. Statistical methods were applied until the problems were found. These sources of variance are called assignable variance, according to Shewhart.

Some variance is beyond the scope of statistical analysis. It is called chance variance and occurs in every process. It happens because nothing is perfect: Machines vary because of use; climate conditions change; people get tired; and complex subsystems are integrated imperfectly. In any man-made process there are plenty of imperfections that create assignable variance, however. There are plenty of opportunities to use statistical analysis.

Sampling and variation work when the assembly process is under control. Under control means the interactions between machines and between machines and people are well understood. Sources of variation can be pinpointed under these conditions and measured. Most important, sampling is based on statistical theory that results in confidence that limited data can tell a person something about the behavior of the entire universe.

Shewhart's insights are the basis for many other applications that are part of every-day 20th century life. For example, during election periods many polls are taken of the attitudes of people toward the candidates. These are flashed on TV and are the subject of many talk shows. As few as 300 scientifically selected people might represent millions of people. Based on the sample size, the pollsters might say if the election was held now, Candidate A would get 60% of the vote versus Candidate B's 40%. The error rate is about 5%. This means that the pollster has confidence that Candidate A would get between 55% and 65% of the vote. Obviously, if the sample size increases the variation would decrease. If all the people in the country were asked, the pollster would have a census and could say the 58.75% of the people in the group are going to vote for Candidate A.

A young man named W. Edwards Deming achieved a Ph.D. in Physics just prior to working under Shewhart at Western Electric. He enthusiastically studied and expanded these ideas. Later, Deming became a prolific author, spokesman, and power in the development of worldwide quality. He worked with the U.S. Census Department prior to going to Japan at MacArthur's invitation to teach the Japanese statistical techniques. Later, he would greatly influence the direction of business in Japan and be given numerous honors. It wasn't until the 1980s that Americans accorded him the attention that his many accomplishments deserved.

W. Edwards Deming: W. Edwards Deming, the quality titan, was born in 1900 and earned a PhD in physics at Yale in 1928. He worked in statistical capacities for Western Electric and for the U.S. Census Bureau until after World War II. Then Deming was asked to visit Japan to help conduct a postwar census, and also to lecture on quality control.

During the 1950s, Deming returned to Japan at the request of their premier technical society, The Japanese Union of Scientists and Engineers (JUSE), to promote statistical quality control in the rebirth of Japanese industry. His message espoused statistical methods to solve quality problems. Japan's highest quality prize was named after Deming. The Deming Prize has worldwide recognition. Deming gave JUSE royalties from reprints on his book and declined lecture fees while supporting the use of statistical quality control.

Wartime applications: In World War II, quality "went to war." In 1942, the War Department set up a quality control section to support initiatives for increased quality in munitions and ordnance. Personnel from AT&T's Bell Laboratories helped in many aspects of the war effort. They used process control charting and sampling to reduce the defective products that were vital to men at war. The nature and intensity of wartime production enhanced knowledge of the power of these techniques in increasing quality.

Statistics had not been taken seriously by business before the war. Quality concerns were heightened because of the nature of war. Wartime statistical studies promoted the notion of acceptable quality levels (AQL). Those AQL tables prescribed the minimum quality levels that were acceptable for certain classes of commodities. As the war drew to a close, statistical advocates recognized its potential for peace time production. The American Society for Quality Control was the basis for professional development in this area. It started in 1945, and developed into the leading U.S. quality organization.

THE QUALITY ASSURANCE PERIOD

U.S. business came roaring out of World War II with worldwide demands to satisfy, and a domestic consumption-oriented population. The problems of large-scale organization was paramount in this period. On the one side, Peter Drucker, Alfred Sloan, and many others were helping with the strategies and structure of these organizations. On the other, Shewhart, Deming and Juran led a growing group of people who focused on improving operations with statistics.

Business context: In the post-war period business settled into a time of unparalleled demand for products and services. It was a prosperous period when minimal acceptable quality was acceptable to the consumer. America was a giant marketplace and was "the only game in town." The rest of the world was rebuilding. Companies grew large and with no international competition, developed an uneasy set of rules for competing in these giant marketplaces.

The marketplace was dominated by the low-cost company. It established market share through economies that comes with large volume. Volume came because a company maximized output through a factory thus lowering average cost faster than did competitors. Volume and not quality was the game. Quality was the preserve of niche companies that sold to the rich. Companies defended market-share with marketing power, and finance developed sophisticated techniques to increase the returns to capital. Almost everyone understood the rules guiding corporate behavior. If a company tried to improve its market share it was sure to get attacked on price and marketing by the market leader. If the market leader tried to eliminate competitors, the antitrust division of the Department of Justice would file suit. This situation conditioned most organizations to play the game.

A sophisticated, domestic, institutional framework that included Wall Street pressure, bank rules, and government regulations covering labor, anti-trust, international trade, tax, and finance increased the conformity. These factors determined the complex dynamics that in turn determined the structure and culture of these organizations.

The goals of these post-war companies were to conserve capital, minimize costs, and co-opt any market move competitors made. The company was able to maintain its market position if it adhered to these goals. This protected the domestic marketplace, and the accepted way of competing resulted in a consistent way of organizing. The old-design organization was successful as long as these conditions persisted.

While business became prosperous in the U.S. market, work on statistical analysis and reduction of variance grew into a full-fledged managerial philosophy. This philosophy was pushed ahead by Americans. Interestingly, the businesses thriving in America were barely interested. Some technical and regulated industries adapted some ideas. But the ideas were nurtured and grown in Japan. According to David Garvin,[3] four insights marked the growth of the next period of growth of quality. They were: discovery of the costs of quality concept, elaboration of total quality control (TQC), the growth of reliability engineering, and the impact of the zero defects movement.

---

[3] Garvin, *Managing Quality*, p. 12.

Costs of quality: The costs of poor quality dealt with resources "wasted" in manufacturing products. Scrap, repair, and rework are examples. The energy and resource costs of poor quality are said to be the "hidden factory." According to this theory, 24% of manufacturing capacity are lost because of effort and resources required to deal with poor quality.

Joseph Juran is a remarkable individual who understood these things in the 1930s. He started working in Shewhart's unit at Western Electric. Soon after that he got a law degree, and his mind turned to implementing quality control in the organization. Juran published the Quality Control Handbook in 1951. This handbook is still a "bible" to industrial engineers worldwide.

Juran studied the economics of quality. He claimed that investment in quality will minimize scrap, repair, and rework and cut those costs of poor quality. The costs of poor quality (CPQ) include avoidable and unavoidable costs of quality. Avoidable costs were estimated to be from 20 to 40% of total costs, depending on the situation. The important idea is to work to prevent these costs. Prevention has become a code word for setting up elaborate procedures to increase the quality of the goods going to customers, driving down CPQ. The effort is a preventive approach.

In later work, Juran distinguished between big "Q" and little "q" quality.[4] Big "Q" quality refers to organization-level problems like marketing processes, business problems, and a business plan. Little "q" problems are those related to operations like a technological problem, factory goals, and manufactured goods. Addressing little "q" problems successfully anchors the development of high quality organizations. The quality revolution started with such successes.

Solutions to little "q" problems generated questions about the rest of the organization's focus on quality. It became clear that quality in operations had to be followed through by quality in marketing and the executive suite. Human resource selection, training, and development had to support the development of quality in operations. Consequently, big "Q" problems became important. Deming also had insight into this concept, but the Juran approach provided the stimulus for a lot of development in Japanese firms as they built their quality organizations in the 1950s and 1960s.

Total quality control: Another giant in the quality area, Armand Feigenbaum,[5] coined the term total quality control (TQC) to reflect his views on the organization. He was head of quality at General Electric during the

---

[4] Joseph M. Juran, *Juran on Quality By Design*. (New York: Free Press, 1988) p.12.

[5] Arnold V. Feigenbaum, *Total Quality Control*. (New York: McGraw-Hill, 1961).

1940s and 1950s. Total quality control was a scheme to broaden the control managers had over the sources of variation in the operations area. This includes purchasing, design, and managerial components. These are components that precede or support operations.

Both Feigenbaum and Juran began to talk about the organizational, nonstatistical aspects of quality in the late 1950s in Japan. Feigenbaum's term of total quality control was used by the Japanese until the late 1960s.

Armand Feigenbaum: Armand Feigenbaum spent most of his career as the quality expert for General Electric. A PhD from MIT, Feigenbaum achieved prominence after publishing Total Quality Control *in 1961. His approach fundamentally influenced the Japanese approach. As a result, he is given credit for introducing the term total quality control, or TQC, in the manufacturing arena. His approach to quality involved the pursuit of excellence, rather than merely reducing defects. His work endorsed three steps to quality: quality leadership, modern quality technology, and organizational commitment.*

Reliability engineering: Reliability engineering combines the rigorous scientific backgrounds of statistics and engineering. It focuses on the prevention of defects by a broad approach to operations. Reliability engineering was and is important in defense industries which had government mandated quality standards to meet. The mean-time-between-failure (MTBF) is a key quality indicator for technical manufacturers.

Zero defects process: The Martin Co. (now Martin Marietta), a large defense manufacturer, began to work with the human side of the quality effort in the early 1960s. Experiences in their missile program showed that motivated workers could reach exceptionally high levels of quality output. The level of motivation was correlated with the expectations of Martin Marietta. If the company had the right attitudes and culture, the level of defects would be low.

In effect, the only acceptable level of performance with this philosophy is no defects. Workers respond to these expectations. These expectations can be enough to focus and motivate the employee.

Philip Crosby was part of this effort at Martin. He later became an officer there, and an enthusiast of what is called zero defects. Zero defects is the feature of a book written by Philip Crosby in 1979, titled *Quality Is*

Free.[6] His logic was that if products met design specifications, costs of quality would be saved, thus making the entire zero defects efforts free. Most managements, according to Crosby, don't set the expectation of zero defects. Employees, then, aren't motivated to prevent defects and continue relatively sloppy work. Crosby's approach emphasizes the behavioral approach. Juran's approach is much broader, including many problem-solving techniques.

Philip Crosby: Philip Crosby, born in 1926, began his quality career as a reliability engineer. He later participated in the Martin missile experience that spawned the genesis of the zero defects movement, and then worked in a quality capacity for ITT. Later he founded the Crosby Quality College. At one time General Motors held a minority interest in the company.

Crosby's approach to quality differs from his contemporaries. He pursues quality by preventing defects. Defects are nonconforming to standards, and thus are to be eliminated; hence, the zero defects view. The only acceptable level of performance is zero defects. If we don't accept defects in financial management, why should we in manufacturing?

THE JAPANESE AND QUALITY

During the immediate post-World War II period, competition among American companies was not based on quality. Quality was thought to be the province of exclusive, and expensive, products. Cost was the major feature of competition in mass markets. Financial and marketing theories were thought to be key to the functioning of a successful enterprise. Some regulated industries had to meet quality standards set by the government, but most firms intended to produce minimal acceptable quality. Marketing efforts put a facade on the relatively poor quality of the goods coming from American companies during this postwar period.

During this time, ideas on quality still flowed from American thinkers. They influenced the defense and space efforts in the United States. and most of Japan's consumer industries. Deming, Feigenbaum, and Juran influenced thought in both Japan and the United States. Crosby's approach is pure American; he had minimal influence in Japan. The hard-core statistical approach espoused by Deming, Feigenbaum, and Juran provided the core element of Japanese quality.

---

[6] Philip B. Crosby, *Quality is Free.* (New York: McGraw-Hill, 1979).

Many of the insights generated by the quality leaders had minor audiences in consumer industries in America during the postwar period. The quality leaders had to lay in wait until the 1980s, when American industry, after failing many times, was looking for a silver bullet to save them. Businesses seemed to hold the unfortunate belief that they could buy a canned program that would make them competitive. In the old marketplace this approach seemed to work. When the Japanese entered this marketplace the old rules didn't work any longer. For most of the 1970s and the 1980s, American companies learned that the old ways of responding to competitive pressure were ineffective. The American consumer had been introduced to quality and would demand it before buying a product. Slick marketing wouldn't help. Lower price wasn't the only factor.

Japanese quality before the war was good. This report by the allies on the results from a test of a captured a Japanese zero (World War II fighter) gives an indication: "The captured fighter was test flown against the best U.S. fighters. During these tests, it was found that the fighter would outclimb all allied aircraft... It was more maneuverable in turns and even outperformed the Spitfire... It is interesting to note that in all the long hours the fighter was flown, under all conditions, no serious faults were experienced with the airplane" From R. E. Cole, "Large-Scale Change and the Quality Revolution," in A. M. Mohrmann, et al. *Large-Scale Organizational Change*, (San Francisco: Jossey-Bass, 1989), p. 231.

The next section explains the critical role that statistical analysis played in the development of these successful Japanese organizations.

POST-WAR JAPAN

In the decades after World War II, Japanese accomplishments increasingly became the driving force in the quality revolution in America and Europe. This happened in spite of an inauspicious beginning. The Japanese had no resources and few manufacturing plants after the war. They did have an educated class of engineers and scientists and a hardworking labor force. Most important, they had an enlightened occupation army.

General MacArthur was in charge of Japan's development. He provided an unusually enlightened period of occupation. He helped develop a revolutionary constitution that improved the rights of common Japanese, granted rights to women, and positioned bright people to take over educational and industrial initiatives irrespective of their pre-war social class. He removed the five pre-war zaibatsu (ruling families) from power to do so. The American ethos was built into the constitution and modeled for the Japanese constantly.

Early in the occupation, MacArthur's headquarters at the Dai Ichi Hotel in Tokyo had the status of a tourist attraction. The Japanese people would gather to view MacArthur and other Americans begin the work of overseeing the rebuilding of war-torn Japan.

A basic element of a viable economic infrastructure is communications. Japanese communications were a shambles. In the Occupation Headquarters, the Civil Communications Section (CCS) restructured the communication infrastructure. They called in visiting experts from AT&T's Bell Labs and the U.S. government to help get this work done.

The CCS organization began working with laboratory standards and quality instruction for industrial managers. In fact, CCS started seminars on industrial management for Japanese executives in 1949. These courses were so popular that they continued for 24 years after the end of the Allied occupation period in 1951 [7].

During the first couple of decades after the war, the reputation of Japanese products in world trade was low quality. However, the reputation belies the work going on within the country focussing on quality. Because of the severity of Japan's problem, people worked closely together on the solution. Associations worked together on the practical goals of developing industry and improving its competitiveness. A primary enabler of their successes was the drive for quality.

Ishikawa: *Kaoru Ishikawa (1915-1989) was a pioneer of the Japanese quality movement. Educated in applied chemistry before World War II, Ishikawa formed, and then led, Japan's powerful quality association, the Japanese Union of Scientists and Engineers (JUSE). JUSE continues to lead the efforts to build the quality process into Japanese industry. He wrote widely on Quality Control. The fishbone diagram for diagnosing root causes of problems is often referred to as the Ishikawa diagram. His legacy is an emphasis on preventive aspects of quality and the notion that the next process is your customer.*

---

[7] K. Hopper, "Creating Japan's New Industrial Management: The Americans as Teachers" *Human Resource Management,* Summer 1982, pp. 13-34.

THE JAPANESE UNION OF SCIENTISTS AND ENGINEERS (JUSE)

The Japanese Union of Scientists and Engineers (JUSE) became the foundation for Japanese quality efforts. It started in 1946 as a nonprofit foundation, maintained directly by corporate members. Assembling university, government, and business engineers and scientists, JUSE promoted the study of technology. The mission evolved to support reliability and quality ventures with educational and training activities. Ichiro Ishikawa, soon to be a power in Japanese quality efforts, was the founder and first chairperson of JUSE.

JUSE utilized the early lectures by Americans to become an early adherent of statistical methodology. In 1949, JUSE created a Quality Control Research Group. In 1950, JUSE began publication of the magazine *Statistical Quality Control.* Even more significantly, starting in 1950, JUSE supported the frequent visits of W. E. Deming, J. M. Juran, and A. V. Feigenbaum for lectures. Deming taught his first 8-day seminar on statistics that year. Deming's thoughts on statistical theory influenced the Japanese. Deming himself seemed to have a particular sensitivity to the Japanese and their plight and became a favorite with them. He made a famous prediction that year about Japan soon flooding the world with quality products.

Although the Japanese were always humble and respectful to all the visiting scholars, they voraciously looked for new ideas to expand their horizons. J. J. Juran and A. V. Feigenbaum had vital ideas that expanded the Japanese understanding of organization quality. Juran's first lecture in July 1954, was about quality management. In all cases, the Japanese refined these ideas from the practical lessons that come from trying to apply ideas. Feigenbaum began to lecture in the late 1950s on his concept of total quality control.

JUSE widely disseminated these ideas to the business community. Publications, radio, and training seminars were primary ways that managers and workers kept up with the basic ideas of improving quality. An essential part of the success of this effort was the close connection between the intellectuals in JUSE and the pragmatic businessmen in their association, Keidanren. Ishikawa's father was head of Keidanren. This fortuitous father-son relationship increased the cooperation between the two associations. The two Ishikawas set the precedent that the president of JUSE would be the current, or former, president of Keidanren. This ensured the constant improvement in new ideas by JUSE and their implementation in the business community.

JAPANESE EXPANSION

Over that early period Japan struggled in the world marketplace. It had little hard capital with which to establish new industry or expansive export initiatives. Central planning was required to ensure an orderly expansion and judicious allocation of capital. The Japanese had to leverage the use of human resources, the only resource they had in abundance. Kenichi Ohmae says of these early companies: "In a way, these embryonic companies were more like communes than corporations."[8] These beginnings set the scene for the unusually cooperative relationship between Japanese employees and managers. Contrast these norms with the U.S. adversarial industrial relations climate. During the 1930s, the unions and management in the U.S. fought a "war" that was settled by a National Labor Relations Act that, in addition to outlining rules regulating how a business and union interacts, unintendedly perpetuated those adversarial feelings. The law was set up assuming that management can't be trusted to treat workers fairly and the union is necessary to ensure fair treatment.

Takeo Fujisawa, cofounder of Honda Motor Co.: *"Japanese and American management is 95 percent the same and differs in all important respects."*
From R. T. Pascale, and A. G. Athos, *The Art of Japanese Management,* (New York: Warner Books, 1981), p. 131.

The Japanese government helped by designating November as Quality Month in 1960. Other laws followed requiring exported goods to be inspected which increased the quality of those goods. JUSE kept training and experimenting with ideas. In the factories of Toyota, Honda, Komatsu, Mazda, Matsushita, and others, the ideas took root and were refined. In the mid-1960s, many companies discovered that the quality effort had the effect of lowering costs. This was the turning point for quality. Most organizations enthusiastically endorse the quality effort.

Feigenbaum's notion of total quality control (TQC) appealed to the Japanese in the late 1950s. During the 1960s, the Japanese refined and broadened the concept. In 1969, they changed the name to Company-Wide Quality Control (CWQC), to differentiate it from Feigenbaum's work. CWQC, they discovered, worked exceptionally well if workers were involved. The discovery that people were a necessary part of the quality effort was key to the Japanese success.

[8] Kenichi Ohmae, *Mind of the Strategist* (New York: McGraw-Hill, 1982), p. 217.

Worker involvement, when equipped with problem-solving and decision-making knowledge, is motivational. Participation and democratic leadership styles were timidly applied by American companies. The job-simplification, authority-oriented American organization wasn't a suitable home for participation schemes. The Japanese were starting organizations and creating new ways of working. The most plentiful resource in Japan was people. They had to find a way to use workers effectively. The organization design optimized the use of people and had minimal levels in its hierarchy.

Genichi Taguchi: *Genichi Taguchi was a Japanese statistician who spent much of his career working for the Japanese Telegraph and Telephone Company. He was the first winner of the Deming Prize for individuals in 1960, for his developments in statistical process control (SPC). Taguchi's method was concerned with product development as well as manufacturing improvement.*

Taguchi explained quality in a loss function, which attempted to reduce variance from a target value of quality. Any deviation from an optimal level of performance carries a loss to the producer, the customer, or both. This technique is controversial, but still used by many companies in reducing product and process variation. By reducing variation, better quality is enhanced.

In 1962, JUSE started another magazine called *Quality Control for the Foreman.* The first QC (Quality Circle) was started that year as well and registered with JUSE. The QC circle is a voluntary group of employees focussing on quality control on the job. The QC circle is part of an overall TQC or PWQC program of the organization. The circles enable workers to continuously address company productivity, cost, and safety problems.

QC circles became a cornerstone to philosophy that dominated the Japanese society. This philosophy is called kaizen.[9] Kaizen means continual improvement. In Japan it means continuing improvement in personal, home, and social life, in addition to working life. It became an organizational strategy with implications for every level and person in the organization.

Deming introduced the Shewhart cycle in his early lectures. The cycle refers to the steps: plan, do, check, act (PDCA). PDCA is the underlying process for kaizen. The cycle guides people through an extensive planning process, doing the project, checking the results, and

---

[9] See Masaaki Imai, *Kaizen* (New York: Random House, 1986).

acting, or implementing the idea through the rest of the organization. The Japanese began referring to the cycle as the Deming Cycle.

Deming contributed his lecture fees and his Japanese book royalties to JUSE to continue their work after 1951. This gesture was deeply appreciated by the Japanese. They determined to offer multiple prizes for those firms and individuals that exemplified the highest quality. They named the prizes the Deming Prizes in honor of the American. The first Deming Prize was given in 1951.

JUSE administers the Deming Prizes which became notorious for the exacting standards for its winners. Counselors (senseii) from JUSE help companies prepare to compete for the Deming Prize. A who's who of Japanese industry has won the Deming.

☑ Chapter 8 covers the Deming prize and other quality awards.

The momentum of CWQC had an uncommonly rapid impact on Japanese industry. It fueled an international expansion that made Canon, Sony, Toyota, Mazda, Matsushita, Komatsu, Seiko, and Honda worldwide brands by the mid-1980s. The success of these companies devastated competitors and penetrated markets worldwide. People bought Japanese goods because the products met their needs. Advertising for these goods highlighted the quality dimensions. People listened to this advertising versus the advertising that tried to con people into buying minimally acceptable quality goods.

In the early 1990s, the Japanese still exported over $60 billion more goods to the United States than they imported. This is, in large part, testament to the quality of their goods. In part, there is some controversy over the aspects of the Japanese economy that appear closed to imports from other countries.

THE STRATEGIC QUALITY MANAGEMENT PERIOD

In 1979, a Japanese observer of American business put the problems in focus:

"Somehow or other, American business is losing confidence in itself, and especially confidence in its future. Instead of meeting the challenge of the changing world, American business today is making small, short-term adjustments by cutting costs and by turning to the government for temporary relief... *Success in trade is the result of patient and meticulous preparations, with a long period of market preparation before the rewards are available* (italics added)... To undertake such commitments is hardly in the interest of a manager who is concerned with his or her next quarterly earnings report."[10]

The comment described American business as it was reeling from Japanese competitive successes. However, even as this was written, changes were underway. The 1980s saw dramatic adjustments in the leading old-design firms. The total quality management (TQM) and zero defects movements had gathered steam and supported the changes. The term *quality revolution* applies to this period. Businesses were looking for any way to stop the loss of markets. Deming, Juran, and Crosby attracted many followers. Books, tapes, programs, and training sessions increased in volume as the 1980s went on. The focus on the shop floor with TQM resulted in turmoil in some organizations, and radical change in others.

A business group worked to establish an American award similar to Japan's Deming Prize. Congress institutionalized this effort by passing an act establishing the Malcolm Baldrige National Quality Award in 1987. The overall goal of the prize is to increase America's competitiveness by focussing business minds all over America on quality. The award recognizes the Japanese prize, but the thinking underlying the award is distinctly American.

The overall goal of companies trying for the Baldrige is quality leadership in the marketplace. The logic behind the Baldrige is that leadership through intense management of four broad systems yields customer satisfaction. The systems are strategic quality planning, management of human resources, quality assurance, and information processing.

The strategic quality planning system is symbolic of the evolution of the quality movement. The original Baldrige definition of this system highlighted strategies that improve quality or the quality infrastructure. Quality seemed to be an end in itself in the Baldrige. Traditional business planning was specifically excluded from its definition. Its emphasis on competitiveness and financial planning was part of the problem with the traditional organization. Competitive strategies weren't included in the quality plan. The traditional power structure in older bureaucracies favored finance and marketing. Under the quality effort production and human resources became major players. The sensitivity to the old structure is understandable. Most firms established separate quality hierarchies in order to give quality an opportunity for growth.

---

[10] The quote is found in R.H Hayes and S.C. Wheelwright, *Restoring our Competitive Edge* (New York: Wiley and Sons, 1984), p. 7.

As the Baldrige competition matured, it became obvious that strategic quality planning and the firm's business planning were tightly integrated. The object is for the firm to be quality leader in the market place, and that depends on competitive strategies in partnership with quality strategies. Financial and accounting activities become partners in the drive to quality leadership. The organizing required to ensure a partnership between these traditional adversaries is sophisticated.

The topic of finance and quality will arise many times in this book. There are many pressures on the modern organization to regress to a "bottom-line" orientation. It seems perfectly logical to cut costs in order to improve the bottom line. This often means diminishing quality, eroding the brand name, cutting training, letting people go, or emphasizing the present over the future. These are often unintended outcomes, but inevitably occur. An executive management of a public firm has to face quarterly Wall Street pressures and institutional shareholders putting additional emphasis on the short term. This issue is a constant balancing act in organizations.

David Garvin's book *Managing Quality*,[11] signaled the broadening of the American movement to a strategic approach from the TQM of the mid 1980s. The Japanese approach to total quality control included a powerful planning process they called Hoshin planning. This planning increased the organization's adaptation to market changes. Hamel and Prahalazad and others in strategic management contributed concepts like strategic intent and core competencies which supported the investment of resources in order to establish competencies that translate into competitive advantage.[12] Quality strategies result in competencies that translate into competitive advantages. These ideas from other fields added precision and utility to quality, because they focused quality resources on goals that would result in competitive advantage.

It's been clear from the beginning that the old-design organization couldn't respond to the changing marketplace. The old-design firms that were competitive generally were threatened with survival before they radically changed. Xerox was nearly put out of business by Canon in 1979 before it changed. Motorola was nearly extinguished by Sony and Matsushita in the 1970s. Both companies came back to win the Baldrige

---

[11] Garvin, *Managing Quality*, see Chapter 2.

[12] A. A. Thompson & A. J. Strickland, *Strategic Management* (Homewood: R.D.Irwin, 1992). p. 37.

quality award in the late 1980s. In order to compete effectively, they radically altered their organization designs to reflect the world-class principles that the Japanese firms used. Other firms, faced with similar survival decisions, changed successfully to the new-design. Organizations just starting during the 1970s and 1980s generally adapted new-design principles from the start and were immediately competitive with the Japanese.

TIMELINE OF QUALITY HISTORY

The following timeline describes the flow of events that resulted in the quality revolution being experienced around the world.

1750s
INSPECTING-IN QUALITY
1900s
- Scientific Management (Taylor)

BUILDING-IN QUALITY
1930s
- Economic Control of Quality of Manufactured Goods (Shewhart).
- Bell Labs and Western Electric in SQC.

STATISTICAL QUALITY CONTROL
1940s
- War Department sets up Quality Control Section.
- Industrial Quality Control Journal published in U.S.
- Civil communications Section (CCS) set up in Japanese Occupation HQ.
- American Society for Quality Control formed.
- Japanese Union of Scientists and Engineers (JUSE) begun.

1950s
COSTS OF QUALITY
- Deming, Juran and Feigenbaum present quality seminars in Japan.
- Deming Quality Prize established by JUSE.
- Quality Control Handbook (Juran).

◆ Japanese Shortwave Broadcasting Corporation airs a
  Quality Control correspondence course for foremen.

TOTAL QUALITY MANAGEMENT
◆ Total Quality Control (Feigenbaum).

1960s

◆ "Total Quality Control" (Taguchi).
◆ Quality circles (Ishikawa).

RELIABILITY ENGINEERING

1970s

ZERO DEFECTS
◆ Quality Is Free (Crosby).
◆ Beginning of Japanese business success in the
  United States.

1980s

◆ Quality, Productivity, and Competitive Position (Deming).
◆ In Search of Excellence (Peters and Waterman).
◆ Baldrige Award instituted.
◆ Service America (Albrecht and Zemke).
◆ Federal Quality Institute established.

STRATEGIC QUALITY
◆ Managing Quality (Garvin)

1990s

◆ Customer Service Quality.

2000s

◆ Organizational Quality

SUMMARY

The quality revolution is a result of many complex forces coming together in the latter half of the 20th Century. The urgency of the world wars resulted in the invention of new technologies. Other outcomes included nations coming together, international responsibilities being nurtured, and new possibilities being discovered.

In and around these cataclysmic events men nurtured ideas. Ideas whose time had come. The barrenness of the island of Japan after World War II set the scene for a parsimonious and hard-working people to build an economic fortress. Unique uses of human resources, a unique culture dominated by a philosophy of <u>kaizen,</u> and creative supply chain management resulted in a dynamic world-class competitor. A unique organization of technical professionals, the Japanese Union of Scientists and Engineers, played a key role in instilling quality in organizations all over Japan. They provided training, magazines, and lectures to managers, foreman, and workers all over Japan. Kaoru Ishikawa and Genichi Taguchi are two of the many Japanese who mastered and refined these concepts.

Interestingly, the intellectual seeds that started the Japanese on their road to superior organization came from Americans. W. Edwards Deming, Joseph Juran, and Armand Feigenbaum were key lecturers during the 1950s in Japan. In America, their influence was limited as industry lapsed into a set of rules that governed competition. Outcomes were expressed as returns to capital, quarterly earnings, average cost, and market share in this marketplace. These took precedence over quality.

During the 1970s, the market losses to the Japanese started to mount. Until these devastating losses, the quality theorists were minor players in America. When American businesses realized they were going to lose it all, they searched for the solution. It took until the 1980s before the Deming, Juran and Crosby movements were highlighted. Philip Crosby joined the quality revolution with his unique concept of quality.

With the establishment of the Baldrige National Quality Award, quality assumed its place in the hierarchy of goals for business to achieve. During this period, the maturation of the quality movement introduced a strategic element. Strategic quality planning began to broaden to include competitive strategies and profit implications.

◆◆◆

POINTS TO PONDER

1. Many organizations have responded to different quality leaders. Which of the major figures of this chapter impresses you the most, and for what reasons?

2. Why would the Japanese have made their notable advances in the quality field, compared to the British, Germans, French or the Americans?

3. Given other social and economic revolutions you know about, how do you think the quality revolution will end? When will it end?

Please see the additional question at the end of the reading.

◆◆◆

READING

The Biggest Name in Quality in Japan is American

"The goal of leadership, should be to improve performance, increase output, and simultaneously bring pride of workmanship to employees. The goal of leadership is not merely to find failures, but to remove the causes of failures-- to help people do a better job with less effort."
W. Edwards Deming, "Deming", World, (New York: KPMG Peat Marwick, 1991), p. 19.

In his last lectures W. Edwards Deming was so frail that he was in a wheelchair and tethered to oxygen. He wasn't as energetic as he had been in the past, but he was as irascible. Most importantly, he was as determined as ever. He gave 30 four-day lectures before his death on December 20, 1993 at the age of 93. I'm sure he wasn't satisfied with the progress of business and would have liked to live and lecture many more years.

Deming's life spans the years of the modern quality revolution. He was a catalyst for many events in this movement. His ideas influenced the direction of the movement in Japan and in America.

♦ Deming started with Shewhart in the quality labs at Western Electric in the 1920s.

♦ He took statistical quality control to Japan as part of MacArthur's plan to help the Japanese get on their feet starting in 1947.

♦ His message on statistics and quality was enthusiastically received by the members of the Japanese Union of Scientists and Engineers (JUSE).

♦ Deming donated the proceeds from the Japanese editions of his books to JUSE to continue with their work.

♦ JUSE named their national quality prize, the Deming Prize, in his honor in 1951.

♦ He continued to lecture in Japan as the Japanese improved the total quality control system that powered their industrial might. He was called the Great American senseii.

♦ He also grated under the lack of respect his work got in America while U.S. business was getting trounced in the marketplace by the Japanese. The fact that the victors were using statistical quality control further frustrated Deming.

♦ Nashua Corp. gave Deming his first consulting job in America in 1979. It came because the CEO of Nashua went to Japan to see why his competitors did higher quality work than Nashua did. He said "All they talked about was Deming." So he called Deming to help.

♦ The 1980 NBC documentary, "If Japan Can, Why Can't We," detailed the Nashua turn-around and Deming's contribution to Japan's resurgence.

♦ He became consultant to many major American companies during the next decade.

♦ In 1982, a Japanese company advertised "The biggest name in quality in Japan is American." He was, of course, referring to the Deming Prize. This advertisement stimulated the idea to develop America's version of Japan's Deming Prize. The Baldrige National Quality Award was commissioned in Congress in 1987.

Deming's work was in statistics, but one of his most potent lessons was on respect for people. He said this about the Japanese, "Their success hinges on the esteem they have for themselves and others... The Japanese understand you can't separate the performance of an individual from the effects of the system in which he or she works." He felt that the U.S. economic decline was directly related to adversarial competition. He said the problems faced by companies is related to the systems in the company and not to the workers. He advocated unleashing the power of the people to solve those systems problems with the power of the statistics. Adversarial systems like performance appraisal would have to be dismantled.

A lot of attention is paid to Deming's personality. He spoke in short staccato sentences and asked more questions than he answered. Many executive groups found it difficult to get over the personality barrier to hire him. His disrespect for U.S. management theory is legend[13]. He said,

> ◆ "Most management today is reactive behavior. You put your hand on a hot stove and yank it off. A cat would know to do as much."
> ◆ "I gave some lectures to the State Department and I told them do not export North American management to a friendly country."
> ◆ "Just choke off the competition. Never mind about the customer, he doesn't enter into this at all."

He taught at Columbia University. The director of the Deming Center at Columbia recalled Deming's answer to his occasional question on how things were going. Deming would say,
"I'm desperate. There's not enough time left."

4. Why do you think Deming was recognized so late in his career? Would things have been different for U.S. business if Deming were acknowledged ten or fifteen years earlier?

5. Was Deming the Godfather of quality? Comment on the impact of a single person on a movement driven by so many forces.

◆ ◆

---

[13] Andrea Gabor, *The Man Who Discovered Quality*, (New York: Random House, 1990), p. 67.

CHAPTER 3
ORGANIZING FOR QUALITY

♦♦

The objectives of this chapter are:
1. To understand the basics of the traditional, old-design organization and the new-design required by the changing environment.

2. To understand the essential systems and processes that make up the new-design organization.

Key Words introduced in this chapter:

Culture
Closed/open
  systems
Cycle-time
Front-line teams
Information
  systems
5 Quality Points:
  Design, Build,
  Inspect, Fix,
  Educate

5 Key Quality
  Systems:
  Benchmarks,
  Product/Service
    Design,
  Partnerships
  People
  Integrated Core
    Technology
AMT--advanced
  manufacturing
  technique

EDI--Electronic
  data interchange
Intelligence
JIT--Just-In-Time
Kamban
Norms
Organization
  design
Statistical process
  control (SPC)

♦♦

INTRODUCTION

Dear Charley:
I have a 1986 Audi. I brought the car back to your garage because it had some problems. Before the car was completely fixed, I had to bring it back several times. The problem was one of those intermittent types that was difficult to diagnose. Soldering a relay eventually solved it. Your service manager, I think his name is Rolf, was excellent. He was courteous and

worked with me in solving the problems. I thought the costs were fair. My experience in maintaining and fixing my car with you is good.
Thanks, Mark.

It's the little things, like this letter, that count in organizations. And these little things cumulate to build sustaining businesses. Easy to say but difficult to do. The testimony comes from the 40% of the nation's 500 largest businesses that fell off the list during the 1980s, or the seven out of ten small businesses that failed. Confident front-line behavior from service managers, clerks, salespeople, and line workers is an outgrowth of a carefully nurtured culture. This carefully nurtured culture is what the rest of this book is about. Confident frontline people are evidence of well designed organizations. Good organization design is the major challenge.

Producing something of value for a customer is the primary strategy of an organization. That customer, and many more, have to feel what they get from your company has value to them. If they don't get value, they don't come back.

Value is added by all organizations by taking inputs and transforming them into some output. For example, a manufacturing plant takes parts and turns them into products that can be used by customers. A comedian takes experiences, and uses them to transform 60 minutes of silence into a fun-filled time for customers. A retailer takes space, goods, employees, and systems and transforms them into a store that satisfies customers who can find what they want conveniently.

> *The term "product or service" is used throughout the book. Where this term is used, the discussion applies to either a service or a manufacturing operation. Chapter 5 details the distinctive aspects of the service firm.*

All organizations are organized similarly. They take inputs and transform them into outputs to meet customer needs. The manufacturing organization finishes the product before it goes to the customer. The service organization often transforms its inputs to outputs in front of the customer. If the store runs out of a product, the customer is dissatisfied. If a comedian isn't funny, his or her performance is a failure. If the sports team continually loses ball games, the players will get booed by the fans as they transform the inputs to output (play the game). If one firm's manufactured goods aren't as good as another company's, they get left on the shelf.

It was the core technology activities done well that caused Mark to write to Charley. Rolf is part of the agency's core technology. Other examples of core technology actions are:

♦ A consultant solves business problems based on tools and experiences.

♦ An auto company manufactures cars.

♦ The post office picks up, sorts and delivers letters and packages.

♦ A library lends books.

♦ A company makes ice cream.

♦ A school educator teaches students.

THE QUALITY ORGANIZATION

The intent of this section is to introduce some concepts that help analyze the design of an organization. Organization design is a term that represents the layout of components like hierarchy, systems, processes, and relevant parts of the value chain, in a configuration that reflects the nature of the task environment and the core technology. The task environment includes the elements in the environment that demand action from the organization. The marketplace, government, and community are three elements in the task environment. The core technology is what an organization does to add value. A value chain is a depiction of the suppliers and customers of an organization's core technology.

CUSTOMER SATISFACTION

Understanding customer needs is difficult. Some firms make product decisions based on hearsay and common sense judgment. Other firms allocate resources based on facts about customer needs. Some understand their present customers needs, but don't have facts about the needs of its competitor's customers, or its own future customers.

Customer satisfaction is the key term in the quality organization. Figure 3-1 shows how diagnosing customer needs translates into customer satisfaction because of a demanding design process. Through focus groups, surveys, and interviews, organizations get the facts on who their customers are and what they need. These needs translate into customer requirements by the product and process design system. The design system takes customer needs and translates them into the technical language of the product requirements. Manufacturing engineers then design a manufacturing plant that will produce this product. To the extent that customer needs are reflected in the product produced in the plant, the product has high quality and the customer will be satisfied.

Customer satisfaction is not easy to achieve. There are potential traps every step of the way, from diagnosing customer needs to building

FIGURE 3-1
Translating Customer Needs

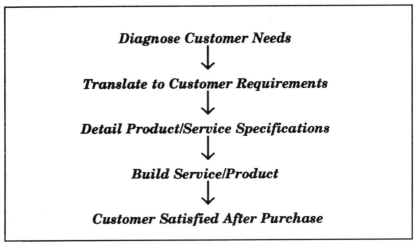

the operations area. Mistakes, poor process, pressure to hurry, jealousies, lack of communication, power plays, and lack of resources are just some of the problems. The design of the organization delivering high-quality goods or services is difficult.

*A **quality product** and process results from accurately reflecting customer needs in the design of product and operations areas.*

ORGANIZATION HIERARCHY
Figure 3-2 is a familiar picture of an organization, illustrating the three levels of an hierarchy. The core technology is the base of the triangle. The middle management translates needs both up and down the hierarchy. It has traditionally handled many communication, coordination, and control functions.

The size of any of the units in the organization depends on the nature of the demands made on the organization by task environment elements. For example, if the anti-trust division challenges the organization, the legal division will be expanded. If the organization is in the growth stage of a high tech marketplace, the R&D unit will be large.

The term <u>core technology</u> applies equally to manufacturing and service firms. A manufacturing firm takes parts and materials and adds value through changing the form into a product that satisfies customer needs. Service firms add value through personal services (cleaning, psy-

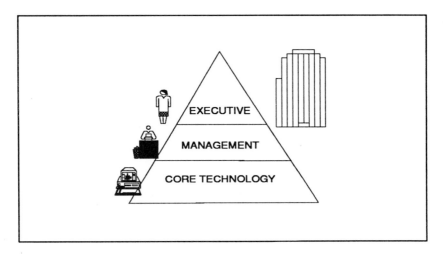

FIGURE 3-2
Organization Hierarchy

chological/medical/legal advice, and through distribution (banks, brokers, stores, delivery of packages). The nature of the technology is different. Hospitals don't, and shouldn't, have the same productivity requirements as do auto manufacturers.

Wal-Mart's information technology made their service efforts very responsive to customers' needs. Just-in-time inventory and supplier partnerships are as relevant to a manufacturer like General Motors as to service stores like Wal-Mart and Sears.

☑ Chapter 5 is about the unique aspects of service stores.

All organizations look alike at this level of abstraction. They all have executives running the organization. They deliver something to customers. The managers of all organizations have similar roles in communicating, coordinating and controlling. Finally, all organizations have core technologies that take inputs and transform them into outputs.

Core Technology: *this represents all the systems and processes that directly transform inputs into outputs, or performs the service. It is the manufacturing operations or service delivery efforts.*

QUALITY/VALUE CHAIN

The firm's core technology is part of a complex value chain where there are many suppliers in the network and many intermediate customers that add value to a product and process. This value chain is similar to an industry map.[1] Value is added in every step along the value chain. Figure 3-3 represents a basic value chain. It depicts one supplier, a core technology where value is added, and an output that a customer buys.

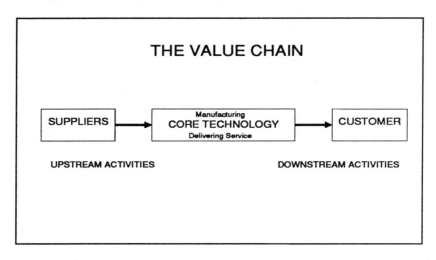

FIGURE 3-3
Value/Supply Chain

The value chain (also a quality chain or supply chain) is an industry map of a firm's supply network and the flow of parts and supplies through a core technology to create a product and process. A product is distributed to customers either directly or through some retail network. A service is often "made" right in front of the customer. Upstream activities refer to activities further from the final customer. Downstream activities refer to activities toward the final customer. Each step must add value or the organization fails.

---

[1]   Michael E. Porter, *Competitive Advantage: creating and Sustaining Superior Performance*, (New York: Free Press, 1985).

In the supply chain everything starts with a raw material. It might be raw copper or iron ore that eventually is made into copper wire or steel pots and pans. There are intermediate steps as the ore is turned into a final product. These steps might take place in one business or several businesses.

Figure 3-4 illustrates a familiar example. A McDonald's hamburger has both a hamburger and a bun. Figure 3-4 tracks the bun back to the field where wheat is grown. McDonald's puts freshly cooked hamburgers in buns (part of its core technology) and sells them to customers world-wide. One of their suppliers, among many, bakes buns (which is that firm's core technology). One of the bun maker's many suppliers makes flour (its core technology), which comes from farmer reaping wheat on their farms (their core technology).

This is a value chain for buns in McDonald's hamburgers. Notice how there is a value added to each step from the raw material (wheat) through each change until it is eaten as a hamburger by some customer. Growing, baking, making, and assembling are the value-added steps in this value chain. This is the basis for the name. If value isn't added at a step, then the firm goes out of business-- it can't sell its product.

FIGURE 3-4
Value/Supply Chain of a Bun

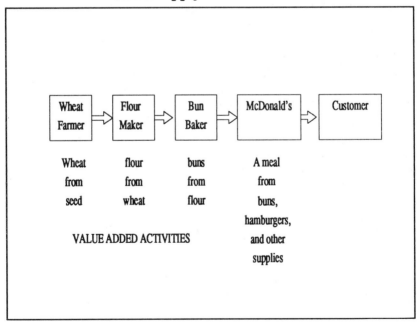

Value chains are complex. Each organization has many suppliers. McDonald's has hundreds of suppliers for items such as catsup, napkins, play equipment and sanitation supplies. Suppliers of suppliers of suppliers of McDonald's are in every corner of the world. For example, McCormick and Co. is a supplier of spices to McDonald's. McCormick buys its spices from many Asian and African countries. Each of these inputs all along the value chain has to be transported by truck, airplane, railroad, or boat to its destination. The logistics of sending supplies is a major factor in determining plant locations and sizes.

Strategies for a firm become evident after an organization maps its own value chain. More value might be added with strategies that integrate a supplier or distributor, or perhaps merge with a firm that is in the same industry. The former strategy is vertical integration and results in integrating an upstream supplier or a downstream distributor. The latter strategy is a horizontal diversification and can result in increased strength in the core technology. A newspaper might buy some magazines as an outlet for news it already collects, as a means of increasing its audience, and as a means of fully utilizing its presses.

There are many variations on this theme of horizontal integration. IBM and Apple Computer, for example, have a joint venture to develop a new operating system called Taligent. Operating systems are software that translates between application programs and the hardware of the computer itself. A powerful operating system might be used by every manufacturer of computers. IBM and Apple are creating a jointly owned supplier in the value chain. They think the feature of their jointly developed operating system will be a superior competitor in the market-place that gives them a competitive advantage.

Some companies with distinct industry maps are joining in alliances and joint ventures because of a threat to their present market. For example, in the future people will be able to sit in a room in their houses and communicate to others, watch a movie, shop in virtual reality, and play video games. This is a result of the multimedia explosion and the information highway. Presently, the telephone company (telephone), movie producers (theater, cable, pay-per-view), retailers (stores), and video game manufacturers (video parlors, special computers) supply these services separately. The market is converging and threatening a portion of each company's market. The threat is causing a number of mergers and joint ventures. What used to be separate industry maps appears to be merging into one map to meet the opportunities in the emerging information highway.

Strategic quality and managing-in quality were previously introduced. The complexities inherent to these concepts are developed in this and ensuing chapters. The value chain is a core model in developing strategies to achieve quality leadership. Quality leadership is constantly challenged by marketplace changes.

QUALITY POINTS

Quality is a major means of differentiating firms in the marketplace. The operant definition of quality is meeting/exceeding customer needs. The quality result is customer satisfaction. As straightforward as this sounds, it is very difficult for organizations to accomplish. This section outlines the standard points in the technical core where organizations build quality into their product and process.

There are five points by which an organization manages quality into the end product and process. Organizations can:

1. Design-it-in• An R&D process creates new product and production plans from customer need information. This unit is a major factor in modern quality. Not only is the product designed, but the process of manufacturing or delivering the service is also designed simultaneously. Product R&D and Process R&D are critical to building the product or delivering the service right. For example, headlights in a Japanese auto are square. To ensure that the installation is correct, the Japanese put a groove on top of the light. The grooved product resulted from intense study of minor details. Ford and Mazda co-developed the Escort. The level of sophistication in the product design required a new factory using up-to-date just-in-time manufacturing techniques. Both product and process R&D were part of the Escort's design.

2. Build-it-in• Factory designs for products and facilities for services carry out the design product and process specifications. The configuration of machines, space, methods, and people and the precision of each variable make up the core technology of the organization. The core technology is made up of a complex of processes and subprocesses. For example, a team of workers in a pizzeria realized that the humidity in the kitchen caused pizza dough to cook unevenly. After keeping the dough in a controlled environment, the problems with the final preparation disappeared. Quality in the final product was built-in the process.

3. Inspect-it-in• Inspection of final or intermediate inventories can identify defects. Data provides the basis for correcting the process, or fixing the product. Inspection is used for certification programs from governmental and professional agencies. For

example, the Nuclear Regulatory Commission requires a visual inspection of nuclear generating plants. The inspection includes every component in the plant.

4. Fix-it-in• At the end of the manufacturing process, or after a customer buys the product, a problem is sometimes discovered. The company then reworks, or fixes, a defective product so that it meets customer needs. Products with defects are fixed under the company's warranty. In a service context, intangible services delivered poorly can simply be performed again, or customers can get their money refunded. For example, Mercedes, Jaguar and other fine automobiles are often reworked after production to attain their refined features. Mercedes puts about 102 hours of labor in their cars before it is shipped to a customer. GE has a large centralized service center to take care of quality problems on their many products. It's not uncommon to hear of massive recalls of automobiles so auto manufacturers can fix-in quality. Using fixing-in as a marketing advantage is more characteristic of older bureaucratic organizations.

5. Educate the customer to appreciate it• Disparities between consumer expectations and the actual product and process quality can be addressed through persuasive advertising and promotion. If a company has a product that doesn't meet customer expectations, sometimes it increases advertising activities to put a different spin on the interpretation of the product and process features or reliability. For example, Cadillac won the Baldrige National Quality Award in 1991 because it had world-class processes to determine customer satisfaction, track quality during the production process, involve workers in the process, and more. Cadillac's turnaround wasn't finished in 1991. It started the effort in 1985. The automobiles manufactured in 1991 were designed in the early 1980s, and were never considered stylish. Cadillac's advertisers tried to educate consumers by distorting the meaning of the award. They suggested the award meant the Cadillac product got the award and was a superior product. The Baldrige people chastised GM and the advertising agency saying the award is for the process, not the product. The car developed designed under the new processes wasn't ready until 1992, after the award was achieved. It won several "Car of Year" awards and ranks very high on quality surveys.

No matter how a firm organizes, it constructs quality in the end-product by concentrating on these quality points. The emphasis a firm puts on any of these points varies among firms. Many firms find they spend a lot of resources on inspecting, fixing, and educating. They have limited resources to build-it-in or design-it-in. For example, they might not have the worker skills to measure or track production problems to their source and correct them. Thus, these firms have to inspect or fix the problems in order to meet their internal expenses. Internal costs to improve quality are very high. Designing-it-in requires immense market research, and an especially intense design process. If this competence doesn't exist, or a firm can't afford the investment in the process, then it resorts to inspecting, fixing, and educating.

Many firms, designed decades ago, rely on inspecting, fixing, and educating to ensure the quality to the customer. This old-design organization met the demands of the marketplace in past marketplaces. Marketplace competitive rules in traditional marketplaces determined that firms produced for market share, quarterly earnings, and return on investment. Adequate quality was enough.

With the revolution in competition, customers, and technology, the old-design is no longer appropriate. Successful new-design organizations realized the fundamental changes that are required. The adage "do it right the first time" describes the culture of the new-design organization. This adage is meaningful when applied to an organization. For example, if a firm inspects as a primary means of attaining quality standards, it isn't doing it right the first time. If a firm emphasizes designing-in and building-in quality, then almost all the production is done right the first time. Defects at the end are dealt with in the next design or with changes in the operations area.

The pressure in the new-design organization is upstream from manufacturing to the design process. The process of reflecting customer needs through requirements, production and into customer satisfaction is a critical process. The prime focus is on design-it-in".[2]

QUALITY POINTS AND THE CORE TECHNOLOGY

The five quality points occur along the organization's core technology in Figure 3-5. They appear sequentially from the design through the educating point, upstream to downstream. Building, inspecting, and fixing focus on core technology activities, and educating concentrates on the customer.

---

[2] Genichi Taguchi and Don Clausing, "Robust Quality," *Unconditional Quality*, (Boston: Harvard Business School, 1991), p. 53.

Organizations can be described in one of three categories:
1) Firms that developed prior to the 1970s in America have similar characteristics. They are old-design organizations. 2) Organizations that have undergone a radical change, or were developed in the last decade or so are probably new-design organizations. 3) The last category are the firms in the process of a transformational change. They are transitional organizations. Transitional organizations are old-design organization trying to transform themselves into new-design organizations.

☑ *Change and development is the subject of Chapter 7*

All organizations are quality conscious to some degree. Some can't attain the level of quality that is possible and most are limited by their organization design.

FIGURE 3-5
Quality Points on the Value Chain

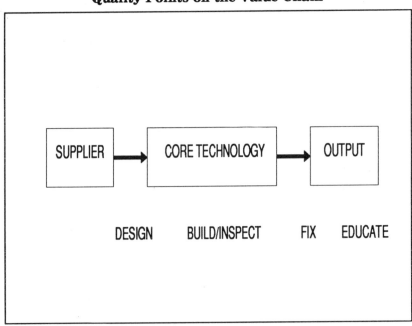

OLD-DESIGN ORGANIZATION FOR QUALITY

This section highlights the development of the old-design organization. An understanding of this development is necessary to appreciate the different assumptions that characterize the new-design organization. It also sets the stage for discussion of the challenges in changing these old-design organization to remain competitive.

OLD-DESIGN DEVELOPMENT

Old-design organizations made important contributions to the development of the wealth of the world. Large-scale manufacturing and equally large service organizations characterized the competitive world as the 20th century moved past World War II. These organizations concentrated thousands of people in a single location to produce millions of items. Within the constraints of communications, transportation, and understanding of the time, the bureaucratic organization was effective.

Many of the principles of the old-design era are in books, business schools and the heads of today's executives. Some organizations are still influenced by old-design principles. These influences are part of the web that causes resistance to change in societies and organizations. Europe's and America's unions are additional influences sustaining the old design. These organizations, however, are slowly beginning to reflect the new influences and change how they approach collective bargaining.

The trials and tribulations of many organizations, including General Motors, IBM, Kodak, Sears, Macy's, and many small and medium-sized organizations, are in the business press daily. They tried to rationalize, then adjust, to the change. Only when faced with survival did they radically change their structure and their management philosophy.

What is deceptive about the change is that the tools of modern quality are accessible to the old-design as well as the new-design organization. The old-design company usually adopted new techniques rather quickly. This tactic didn't give the old design any lasting strength.

These tools were often copied superficially and were referred to sarcastically as the "gimmick of the week" or the "quick fix response" by employees. These same techniques, though, are design variables in the new-design organization. They didn't work in the old organization because the design and resulting culture weren't supportive. These same systems, though, are basic elements of the new-design organization and help form the new culture.

It dawned on the old-design managers that the technique wasn't the reason for marketplace success. It was the quality philosophy that determined the difference in impact.

A basic design principle of the old-design organization is to increase control. The intent of management is to minimize the impact of outside influences on the organization. The practical effect is to formalize relationships with outside elements and control the actions of insiders. Contracts and policies characterize ways to minimize variations in outside company's affecting internal actions. A major focus of the control policies are humans. Humans are controlled by simplifying jobs and regulating the surrounding environment through rules and regulations. This setting is designed to increase control.

In manufacturing settings, jobs were simplified to increase reliability and minimize any potential for variation.[3] Union strategies complemented the management approach. Work rules and seniority reduced other options of management in the operations area. The operations area of most plants were closed off to outside influences. Even service positions in these organizations were shrouded by policies, rules, and regulations. The customer had to deal with these layers of policies to get any satisfaction.

OLD-DESIGN AND THE QUALITY POINTS

Figure 3-6 illustrates the design of the old-design organization. The core technology design limits the influence of outside value chain variables. The design-in, build-in, inspect-in, and fix-in quality points are in the closed core. Customers and suppliers are outside the processes and controlled by contract or policy. By following this logic, the core technology is under control.

The characteristics of the old-design system are:

Design-in quality:[4] The design of the product and process reflects the organizations understanding of the customer. The internal process is sequential and impersonal and reflects the functional management style. This approach minimizes cross-functional communication.

The steps of the process result in separate groups handling each step. A typical sequence is product definition, feasibility studies, detailed design and engineering, prototyping and product tests, then full scale mass production tests. Responsibility passes from one group of engineers to another group of engineers sequentially through the process. Conservative

---

[3] Mark S. Young, "A Framework for Successful Adoption and Performance of Japanese Manufacturing Practices in the United States," *Academy of Management Review*, 17, no. 4 (1992), p. 679.

[4] Warren B. Brown and Necmi Karagozoglu, "Leading the Way to Faster New Product Development," *The Executive*, 7, no. 1 (February 1993), p. 38.

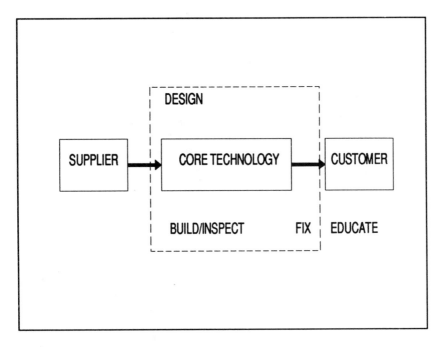

FIGURE 3-6
Old-Design System Logic

engineering standards are used, which requires ample safety standards. Avoiding the potential for unexpected problems, conservative engineering units over-built or specified in certain parts to insure they didn't give any problems.

*The phrase "**throw the design over the wall**" was used to describe the insularity of the various engineering groups. They would finish their portion of the design and "throw it over the wall" to the next group.*

Suboptimizing: Organizations are departmentalized for control purposes. Often these are functional departments like marketing, finance, operations, and human resources. They each have an authority hierarchy. Each unit has cost and performance goals to accomplish. The top-down objectives system is supported by an incentive system based on performance.

With each manager responsible for the performance outcomes the result is that each functional unit is managed like a personal unit. The responsibility of the unit head is for the unit's goals to be met. The idea is that if the unit's goals are met, the organization's goals will be met. The unintended result is that communication is minimized between units. The unit's goals are frequently met at the expense of the organization's goals. Some examples are:

♦ An accounts receivable unit minimizes its cost by batching orders, but customers get angry because their orders are processed slowly. The unit suboptimizes at the expense of organization goal of satisfying customers.

♦ A purchasing unit minimizes costs by establishing a rigorous bidding process.[5] Purchasing meets its goal, but the organization gets no cooperation from suppliers on design or manufacturing problem-solving.

Customer needs are secondary goals: Regardless of intent, the systems and goals relegate outside interests to secondary importance.

♦ Marketing's customer knowledge supports its goal of selling product.

♦ Customer service's customer knowledge focuses on pacifying the customer and fixing the problem.

♦ The product and process design process is initiated on the basis of customer data, but that soon gets subordinated to technical and departmental goals.

Inventory buffers: Inventories create slack so material is ready when the machines in the core technology need them. Some examples of inventories include:

♦ Inventories of inputs for inspection and economies.

♦ In-process inventories of partially done product allow inspection, and

♦ Output inventories to buffer the production from sales

---

[5] A. Ansari and B. Modarress, *Just-in-time Purchasing*, (New York: Free Press, 1990).

cycles and quality problems.

Production Process: Keeping average cost low through continuous production is the goal of the traditional organization.

♦ Input inventories ensure the process can keep producing at an optimal rate. Inventories can be stockpiled, if deals are found.

♦ Subprocesses within the production process have their own in-process inventories to allow inspection and to suboptimize its own production costs.

♦ An output inventory absorbs any difference between sales demand and factory output. This logic optimizes the production process and pressures the sales unit to sell the product. Each preceding unit pushes the next unit to meet its output regardless of the environment it is facing.

The "push" strategy was characteristic of large-scale manufacturing in the United States. One unit produces for inventory at a rate that satisfies its efficiency goals and the next unit is compelled to take its production from that inventory.

The Japanese system is a "pull" system. Demand from the customer triggers production work. The *Kamban* system is a signal from a assembly to its supplier units to start producing. This process continues upstream to the outside suppliers. These suppliers deliver input just-in-time for the production. Inventories are minimized in the "pull" system.

Simplified jobs: Simplified design of jobs in organizations reduces human error. Automation of jobs excludes humans and the potential for error. Where automation isn't feasible, performance, supervision, and reward systems support high performance from these narrowly defined jobs.

Inspect-in quality: The logical place to ensure quality items in the old-design organization is through inspection. The closed nature of the design results in the inability to get more than superficial upstream support for better design or downstream customer participation.

NEW-DESIGN ORGANIZATION FOR QUALITY

The new-design organization is focused on changing customer requirements and marketplace competition. This results in more information guiding decisions made in the organization. The changing information from outside the organization makes internal systems and processes continually adjust. A mature relation with outside customers and suppliers into current production efforts, product and process design, and service strategies increases the quality of the product and process. The organization is flexible in relation to these changing conditions.

The old-design organization creates certainty because it closes off the system with inventories, policies, and rules. It minimizes errors on the inside by automating and simplifying human participation and emphasizing the authority system. The new design includes outside stakeholders and information in the organization, making it more open and flexible in the short term. It counts on the use of intensified communication, information systems, and training systems to keep the organization competitive. The core technology is organized to use decision-making teams of individuals. Flexibility characterizes behavior in the new-design culture. Old-design organizations traditionally change reluctantly. All the systems and the culture are managed for certainty.

"Intelligence" is a metaphor describing a major outcome of new-design strategies. Flexibility means that many parts of the organization that processes information begin to change as a result. They don't wait for an order through the hierarchy. If an organization relies on this kind of action, frontline people need appropriate information. They also need skills to solve problems and make reliable decisions. Where they have the skills and information, the organization builds intelligence. The authority hierarchy isn't required for action. Training systems ensure employees have decision-making and problem-solving frameworks. Teams of trained employees increase the intensity of problem searches and innovations. Information and planning systems are also involved. These systems and the structure of the organization are designed to build intelligence throughout the organization to absorb information, make decisions and problem-solve. This design insures flexibility in responding to environmental changes.

> The new-design organization builds in *intelligence* so that it flexibly and reliably responds to the changing environment.

Front-line workers like clerks, service technicians, and employees on the assembly line have the information and authority to respond to the problems they face. Designers of products or services have the continuing input of suppliers and customers to help them make good product design decisions. Customer participation ensures the product meets its needs. Supplier participation ensures the needs parts can be supplied.

Information systems are key to the new-design organization. They are a necessary condition to creating a new-design organization. They enhance delivery of products and services; they provide the means of involving teams in the production of a product or service; and they provide the basis for reshaping middle management and the executive level.

Maintaining intelligence throughout the organization is a major undertaking. Maintaining the systems that update databases and ensuring that they are in a form to be used is complicated. This effort is reminiscent of learning. The learning organization is another metaphor for the dynamics of sustaining intelligence inside the new-design organization. Arie De Geus, head of planning at Shell, said, "The ability to learn faster than your competitors may be the only sustainable competitive advantage."[6]

The approach is to use the full potential of all the organization's resources in meeting or exceeding customer requirements. This requires

- all the potential contribution of suppliers,

- active participation by customers or customer information,

- focused energy by employees and

- effective management systems to organize this energy.

The result is a design that requires constant managing of the boundaries of the system because its outside elements are interacting so frequently. The means of managing are through building-in intelligence throughout the organization.

---

[6] Peter M. Senge, *The Fifth Discipline*, (New York: Doubleday, 1992), p. 4.

KEY QUALITY SUBSYSTEMS

This section develops the key systems that support the new-design organization's pursuit of higher quality. Higher quality means more flexibility from the organization. Flexibility is built in by design. These systems are necessary to the successful implementation of the new-design model.

These key quality systems are:
- → *Product or Process design system*
- → *Supplier partnership system*
- → *Benchmarking system*
- → *People systems*
- → *Integrated core technology system*

There will be many discussions of the implementation or impact of these systems throughout the text. These systems and the supporting hierarchy create an organization that is responsive to most customer pressures and competitive demands.

Combining the subsystems with the value-chain model developed earlier illustrates the complexity of the overall organization. The new design is a combination of the interaction of several subsystems. Each of the subsystems can be built, to a degree, as a standalone system. Flexibility results from all the subsystems to increase performance.

Figure 3-7 illustrates all 5 subsystems. Benchmarking is used to help improve all elements of the core technology and the administrative systems. The product and process design cycle is the partnership between the supplier, customer and organization. The supplier has a second relationship with the core technology. People systems are complex and affect all the other subsystems. The integrated core technology indicates the closeness of the supplier through the customer in delivering a high quality product and process.

The discussion about each of the systems emphasizes the impact of that system. There is discussion on the interface between systems as well.

Product and Service Design and Development System (R&D):

Before any production or delivery of service, the product or service is designed. New-design organizations place pressure on these units to (1) design quality into the product; and (2) respond quickly to the changing needs. Cycle time measures how quickly a company can respond to changes in needs through design and manufacturing to delivering a new product to the customer. For example, until recently it took American auto

FIGURE 3-7
Key Quality Systems

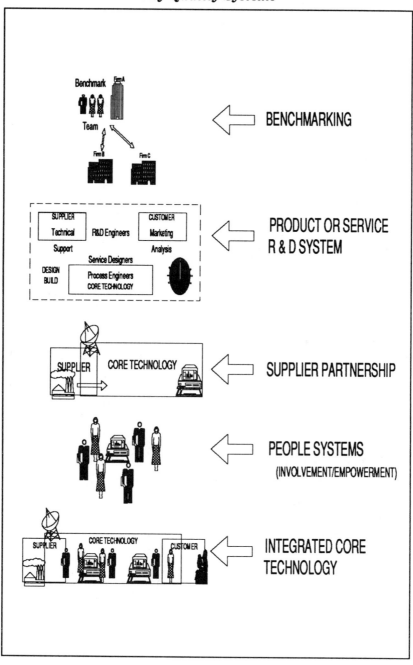

companies nearly five years to design and build an entirely new automobile. The Japanese design cycle is about three and a half years. This was a tremendous competitive advantage for the Japanese. Recently, Chrysler finished the design to production cycle for the Neon in less than 3 years.

The logic applies equally to a service. What is the cycle time on rebuilding a professional football team, or developing a new comedy routine, putting out a new insurance product to the sales team. R&D isn't as evident in services because there is not an R&D center filled with exotic equipment. However, sales people are constantly redesigning a sales floor, or adjusting a sales spiel. The meetings surrounding these changes are service equivalents to product R&D.

The challenge is to organize such that the resulting system supports faster and faster responses to customer and competitor changes. The goals of such a system are to increase communication, increase accuracy in reflecting customer requirements and design it with production and suppliers to ensure its manufacturability. Intelligence is built into this process by increasing the amount of information available to the front-line teams which make key decisions.

Cadillac knew it had to develop an engine that could beat the Lexus, Infiniti, Mercedes, and BMW. Their engineers studied BMW V-12s and Honda 4-cylinder engines. Using computer simulations they decreased trial and error efforts. Design-for-manufacturability efforts resulted in only 1,200 parts (versus 1,700 for the Lexus). This reduced the manufacturing time by 60%, and a tune-up to once every 100,000 miles. The new Northstar engine required a special suspension that has computers on each wheel reading the road to adjust for bumps. At 60 mph, there is a reading once every inch.

☑ *Chapter 5 details the service design process*

Front-line teams in manufacturing design include customers, suppliers, marketers, and design and manufacturing engineers. A service organization such as an insurance company would have a team involving customers, underwriters, marketers, and actuaries work as a team to develop a new product that could roll-out rapidly. These teams are cross-functional. The vertical hierarchy is subordinate to the needs of the cross-functional process.

An approach describing this system of product design in manufacturing is concurrent engineering.[7] The next section describes the complexity of this process and how it results in a higher level of quality designed-in more quickly than do other methods.

Designing customer needs into the product is difficult. Even with information from, and participation by, the customer there is a chance that something important is missed, or that the customer needs can't be met. The ideal is when customer needs are accurately reflected in the final product and process. These products or services will be purchased over others. Building that capability into a business unit requires extensive customer, marketer, supplier, and manufacturing information as the design progresses. There is no "over the wall" interaction. Teams arduously work out the design.

> *Genichi* Taguchi *developed the Taguchi method, which postulates that quality is a product of design. Most product failure occurs after its sale and during use. No matter how stringent the on-line manufacturing control, the robustness of the product during use won't change. The only reason a product lasts long during use is that its design reflects requirements and allows a consistent manufacturing process.*
>
> From Genichi Taguchi and Don Clausing, "Robust Quality" in *Unconditional Quality* (Boston: Harvard Business School, 1991), pp. 53-63.

A master project plan details activities that result in the product and process design. The plan coordinates concurrent activities, and adds a time requirement to it. For example, the cabinet for a television set can be designed and approved simultaneously with the design for the electronics. The key is that it complements the size and acoustic requirements of the electronics. Alternate experiments with audio technology goes on simultaneously with the video electronics. A master schedule requires interaction between these concurrent activities at key times to work out possible conflicts. Customer and supplier input is obtained at points on the process. Manufacturing engineering begins to explore the feasibility of manufacturing the design early in the process and recommending design changes that would make the production process more effective and efficient.

Explicit discussions of reliability throughout are important in

---

[7] David Brazier and Mike Leonard, "Concurrent Engineering: Participating in Better Designs," *Mechanical Engineering*, January 1990, pp. 52-3.

ensuring that quality is designed-in the process.[8] Reliability demands on the product comes from customer needs. A product that is used in wartime requires demanding reliability. Products used as part of a commercial airliner are required to have high reliability. A consumer product has different demands made on it than a commercial or defense product. The key is for the product to be designed for the particular user environment and to reflect those needs. Reliability engineering deals with the reliability demands on a product. A key measurement where reliability is an important requirement is mean-time-between-failures. It measures how often, under field conditions, that a product fails.

Most design systems involve sophisticated computerized information systems. Computers build-in intelligence into systems. For example, computer-assisted-drawing and computer-assisted-manufacturing (CAD/CAM) and rapid prototyping are useful in exploring alternatives quickly and applying what-if questions to the approach. Quality function deployment (QFD), design of experiments, project management, and team building are three examples of tools that make the design process more effective.

☑ Chapter 6 details these techniques.

In the late 1980s, Chrysler had to make a dramatic change or risk putting the corporation into bankruptcy. Stuck with an outmoded car line, it was faced with the challenge of designing a new car in a much shorter time than the American industry average of five years. President Bob Lutz put a large team of designers, marketers, and manufacturing engineers in an abandoned factory north of Detroit with the charge to "do it right." No interference from headquarters. Close quarters, no privacy, and constant interaction resulted in the new LH series of cars in about three and a half years. The LH was immediately successful in 1992. The cars won several "Car of the Year" awards in 1992. Consequently, Chrysler christened its new billion dollar design facility in Detroit to support concurrent design.

Customer and Supplier Partnerships-- The degree of sophistication of product and process design increases because suppliers and customers play a key role. A sophisticated design entails close relationships with the value chain. The level of sophistication of a product or service design can't exceed the capability of the value chain to supply appropriate parts and

---

[8] David A. Garvin, *Managing Quality*, (New York: The Free Press, 1988), p. 136.

services. This often requires a firm to work closely with suppliers to increase their quality through active participation in the design process.

Business is full of horror stories about the variation in quality of key components in machinery. Even when some parts are within specification, it's possible a condition called "stack up" can emerge. Each part might pass initial inspection. However, during assembly, they become out-of-balance, noisy, and perhaps dangerous.

Partnerships with suppliers and customers require intense communication and a heavy flow of information to work. Outside the normal flow of information, there are problems to work out. The following questions focus the parties to the partnerships on the right areas.

Supplier Questions
→ Does my supplier know my requirements?
→ Does my supplier know what I am getting?

Customer Questions
→ Do I understand my customers' requirements?
→ What is needed to meet my customers' requirements?
→ Is my customer satisfied?

♦ For example, a small machine tools manufacturer developed a sophisticated computer-assisted machine that increased manufacturing flexibility. His hand-made prototypes of the new machine worked perfectly. However, when he began using outside suppliers for parts to assemble the machine in quantity, he had a nightmare. The machines were noisy and of questionable quality.

He tracked the problem to tolerance in a key part. In general, specific design requirements meant little to the suppliers as long as they could stay within specifications. The supplier didn't have the tools for measuring the precision of his part and wouldn't adjust his production. His defense was that his other customers didn't demand it and he wasn't about to change it.

The machine-tool manufacturer didn't have any option but to deal with this supplier. He supplied the precision measuring tool and paid for any extra work the supplier did on the order. Establishing higher quality in the supply chain took many months. As a small company, he had little leverage.

♦ Ford jointly engineered an upgrade of the Escort with Mazda during the 1980s. The Escort price point was in the $10,000- $12,000 market range. The Japanese took the engineering lead with Ford engineers as partners. The final design turned out to be far more sophisticated than Ford would have undertaken on its own. When Ford involved its American suppliers to actually cost out the car, they refused to cooperate. The responses were: (1) very high prices because the parts required higher quality; (2) suggestions to use off-the-shelf parts; or (3) they refused to bid to supply the parts.

None of the alternatives are acceptable. Off-the-shelf parts wouldn't yield an good automobile. Keep in mind, Mazda would produce the sister car, Mazda 323, to these specifications and at that price-point. The Japanese supply chain were partners in the Mazda manufacturing process. American suppliers weren't used to these quality standards nor to the rigors of participating in the design process. Adding up the American suppliers estimates for the Escort parts resulted in a consumer price of about $25,000. Clearly unacceptable. Ford "twisted the arms" of key suppliers to gain cooperation. Eventually, they produced the car at the price points they intended.

These examples highlight a critical issue in product quality. The final manufacturer of a product is limited by the capabilities of its supply chain. Working with suppliers to increase quality is a worldwide concern. Encouraging, even demanding, that suppliers engage in quality efforts is heard more frequently. Certification of operations by a professional certification boards is one means of proving a level of quality. ISO 9000 is an international quality standard for certifying operations processes. Companies involved in competition for quality awards like the Deming or Baldrige work closely with their supply chains. They recognize the limitation of their quality efforts if the supply chain is inadequate. For those firms that can sustain quality over a longer term, many buyers have special partnership programs. The programs focus on prevention, improvement and process controls. AT&T's Quality Leadership Program[9] sets up a long-term partnership between qualified suppliers and AT&T.

☛In Chapter 9, ISO 9000 certification for suppliers is addressed.

Supplier process control[10] focuses on the processes within the supplier's plant. Once the customer requirements are known then the supplier uses statistical quality control to ensure that the process conforms

---

[9] Brian Leary, et al., *Quality Manager's Handbook*, (Indianapolis: AT&T, 1990), p. 64.

[10] J. M. Juran & Frank M. Gryna, *Juran's Quality Control Handbook*, 4th Edition, (New York: McGraw-Hill Book Company, 1988), Chapter 15.

with the requirements. Juran suggests a nine-step approach to set up a
good supply chain:

1. Define product and program quality requirements
2. Rate alternative suppliers
3. Select suppliers
4. Conduct joint quality planning
5. Help with the supplier during the execution of the contract
6. Get proof of supplier conformance to requirements
7. Certify qualified suppliers
8. Conduct quality improvement programs as required
9. Create and use supplier quality ratings

Just-in-time[11] (JIT) purchasing tries to coordinate the production of
the supplier with the needs of the buyer's organization. If supplies arrive
just as they are required in the production process, the inventory is
unnecessary. Costs go down considerably.

The demands such a system makes on both the company and its
suppliers are very high. Parts arriving just in time have to meet quality
standards without fail, otherwise the production process stops. The two
companies require intensive communication links for all the information
about orders, delivery and payments.

JIT is a "pull" system. When the production system needs the input,
the supplier will deliver it. This contrasts with the old-design system in
which the inventory "pushes" the organization to produce according to
schedule. JIT complements a production system the Japanese call
kamban.[12] This is a signaling system in which each downstream unit
signals upstream units when it needs parts. The results are that actual
sales pull production from each preceding upstream unit back through the
supply chain.

Electronic Data Interchange (EDI) is an electronic communications
linkage between suppliers and manufacturers. Computers link buyer and
seller so all ordering, distribution, payables and receivables information is
electronic. This link can be as simple as a modem and compatible programs for electronically ordering. Or it can connect suppliers into the
producers computer to verify production runs so the supplier knows what
parts to supply and when. Further activity might include transmission of

[11] Richard J. Schonberger and James P. Gilbert, "Just-in-Time Purchasing: A Challenge
for U.S. Industry," *California Management Review*, (Fall, 1983).

[12] R.J. Schonberger, *Japanese Manufacturing Techniques: Nine Hidden Lessons in
Simplicity*, (London: The Free Press, 1982).

CAD/CAM technical drawings to the supplier for their input.

Wal-Mart, Motorola, General Motors, and many others are making EDI a precondition to doing business with them. At one level, this is a strategy focussed on the value chain relationship between any buyer and seller. It creates value out of a previously burdensome process.[13] At another level, it is a clear indicator of the difference between the old-design and new-design company. The old-design approach was to take the low bidder and manage the relationship by contract. The new-design relationship gives both suppliers and customers broad access to both facilities requiring infinitely more trust. Suppliers are selected based on quality as well as cost of parts. Instead of multiple suppliers, a company might select only one or two companies to establish a partnership.

Benchmarking-- Benchmarking is a system for establishing comparative performance on internal processes. The intent is to benchmark companies that developed world-class performance on processes and sub-processes to judge performance.[14]

Whatever is measurable can be compared to other firms. Quality efforts are fact based, so measurement holds a central role. External benchmarks stimulate a problem-solving focus on internal processes. With the benchmarking system constantly searching for firms doing processes better, it is hard for the firm to become complacent. Table 3-1 gives some examples of the variety of competitive benchmarks. The organization is always improving some process that will result in a product that meets customer requirements a little better, a little faster, or a little less costly.

Baldrige winner Xerox championed benchmarking.[15] The Baldrige encouraged its use through publication in award guidelines.[16] Firms winning the Baldrige actively use the system. After winning, each firm is obligated to encourage others through benchmarking.[17]

The intent of the program is the achievement of a competitive

---

[13] Johnston, H. Russel and Michael R. Vitale, "Creating Competitive Advantage with Interorganizational Information Systems," *MIS Quarterly*, (June 1988), p. 152-165.

[14] Robert C. Camp, *Benchmarking-- The Search for Industry Best Practices That Lead to Superior Performance*, (Milwaukee, WI: ASCQ Quality Press, 1989).

[15] Camp, Benchmarking-- *The Search for Industry Best Practices....*

[16] National Institute of Standards and Technology, *1993 Award Criteria*, (Washington, D.C.: U.S. Government Printing Office, 1993), p. 6.

[17] AT&T, with two division Baldrige winners in 1992, felt that benchmarking applied to 270 of the 1000 points on the Baldrige.

Process Benchmarks
→ Assessment
→ Performance
→ Financial

Product Benchmarks
→ Development
→ Features
→ Availability

Development
→ Goals
→ Countermeasures

Marketing
→ Target Markets
→ Price Strategies

Improvement
→ Gap Analysis
→ Targets

Sales
→ Bid Responses
→ Customer Talks

Comparisons/ Competitive Analysis
→ Scope
→ Complexity
→ Cost

→ Features
→ Architecture
→ Availability

ADAPTED from "A Summary of the AT&T Transmission Systems Malcolm Baldrige National Quality Award Application" p. 4.

TABLE 3-1
Examples of Uses of Competitive Benchmarks

advantage in the marketplace. Benchmarking competitors might be a little sensitive unless both members can benchmark.[18] Where one firm has a particularly sensitive process, they might exclude it in a benchmarking exercise. Benchmarking in the hands of one organization might be shameless stealing; in another, it might be creative imitation; and in another, a learning experience.

In the learning experience the study to pinpoint processes to benchmark is long and arduous. Then appropriate benchmarking companies need to be selected. This might be a long process because (1) only winners should be benchmarked; (2) the benchmark company might be in another

---

[18]. The American Productivity & Quality Center in Houston has organized the International Benchmarking Clearinghouse. About 100 large firms pay a fee to belong and share information. This ensures information sharing and some protection against blatant stealing.

industry. The organization learns because benchmarking teams are plugged into the new-design organization's team network and planning system. These systems insure changes inside the organization.

Stealing and imitation seldom result in a long-term competitive advantage. Stealing and imitation are, by definition, superficial. No fundamental change results from the exercise. There are seldom any systems available to implement the information.

Benchmarking success is dependent on how well the organization's overall business strategy is working. Motorola and Digital Equipment are part of the same benchmarking consortia and get high marks in their efforts. Yet, Motorola constantly makes breakthrough changes and leapfrogs the competition. Digital is in a multi-year turnaround from being a high-cost, rather slow-acting company. The effectiveness of a strategic planning system in the organization is important in giving direction to benchmarking.

Organizing for Benchmarking-- Benchmarking teams are the core component of an effective benchmarking system. The teams become part of the team network (discussed under people systems) and the planning system (discussed in the next chapter). The team network is necessary to both supply the benchmarking direction and implementing the benchmarking results. The planning system integrates the benchmarking information in a formal system and is the means of planning and approving changes based on benchmarking information.

The key steps are of a benchmarking system are:

♦ Step 1. The team-- A benchmarking process requires a disciplined team of employees. These characteristics ensure intensity and psychological ownership of the benchmarking projects. The members of the team include people from the process being benchmarked plus any technical or managerial personnel that add to the analytical or implementation power of the team.

♦ Step 2. The self-study-- A target for change is determined in a number of ways. A process might be important, it might block achievement of customer satisfaction goals, or an outside organization's performance might unexpectedly highlight an internal process that needs attention. The self-study is designed to enable the team to understand all the subtleties in the process as the organization implements it.

♦ Step 3. The outside study-- Outside organizations that do the targeted process well are visited by benchmarking teams. The study is set up in advance with precise questions gleaned from the self-study.

BENCHMARKS

XEROX CO. used the following firms and processes as benchmarks:
→ *L.L. Bean for order taking and warehousing*
→ *American Express for billing*
→ *Deere & Co. for computer operations*

FIDELITY INVESTMENTS used:
→ *McDonald's french fry making for lessons on consistency*
→ *Walt Disney World Resort training for lessons on loyalty*

The team's responsibility is to bring back information to improve a process or sub-process. For example, Federal Express (Fedex), a Baldrige winner in 1990, benchmarked Domino Pizza's system for customer response. Then, Fedex benchmarked on Domino's telecommunications innovations and training intensity. These were systems that gave Domino's a competitive advantage.

♦ Step 4. Making the change-- Another important element in benchmarking is actually making internal changes. Change is difficult for most organizations and employees often resist. Benchmarking is part of the new-design organization that prepares the organization for constant change. Table 3-2 shows the complexity of the internal communications that surrounds a vital benchmarking program.

With the team network and powerful strategic planning system, benchmarking information provides the rational basis for deciding if a change should be made. The benchmark information becomes targets in the firm's planning system. The study provides the understanding of how the benchmarked firms operate the system. This information is the basis for any project planning.

The deployment infrastructure: The benchmarking team is the heart of this system. Employee involvement in the studies increases the chances of a successful implementation. The planning system arrays the bench-marked system against the other strategies and utilizes the team network

Benchmarking Library
Benchmarking Newsletters
Benchmarking DataBase
Network Team Review
Operations Review
Quality Improvement Team Reviews
Management Team Visits

TABLE 3-2
Benchmarking
Communications

to help deploy innovations. The necessary condition is the continuing leadership committing the organization to quality leadership in the marketplace.

Discussion: The new-design organization is different from the old-design organization. Customer partnerships in the design process ensure that customer requirements guide the design of the product and process. The supplier partnership ensures that inputs conformed to design tolerances demanded by customer requirements. Benchmarking insures the systems and processes of an organization lead or emulate world class processes.

> *Frederick Herzberg and others developed the ideas of job enlargement and job enrichment during the 1950s & 1960s. Enlarging a job meant doing more tasks. Enriching a job meant more authority was vested in the job. Enlarging a job is similar to involvement and enrichment is similar to empowerment.*

People Systems: This is an umbrella term for a large part of the infrastructure of the new-design organization. The new-design organization is dependent on a powerful set of people systems.[19] One major system is a quality team network that solves problems, makes decisions, and implements. These teams focus on all aspects of maintaining, improving,

---

[19] P. Block, *The Empowered Manager*, (San Francisco: Jossey-Bass, Inc. 1987).

and innovating processes within the organization. Most processes involve activities that cross a number of functional units.

People play an important role in all aspects of the new-design organization. They run the integrated core operations, staff the bench-marking teams, maintain the partnerships, and turn customer information into product. These systems are the means of building intelligence[20] throughout the organization. Although computers, machines and systems are elements in this intelligence, people are a necessary element in building intelligence. People become a valuable part when the decision making, problem-solving, communicating, and planning become reliable. People systems provide the basis for reliable behavior. Some of the key systems are:

1. Selection systems: Selecting capable employees is important. Employees with a predisposition to learning and cooperation feed an organization infrastructure that requires extensive involvement in teams.

2. Training systems: Extensive training increases knowledge of operations, skills in problem solving, and mastery of interpersonal ability.

3. Role systems: Roles define authority and responsibilities of people in organization settings. In a new-design case, the employees in operations and other front-line positions have expanded roles and commensurate authority. In contrast, in the old-design case, employees have narrow roles and limited authority. In the new-design organization, the intent is to empower employees. In the old-design organization, the intent of management is to control the employee. In the new-design organization, supervision supports the empowered employee. In the old-design organization, the supervision is a key component to insuring the control of employee behavior.

4. Team infrastructure: An elaborate system of grouping people into teams can manage the problem-solving requirements of the organization. Teams develop norms for complete and continuous problem solving that enhance the quality effort. Some of these aspects include continuous improvement, cross-functional problem solving, self-directed work teams, and process management

---

[20] Paul Adler uses the term "knowledge intensity". See Paul Adler, "Managing Flexible Automation," *California Management Review*, (Spring 1988), p. 34.

problem solving teams. As long as the organization maintains its commitment to being a quality leader, the quality team network develops an independent, consistent intensity in diagnosing problems, solving them, and implementing the solutions.

---

*"**We have been told** by process design team members that it is difficult to allocate attention to teamwork unless it comprises at least 50% of their jobs. In other words, a team that meets only one day per week is not likely to succeed." Thomas Davenport, Process Engineering. (Boston: HBS Press, 1993) p. 101.*

Changes in the outside environment requires organization flexibility and reliability. The intelligence required to meet this challenge involves a complex set of systems. People systems trigger action from other systems. Team technology is a way to leverage individual talent and focus it on complex organization issues. Selection, role, and training systems support the effective behavior of people in organizations.

☑ The next chapter discusses people systems in detail.

Teams work in cultures that are supportive. The authority hierarchy interferes with the development of teams. In an authority situation, teams are unable to develop because they are looking outside the team activity for direction. For full development, teams direct their own action based on the facts. Authority comes from the team. Direction comes from the planning context and the facts. In an authority hierarchy there can be meetings, and groups can complete tasks easily. But, these are not teams and can't develop into them.

Teams can't develop in core technologies that were designed with simplified jobs to minimize interaction and factor human intelligence out. Automation, inspection, and close supervision are part of a system that distrusts people and controls behavior. An organization expecting to develop a team network has to expect to change the way the core technology is organized.

*'**The culture** of Federal Express motivates people to take the extra
step and do the extra thing. Our culture and our values say. 'I'm
important, I'm in control. I'm smart and I'm expected to use my mind
to think'. That's where our people really learn to go out of their way to
solve customer problems, and why they keep doing it."* Peter W. Addicott
of Fedex Corporation in Chip Bell and Ron Zemke, "Service Recovery. Doing It Right
the Second Time," *Training*, June, 1990. p. 48.

The next section addresses an integrated core technology. Such
technology has a design that utilizes team decision and problem-solving
power to maintain, improve, and innovate the core technology. In
addition, it integrates the customer and suppliers into the action.
Computer automation and information systems are a reason the integrated
core is possible. This core technology can exploit the full energy and
power of the team technology.

The old-design assembly lines of American auto manufacturers were
designed to minimize the impact of the unionized worker-- simplify and
use automation as a means of control. There are several instances of new-
design core technologies in America: NUMMI (GM/Toyota joint venture),
Saturn (GM Tennessee plant), and several American Japanese plants
(Honda, Nissan, Toyota, Mitsubishi, and Mazda). These companies
illustrate teamwork, cross-training workers, and minimal supervision on
the assembly line. These plants are successful and high quality. Some of
the plants are organized by unions, but in each case they have special
work rules which allow management unprecedented ability to transfer
workers, cross-train them, and use different incentives.

The Integrated Core Technology: The integrated core is a term that
symbolizes the organization of the firm's operations and integration with
customers and suppliers. Specifically it focuses on partnerships of the
customer and suppliers in a just-in-time production or service system.
This is the "pull" system (described earlier in this chapter). The demand
for the product and process by the customer sets off a "pulling" demand for
production in units and suppliers upstream. Toyota's system is the model
for manufacturers. Wal-Mart's system is a good model for delivering JIT
service in their stores.

The core technology refers to the operations area of a manufacturer
or a service organization. There are a lot of similarities between the two
types of organizations. The back office of a bank, insurance company, amd
a stock brokerage, all service organizations, are often managed like a
manufacturing facility. It is a relatively closed system, highly automated,
and has little interaction with outsiders. A life insurance company is

organized the same way. Service characterizes these businesses because the products of these institutions are often customized for the customer while the sales effort goes on.

The retail store is organized so it has the right inventories based on information collected as customers make purchases. The cash register is part of a complex information system that signals suppliers for resupply, updates inventory, pays vendors, and customizes store offerings. This is very similar to manufacturing. The major difference is that the core technology of a manufacturer can finish the product before delivering it to a customer. A service is often made and delivered in front of the customer.

The supply chain is equally important. For example, labor is important in both industries, for example, but the individual is often the major part of the delivery, and perhaps the production, of the output of a service organization. The customer might be seen as an input to many service processes. They are part of the core technology as it operates. The retail store is the core technology and customers come in and out all day. Patients come into the doctor's office (core technology) and have procedures done to them. Students come into the classroom to be educated (the operations area).

Integrated refers to
♦ *integrating the customer and the supplier as partners in operations*
♦ *integrating employees as individuals or in teams with the operations to ensure a flexible system and a continuous improvement environment.*

The integrated core is a relatively open system. Suppliers, customers, individuals and teams intervene in the system as the need arises. The boundaries of the system aren't controlled to prevent outside intervention. Having a manager regulate whether information is important or not (1) discourages spontaneous contributions, and (2) takes extra time as all communication is dealt with several times. Instead, boundaries are managed to encourage communications. The task of keeping up a complex business is difficult without help. It is the accumulation of "little things" done right that results in the high quality output. The more fact-based communications there is, the more likely the organization will meet higher and higher quality standards.

Gunn suggests "This is one continuous spectrum. No activity can be performed along this spectrum without affecting some other part of it either upstream or downstream."[21] Davenport calls this the "virtually integrated enterprise."[22] This enterprise wide view means treating all the firms that play a role in delivering completed services or products to customers as partners.

> *"Change is in the air.... From that pursuit of speed.... came our vision for the 1990s- a boundary-less company. Boundary-less.... describes a whole set of behaviors we believe are necessary to achieve speed. In a boundaryless company, suppliers are not 'outsiders'.... Every effort of every man and woman in the company is focused on satisfying customers' needs. Internal functions begin to blur...."* From the *1990 GE Stockholder Letter* from Jack Welch, Lawrence Bossidy, and Edward Hood.

These are some examples of the ways organizations, people, and teams operate to maintain and improve the system. These interventions are based on the needs of the system and need no more than information to stimulate action:

♦ Suppliers work with the company's engineers to refine the precision and the delivery of the supply parts. Electronics like EDI (electronic data interchange) and CAD/CAM enhance this effort.

♦ Information systems link machines to time the delivery of supplies, provide the basis for just-in-time manufacturing, and provide information for human or team decisions to maintain and improve the operations.

♦ Information is available to internal teams so they can decrease variation in the production process.

♦ Information from customer satisfaction surveys to refine product or service offerings are fed to production units and process teams to solve problems and improve operations.

♦ Computers automate parts of service or production processes that humans can't do, or are boring. Computer integrated manufacturing (CIM) and advanced manufacturing techniques (AMT) are terms capturing the manufacturing use of computers.

---

[21] T.G. Gunn, *Manufacturing for Competitive Advantage*, (New York: The Free Press, 1987), pp. 28-9.

[22] Thomas Davenport, *Process Innovation*, (Boston: Harvard Business School, 1993), p. 169.

♦ Research and development/ design process closely tied into both customer, supply, and manufacturing information for more immediate translation of information into product and production requirements.

> ***Mass customization*** *of products and services is now possible with efficient shorter runs from manufacturing facilities. Quick changeovers to different products are possible in operations because of the computer control, and skilled and empowered employees.*

Integrated core technology refers to the way an organization produces its product and process. It refers to the use of inputs to create an output that meets or exceeds customer requirements. The throughput, or transformation, supports the complex demands the new-design organization for speed and flexibility. These reflect the organization's commitment to responding more quickly to customers with more custom products or services. Shorter manufacturing runs, or more variable services, can only be economic when the core technology has more computer intelligence built-in and takes full advantage of human talent.

Three systems make up the new-design manufacturing advanced core technology: advanced manufacturing technology (AMT), just-in-time purchasing/inventory (JIT), and total quality management (TQM). Each of the techniques are implemented independent of the others, in practice. Integrated together they eliminate "barriers between stages, functions, and goals of production to create a streamlined value-added system."[23]

AMT[24] is "an automated production system of people, machines, and tools for the planning and control of the production process." It takes advantage of technologies like CAD/CAM, materials resource planning systems, automated materials handling systems, robotics, computer controlled machines, flexible manufacturing systems and computer-integrated manufacturing systems.

AMTs support the flexibility that is required for the modern high-quality manufacturing organization. Advanced organizations world-wide

---

[23] Scott A. Snell and James W. Dean, Jr., "Integrated Manufacturing and Human Resource Management: A Human Capital Perspective," *Academy of Management Journal,* 35, no. 3 (1992), p. 470.

[24] Raymond F. Zammuto and Edward J. O'Connor, "Gaining Advanced Manufacturing Technologies' Benefits: The Roles of Organization Design and Culture," *Academy of Management Review,* 17, no. 4 (1992), pp. 701-728.

are building plants that reflect these technologies. The capability of people on the shop floor and in the organization culture are important conditions for success of AMTs.[25] The nature of the AMTs is that they require constant decision making to keep high performance. Information systems provide the data for decisions to be made. Competent personnel decide to stop, start, adjust, change or substitute.

JIT is a system that requires supplier partnerships. It is an integral part of the "pull" manufacturing system developed by Toyota. TQM is designed to control the maintenance and improvement of the core technology through analysis of information and implementation of changes. TQM provides the framework that directs team and individual behaviors to improvement activities. The logic focusses behaviors to intra and inter departmental problems.

☑ Chapter 6 details the key tools.

DISCUSSION

The old-design and new-design organization are fundamentally different. Table 3-3 arrays the new-design and old-design organizations against the five quality points. The two organization designs differ. The old-design organization minimizes cost and achieves economies from the production process. Long runs result in lower cost. The new-design organization is conceived to respond to a highly discriminating customer. The design ensures that products satisfy customer needs.

ORGANIZATIONAL CULTURE

Culture is a combination of all the intangibles that powerfully direct behaviors. Culture is a accumulation of stories that employees, competitors, community members, vendors, and customers tell about the company. It is evident in how the firm makes decisions, solves problems and treats customers, vendors, and others.

---

[25] Zammamuto and O'Connor, "Gaining Advanced Manufacturing Technologies' Benefits," pp. 718-723.

TABLE 3-3
Quality Efforts by Old-Design
and New-Design Organizations

	OLD-DESIGN ORGANIZATIONS	NEW-DESIGN ORGANIZATIONS
	Strategy: Low Cost through economies of scale	Strategy: Quality Leadership in the Marketplace
Design-it-in	This company is under pressure to match a competitor's product or service quality. Customer requirements are given to the unit by marketing. Finished design is given to suppliers and manufacturing to do their engineering.	The company has its hands on the pulse of the buying public and utilizes customers in design teams to confirm the product reflects customer needs. Suppliers and manufacturing personnel are partners in the concurrent design process.
Build-it-in	Production engineers get product design specifications. They design a process that melds those product specifications with available parts from low cost suppliers.	Concurrent engineering results in both product and process design engineers working together to assure the quality is built-in through good process design.
Inspect it in	Cost and time considerations result in modest product and process design. Quality pressure increases on inspection to catch errors. Extensive quality assurance departments raise the quality of the product.	Partnerships in the design system increase the quality and reliability of the product. This emphasis results in designing in quality and minimizes inspecting, fixing, and education quality into the product. Federal requirements and customer requirements
Fix-it-in	Fixing, or reworking, is an important strategy for the old-design firm. ◆ Quality is measured as meeting specifications. ◆ The assembly line is driven by an objective of lowering average cost. ◆ Fixing products or redoing services is often cost justified.	Problem-solving teams, with trained front-line employees, are used to find root causes of defects in the production process increasing the quality built in and decreasing the need to fix-in quality.
Educate-it-in	Marketing and public relations try to get the customer to buy the product or service. At the extreme, it might require doing "whatever it takes." The feeling is that increasing final inventories or returned products result from inadequate marketing and poor advertising.	All front-line personnel, including customer service and marketing, concentrate on transmitting the company's quality message and helping customers expand their enjoyment of the product or service.

Once a firm establishes a way of doing things, it is difficult to change. It doesn't make much difference if a firm is a success or a failure. Unsuccessful firms require more than financing and a solid strategy to succeed. It's the unexpected regression to a losing way of behaving that gets them. Or perhaps a firm doesn't win a contract because of suspicions based on the way the firm performed in the past.

Norms are the way of describing the intangible stories that guide behaviors. Norms result from performances in the past. As these performances, and the glee or frustration that results cumulate, a norm is formed: "We can't compete against BC company," or "No one does a better job than we do." Norms often end directly or indirectly supporting continued success, or, equally likely, behaviors that limits the firm's success.

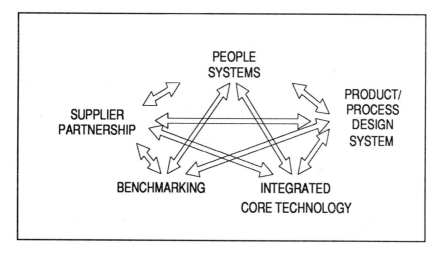

FIGURE 3-7
Development of a Culture

Norms come from people interacting over some organizational activity. Feelings result naturally from the interaction. The interactions and activities are a product of the role a person plays. These roles are part of an organization structure. Sentiments, and consequently norms, are formed through formal and informal interactions. In a high performance organization both types of interactions are likely to yield supportive norms. In a low-performance organization, neither type of interaction is likely to be supportive of high performance.

*"**When speaking** of "quality", one tends to think first in terms of product quality. Nothing could be further from the truth. In Total Quality Control, the first and foremost concern is with the quality of people. Instilling quality into people has always been fundamental to TQC. A company able to build quality into its people is already halfway toward producing quality products."*
Imai, Masaaki, *Kaizen*, (New York: Random House, 1986), p. 43.

The norms of old-design organization are constantly reinforced because the interactions and activities are unlikely to be changed. The norms of new-design organization have to be fundamentally different because the interaction and activities are different.

In a new-design organization the subsystems allow great latitude for interactions with superiors, peers, and subordinates over business activities. The norms developed in this setting are positive if the organizations are successful. Old-design organization set up norms designed to enforce behavior under the control philosophy.

New-design norms evolve from the interactions in the activities set up by the five quality subsystems as Figure 3-7 suggests. Thus, the increased involvement in activities and the authority vested in the role results in far more interactions over many important activities in the organization. Further, the interactions came as individuals and as team members. The team dimension is a new dimension and results in norms that increase the reinforcement for additional performance.

SUMMARY

All organizations fit somewhere on an industry map reflecting the interconnected nature of manufacturing and service companies. Industry maps reflect the value chain of specific companies that flow upstream from their customers through the supply chain to raw materials. The firms transform inputs from the supply chain into outputs of products or services for customers. The transformation process is in the company's core technology.

Quality in the final product is fixed-in, inspected-in, built-in, or designed-in. The philosophy behind the old-design organizations results in more inspecting, fixing and educating quality into the product. The philosophy behind the new-design organization results in an emphasis on design-in and building-in the quality. The design features make the respective designs focus on quality in unique ways.

The old-design organization stresses hierarchial control. Simplified jobs, high automation, and close supervision result in highly efficient operations. The intent is to close off the system for more control. Consequently, communication is limited and information is centralized.

The new-design organization stresses flexibility and speed. The design increases the information flow among closely related stakeholders. These stakeholders are both inside and outside the organization. They are integrated into the challenge through five key quality systems. The systems include a product or process design system, a partnership system, a benchmarking system, people systems, and the integrated core technology. This results in managing a relatively open system. Benchmarking systems span from the organization into the external environment. Boundaries of the new-design organization are constantly flexing as suppliers, customers, and benchmarking teams go in and out and gather, process, or give information for decision making and problem solving.

> **"The need** for faster, more flexible response to changing customer requirements is leading companies to redesign their management systems. This is leading to a major new market opportunity for TI...as we build a profitable billion-dollar software business by the mid-1990s.
> See *1992 Texas Instruments Annual Report*, p. 3.

The following list itemizes the advantages of the new-design form of organization.

◆ Satisfying the customer is a priority in designing new products or adjusting the delivery of a wide variety of existing products.

◆ Cycle time is rapid because of the concurrent activities that result from the team capabilities, partnerships, and information systems in the R&D unit.

◆ A trained employee base, woven into a sophisticated team environment, results in constant analysis and problem solving. The environment of empowered employees results in continuous improvement to the processes and product.

◆ Customers and suppliers contribute as partners to product or service design efforts and operations changes. This results in a more sophisticated response to customer requirements.

◆◆◆

POINTS TO PONDER

1. Why are benchmarking and compilation of "best practices" some of the most widely used quality practices?

2. Indicate some ways in which you see the 1990's as the decade of value. How would that differ from earlier decades?

3. What is value to you? How is this different from your friends or possibly your customers? Is value a personal thing, or can it be generalized to groups of people, such as mechanics, salespersons, builders, or hospital patients.

4. Does an emphasis on core technology help differentiate the new design from the old design organization? How?

Please see the question at the end of the reading.

◆◆◆

READING

IBM Begets Microsoft

IBM and Microsoft are companies in the computer industry. IBM was the dominant company for decades until the advent of the personal computers. They grudgingly offered products but held an internal policy not to let PCs undercut the mainframe business they had with large businesses. As the PC technology got more sophisticated it began to address the needs of these larger companies more effectively than mainframe technology.

Microsoft was born into the PC industry. IBM gave a young Bill Gates control over the operating system (DOS) for the PC. He developed DOS and slowly built a number of applications. By the end of the decade Microsoft was a rapidly growing, very profitable, software firm. The relationship with IBM constrained Microsofts growth and so it became rocky. The significant break came when Microsoft decided not to jointly develop an operating system with IBM.

By 1992 each company was on a different track. Microsoft was growing 30% to 50% per year and was a powerhouse. Its 1992 revenues were $2.5 billion. IBM had declining revenues and began to show significant losses. A 1984 boast that they would be a $100 billion company by 1990 was never realized. Its peak was $69 billion and it now is about $63 billion. The 1984 stock price was the highest its been since. It lost market share in PCs from that date as well.

Ironically, in early 1992 both companies had secret internal memos leaked to the public. They were both critiques of what was happening to the respective companies. The IBM critique came from the perspective of a previously great company in decline. The Microsoft critique came from the perspective of a company still in the rapid growth stage of its industry.

Bill Gates, Microsoft's CEO, takes an annual "think week." He goes off, alone, to read and contemplate the company. His document is a long litany of criticisms of Microsoft's initiatives. John Akers, IBM's CEO, disclosed his sentiments in a meeting of junior executives at IBM. The notes from this meeting were stolen off an internal E-mail system, and published.

The Gates memo was about strategy. Microsoft has some serious legal and competitive threats, including a mounting challenge by IBM in Microsoft's core operating system market. The tone of the Gates memo is cautionary, but positive. "Although the challenges should make us quite humble about the years to come, I think our position is enviable..."

Akers's talks about the market problems resulting from a cozy IBM culture. He complains about the "average IBMer" who is very comfy and not producing and laments the financial implications. He's concerned about IBMers schmoozing around the water cooler and wasting too much time both drinking coffee with customers and doing community activities.

The tone of Akers's diatribe was negative and financial. "What are you doing for me." "The business benefits should accrue therefore WHERE ARE THEY?" " It's no fun in having the stock at a 25% discount." "IBM exists to provide a return on invested capital to the stockholders."

What is interesting about Akers's diatribe is that it features typical bureaucratic problems. He refers to his sentiments being "filtered... with the masses [employees] never getting the full message." He follows up with some threats: "I used to think my job as a rep was at risk if I lost a sale. Tell them theirs is at risk if they lose."

5. Do IBM and Microsoft fit the classic Old-Design and New-Design organization principles?

◆◆◆

CHAPTER 4
ESTABLISHING ORGANIZATION INFRASTRUCTURE

♦♦

The objectives of this chapter are:

1. To elaborate the systems described in Chapter 3.

2. To describe the major levers that managers use to achieve quality leadership.

Key Words to Watch for:

Benchmark	Input	Scenarios
Catchball	Managing by plan	Self-managed
Customer Info Sys	Momentum	teams
Empower/Involve	Network	SWOT
Facilitator	Process Mgmt	Synergies
Hoshin Planning	Team--PMT	Systemic
Improvement Team	Quality control--QC	Team culture
Infrastructure	Reengineer	Transformational
Innovation	Satisfaction	Work group

♦♦

INTRODUCTION

In the middle 1990s, organizations find themselves in a real quandary. They aren't competitive in the marketplace. Germany's Volkswagen recently laid off 30,000 employees world-wide. Their American market-share decreased from about 7% in 1970 to 0.6% in 1993. In order to show a profit, their Wolfsburg, Germany facility has to produce at over 90% of capacity. Most competitors are much more efficient and can show a profit while producing at 70% of capacity. Volkswagen is a strong competitor in Europe today. However, it will have increasing difficulty because European auto companies are more efficient, and the Japanese are just overcoming barriers to entry in Europe.

Volkswagen isn't the only European or American firm to experience the combination of quality and productivity problem. Over the last four years, IBM, for example, has decreased its employee base from over 400,000 to under 300,000 employees. Most old-design organizations are facing a period in which radical change is required to achieve competitiveness.

There is a difficulty in interpreting the reactions by these firms. The old-design traditional reaction to adversity is laying off workers. This doesn't necessarily mean that the firm is building the internal systems that signal a transition to new-design status. More is required. These companies understand a change is required, but it's not clear if the firms understand the extent of that change, the commitment required to enforce the change, or how long it is going to take.

There is more to these firms' problems. It's not known if the firms have viable competitive strategies to emerge from their difficulties. In most industries, there are new-design firms. They have the competitive advantage in the 1990s. The systems are already built. A supportive culture is developing strength. Any firm just starting to change is behind the leaders by several years. This is a substantial barrier. It threatens the survival of many firms.

Novell is a billion-dollar, new-design firm formed in 1983. Its marketplace is the constantly changing computer industry. Novell makes the software that supports local area networks (LAN). LANs connect personal computers (PCs) to increase communication, coordination, and control of the organization. Novell controls about 65% of the marketplace.

Coopetition is a term that joins the words cooperation and competition. It characterizes the culture at Novell. It also captures a characteristic of new-design organizations-- an unusual openness inside the organization that causes people to fight for what they want. But once a decision is made, everyone cooperates to beat the competition.

Novell's mission statement says: "Our mission-- to accelerate the growth of the network computing industry. Our products-- software systems, service, and support. Our priorities-- customers first, employees second, shareholders third. Our commitment-- to be two years ahead and gaining."

Competition underlies the Novell statement. Yet it represents the new-design values of priority on customer and employee satisfaction. Customer satisfaction as a priority has been discussed in earlier chapters. Employee satisfaction as a priority will be established in this chapter and the chapter on service.

The challenge, then, is for old-design organizations to transform to the new design. The five quality subsystems in Chapter 3 set the base for the new-design. There are several other elements. This chapter builds the infrastructure to support the functioning of the subsystems. It also builds the planning system that gives competitive information to the organization. Chapter 6 adds detail to the systems that keep the organization improving continually. Chapter 7 examines change in the organization.

THE REST OF THE STORY

The five quality systems make a clear difference between the old-design and new-design organization. An elaborate infrastructure is required to assure the firm of competitive success.

♦ <u>People</u> <u>systems</u> are central to the success of new-design organizations. The quality network highlights team-based problem solving. Problem solving underlies the continuing improvement culture. Benchmarking, partnerships, design, customer influence, and the operations all depend on participation by humans. Human subsystems need constant maintenance. Supporting systems are extensive and critical to the success of the enterprise.

♦ A <u>customer</u> <u>information</u> <u>system</u> complex enough to supports appropriate decisions in the organization. Understanding these subsystems is important because the firm's success depends on high quality products. Marketing systems play an important role in bridging the organization boundary to the customer. Information systems play a role in getting the information to the right units.

The customer is a priority in the system. It's easy to get wrapped up in the detail of these systems and forget that customer satisfaction determines everything that goes on. It is the customer's selection of products/services that lasted longer, worked better, and made them feel better that caused this radical change period in organization.

♦ The <u>planning</u> <u>system</u> provides the direction and pressure for performance. It is the "glue" that brings the organization together and focused on target objectives. These objectives cumulate to successful strategies that achieve long-term visions. A planning system runs from the environment to every person in the organization. It supplies the direction for every behavior. A basic issue is how to integrate the quality planning and the competitive or business planning processes. Many think business planning drives out quality planning. There is no doubt that this happens often. Leadership is required to insure that quality remains a priority. The new-design organization requires intense management to avoid such problems.

PEOPLE SYSTEMS

The teams[1] network is a central framework for building problem solving, decision-making, and planning competence into the new-design organization. Problem solving, decision-making and planning competence at the front line increases the organizations speedy response to problems in the core technology, and to demands from the customer.

> *The team network reinforces performance behaviors and ensures a disciplined approach to problems.*

Teams are used in two contexts. One is the use of work teams in the manufacturing of a product or a delivery of a service. The test is that the core technology is specially designed to utilize teams. Some technologies are more conducive to teams than others. Some positions can't be organized into teams. The second use is teams as a means to improving quality. These teams take on projects that require special effort. In this chapter we discuss how both types of teams become part of the team network. Work teams report through the functional hierarchy. The quality improvement teams are often associated with a quality network and are accountable through that network.

Team infrastructure complements the design of the integrated core technology. Recall from the last chapter that the core design:

♦ empowers human operators, which in turn are supported by the team infrastructure, and
♦ integrates the components of the core technology and other parts of the value chain.

This situation is very complex. There is some uncertainty involved about whether people can respond to the intensity of decision making and problem solving required in this integrated core. The integrated design

---

[1] This discussion is an extension of the research done on sociotechnical systems. Sociotechnical systems analyzed the symbiotic relationship among technical design of operations, people, and the emergent social culture.

requires competent people. Many resources are required to:

- ◆ put the right people in place (selection systems),
- ◆ give them the right skills to do the job (training systems), and
- ◆ sustain high performance (quality team network, and reward and supervisory systems).

With these support systems in place, it is likely the organization can respond more flexibly and adapt to new environments.

Definitions
◆ *Working Groups rely on "individual bests" for performance with no collective work products.*
◆ *Teams entail risk of conflict, joint work products and collective action. Results in common purpose, set of goals, and mutual account-ability.*
◆ *Success is the reason that teams develop from potential teams to high potential teams. Using the discipline of a foundation of prob-lem-solving skills is the most effective way of progressing.*
Adapted from Jon R. Katzenbach and Douglas K. Smith, *The Wisdom of Teams* (Boston: Harvard Business Schools, 1993), pp. 84-85.

TEAMS AND PERFORMANCE
Katzenbach and Smith[2] suggest a classification of teams. It is based on the phase of development pattern of teams. The phases of development are:

- ◆ Phase I-- Pseudo-teams: Members still have to learn how to be good team members. Learning all the initial team formation tasks is the challenge. These tasks include establishing team purpose, detailing the task, establishing milestones, and determining the inventory of skills required to accomplish the task.

- ◆ Phase II-- Team: With the preliminary tasks out of the way, performance successes start to occur. The team becomes an important factor in the person's career and begins to warrant more time, effort and concern.

---

[2] Jon R. Katzenbach and Douglas K. Smith, *The Wisdom of Teams,* (Boston: Harvard Business School, 1993), p. 65.

♦ <u>Phase III-- Real</u> teams: Improving performance feeds on itself, and the team coalesces. Members value their team and identify with its successes. They increase their attention to team wishes.

♦ <u>Phase IV-- High-performing</u> teams: Only a few teams grow to become high-performing teams. A high performing team becomes a preoccupation with its members. The momentum developed by the importance of the challenge facing the team wraps everyone into the team activities. Members of these teams describe not only team successes, but personal peak experiences.

> *John Scully, the ex-Chairman of $8 billion Apple, explained the radical restructuring the company had to take in 1993. He said that every major computer company had restructured in the previous 18 months to reflect the rapid changes in the marketplace. There was no way to keep up through normal change processes.*

When conditions are appropriate, teams go through the development described above, and then dissolve. The conditions include an organization challenge, adequate resources, and an appropriate culture.

♦ An <u>organizational</u> <u>challenge</u>: Some degree of urgency under- lies the development of teams. The level of urgency can range from a threat to the survival of the firm to the need to show indications of continual improvement. An organization that is used to being a winner generates an intensity for small perfor- mance victories. An organization faced with a rapidly changing environment can generate scenarios of imminent failure, no matter how successful the firm was in the past.

♦ <u>Adequate</u> <u>resources</u>: Resources have to be adequate to encourage a team. Teams have succeeded in survival situations with minimal resources. The key is defining minimal. In many cases, teams start in situations that seem hopeless, but create momentum that attracts the appropriate resources. With some success, for example, outside investors might be attracted. In other cases, teams find resources for projects that companies didn't realize they had. A team finds solutions to inventory or scheduling problems that free up resources the company didn't count on.

♦ A culture that supports an empowered team: A culture that supports the relative freedom of people to work on team projects means authority is not a central value in the culture. Norms supporting empowered positions enhance the development of teams. When an organization can't sustain success in the environment, teams ordinarily can't be supported for long. Whatever the norms of the culture are that support a losing competitive battle, they aren't likely to support successful teams.

Teams in an empowered culture give an organization a major asset in the fight to stay competitive. This next section illustrates why teams evolve and the conditions under which they are successful.

EMPOWERMENT AND INVOLVEMENT

These concepts have played a central role in organization literature for a long time. In Frederick Taylor's days of scientific management, the intent was to deny workers involvement or any degree of empowerment. The illiteracy of the worker and simple tasks seemed to require this approach. The bureaucracy, which still largely dominates government and many private sector organizations, was designed to use people to do a massive number of small tasks reliably. Consequently, empowerment was not required, but modest amounts of involvement were built in. The new-design organization is built for flexibility. Small boring tasks have been automated, and front-line people can be trained and supplied with adequate information to respond to complex problems. Involvement and empowerment are built into the roles.

Frederick Herzberg and others developed the ideas of job enlargement and job enrichment during the 1950s & 1960s. Enlarging a job meant doing more tasks. Enriching a job meant more authority was vested in the job. Enlarging a job is similar to involvement and enrichment is similar to empowerment.

♦ **Involvement** means being asked to be a contributor in significant organization processes and systems. For example, being on a team evaluating proposals during the formal planning is involvement. Meeting with the supervisor weekly to make suggestions involvement. Being in a quality circle is being involved. Control-oriented positions can be loosened to allow limited involvement. Rules/policies can be adjusted to increase the amount of involvement. Involvement doesn't necessarily entail empowerment.

♦ **Empowerment** means the information and authority is available to solve problems and make decisions as part of the role description. Approval from the hierarchy isn't needed except for the rare situation. Some examples of empowerment include workers shutting down the assembly line because of quality problems, or a waitress deciding whether to "comp" a bill because of a customer complaint. Sometimes people assume decision-making authority in spite of policies against it. This is part of the informal culture. Stories about stealing, subversion, and other "games" are prevalent in hierarchial, old-design organizations.

Table 4-1 suggests the use of teams is related to the amount of empowerment and involvement in the organization. Starting clockwise is Block 1 with the highest involvement and empowerment rankings. Block 3 has the lowest rankings on these two variables. Block 3 has active strategies to go to Block 2 or Block 1.

Block 3-- Old Design: The old-design organization is based on a control philosophy that limits involvement and empowerment. At the work level, the core technology minimizes human impact and simplifies jobs. At the middle management level, heavy authority relationships and hierarchial responsibilities don't build a fertile culture for teams or real teams to evolve.

At the extreme, the Block 3 old-design organization is tightly controlled and completely top-down. "Leave your personality at the door and do what you are told" is the philosophy. The worst of tyrannical leadership occurs in this setting. Many stories are told about the reaction to this kind of environment. Block 4, in Table 4-1, illustrates the informal reaction to the extreme authority-driven organization. People informally, and secretly, empower themselves. Involvement in the formal organization is low. People get together for protection. These informal groups might conspire to "get" a supervisor, or to sabotage an assembly line. Perhaps workers secretly organize a union to protect them from the tyranny of the hierarchy. Not all Block 4 organizations are as bad as that, but they all develop informal organizations that empower workers to some degree.

Block 3 to Block 2: This represents an active strategy for many old-design companies. Leading firms have been experimenting with ways to

	High Empowerment	Low Empowerment
High Involvement	1. Only exists in new-design organization. Authority and information is in front-line positions. E.G. Teams, self-managed teams, groupware.	2. Conditions are possible in old-design organizations experimenting with ideas like Quality of work life (QWL); Quality circles (QC).
Low Involvement	3. Exists in informal setting in old-design organizations.	4. Conditions likely in old-design hierarchy with emphasis on simplified front-line tasks and limited group activity.

TABLE 4-1
Involvement and Empowerment
in the Organization

involve workers for several decades.[3] They know they must have the front-line worker on their side to compete effectively. However, a company that is organized by a union, and/or it has a negative climate from past abuses has a challenge-- it is difficult for them to create a changed environment. General Motor's core auto assembly plants are organized by the UAW. Because of distrust between management and labor, the contracts are difficult to change. Eastern Air Line's workers and management created such a distrusting culture that the unions representing their workers stopped cooperating. The company failed in 1991.

There is little opportunity for official empowerment in the controlled setting. Using limited delegation of authority to project groups can

---

[3] In the 1930s, Chester Barnard suggested an upside-down pyramid that involved the workers. Kurt Lewin's University of Iowa studies on democratic leadership impacted many organizations. Sears was noted for its flat structure in the 1940s. McGregor's Theory X and Theory Y ideas are part of this heritage. Rensis Likert of the University of Michigan led the way in highlighting the power of the organization that utilized its employee base fully.

increase involvement. Although the discretion is limited, the results can make a major difference in the old-design culture.

Committees, quasi-teams, and project groups are useful in changing the culture of old-design organizations. They are more useful in middle management projects than on the assembly line. Middle-managers often have more flexible roles than front line workers. Machines require people at all times. A middle manager can pull away from a paper flow for a while to attend a group meeting. None of these jobs are designed for people to work together to complete the task. Work teams aren't possible.

Quality Circles (QC) are collective efforts used in core technologies. They can be relevant to new-design technologies, but are used mostly to increase participation in old-design core technologies. It doesn't require any change in the design of the core technology to implement QC. Workers voluntarily meet after work every week. The meetings, lasting about an hour, focus on minimizing scrap, rework, and warranty problems. These are general problems affecting their units.

Human Resource Departments provide quality circles with facilitators. QCs meet too few hours to work through their own group problems. Facilitators help deal with problems associated with the underlying group or problem solving processes. Group problems include rationalizing differences of opinions, selecting problems, or how to lead. Problem solving include deciding how to collect information, determining the next step, deciding whether a stage of the process is complete.

Quality circles are used for involvement, but don't empower people. In old-design situations, they are used as a powerful suggestion system. Most of the work is done through functional departments with the approval of the supervisory system.

Block 4 new-design organizations are designed for increasing response to a changing environment. This requires full use of employee decision making and problem solving abilities. Positions in the front line have authority to deal with the wide array of activities designed into the position description. The intent, contrary to old-design principles, is to optimize the employee talent and energy. The result is a culture that is characterized as high involvement and high empowerment.

The full development of teams are possible. The core technology might be designed for the full use of work teams. In this case, workers in the team are cross-trained to do a group of tasks or all the tasks on the product. At Harley Davidson, work teams assemble most of the motorcycles. At Harley, the team-based assembly line runs parallel to a traditional line. In some situations, teams aren't required for some assembly jobs (e.g. painting). Problem solving teams are formed to solve problems in that unit.

There is wide use of teams at the middle management level. Authority built-in at the front line and electronic communication have diminished the use of middle managers for communication and control activities. Most roles have enough slack time to devote to team projects. These projects are complex enough, and long enough to allow the teams to develop from quasi-teams to teams, and in some cases, real-teams.

Self-Managed Teams: Some teams advance to the stage where they can manage themselves. Self-managed teams have the authority:

♦ To make significant decisions about allocation of tasks within the unit,
♦ To decide how they go about completing their work,
♦ To decide what resources and relationships are necessary to complete the work and to get them.

Self-managed teams are responsible for the timely performance of the task or project assigned to the team in any assessment.[4]

There is a significant shift in the role of the supervisor where self-managed teams exist. The role of the supervisor was traditionally defined as a "pusher," a person responsible for the output of the unit. In the new-design organization, the supervisor cedes performance responsibility to the team. Regular problem solving is also a team responsibility. The supervisory role shifts to a coaching/facilitator role. The self-managed situation results in the supervisory duties being totally a team responsibility. Teams are accountable for their performance. Supervisors become coaches and facilitators. This enables them to support the front-line worker deal with the exceptional problems.

Self-managed production teams exist when the core technology is designed to use teams. Teams in the design process can be self-managed. In batch manufacturing, certain sales situations and combination sales and service teams are possible areas for self-managed work teams. If the tasks are simple and the production line is designed to separate people, then a team strategy will fail.

Volvo designed a unique manufacturing plant where teams put together an entire car and then assess its quality. This is the classic example of a self-managed teams. Digital Equipment Corp. built a new plant in 1981 in Enfield, Massachusetts to accommodate self-managed teams. Three business units have one to four teams made up of 12 to 18

---

[4] For additional information see Chris Lee, "Beyond Teamwork," *Training*, (June, 1990), pp. 25-32.

members. Every team member is cross-trained in all the steps from raw materials to shipping.[5]

Texas Instruments' (TI) defense division has more than 1900 work teams. By the middle 1990s, they intend to make about 50% of them self-managed. TI has a twenty-year history with teams. In the 1980s, TI had pride in their management in the United States. However, they knew they could improve by competing for the Baldrige National Quality Award. TI's role model was their Japanese affiliate. It was the first American subsidiary in Japan to win Japan's Deming Prize, in 1985. The improvements in quality in that subsidiary were dramatic.

TI started to consider self-managed work teams as part of their American strategy. To their surprise, many self-managed teams had simply evolved over the previous 15 years. Their regular culture supported initiative and over-time groups assumed more and more responsibility. When management discovered them in 1989, they simply endorsed the teams, and built on their success.[6]

In practice, many organizations have difficulty with self-managed teams. The major reason is the core technology can't be organized to accommodate teams. Another reason is a control-oriented philosophy limits the authority allocated to the position. A third reason is that the organization doesn't have the support systems that keep a self-managed team on track. With the appropriate structure, systems and culture, the likelihood of a team being formed, becoming successful, and evolving to a self-managed level.[7] The human resource and planning support systems are discussed in this chapter.

<u>Block</u> <u>3</u> <u>to</u> <u>Block</u> <u>1</u>: Because of the major changes required, the movement to Block 1 is called a transformational change. All the key quality systems in Chapter 3 have to be developed along with the necessary cultural changes.

☑ Transformational change is elaborated on in Chapter 7

---

[5] B. H. Proctor, "A Sociotechnical Work-Design System at Digital Enfield: Utilizing Untapped Resources," *National Productivity Review*, (Summer 1988), pp. 262-270.

[6] Presentation by Texas Instruments at the *Quest for Excellence Conference*, Washington D.C., (February 15-17, 1993).

[7] B. Dumaine, "Who Needs a Boss," *Fortune*, (May 7, 1990), pp. 52-55.

Quality Network: Teams in the organization are woven into the core technology and/or they are associated with the quality strategies in the organization. Self-managed work teams are part of the organization of the core technology. The functional hierarchy manages these efforts. Teams that are part of the problem-solving network of the organization are organized separately to solve problems related to meeting customer's needs. Employees take time from their functional duties to serve on unit or departmental improvement teams.

The teams focused on problem solving in organizations are a necessary component of the strategy of continuous improvement. Another component is the quality network which ensures momentum and organization for the quality effort.

Quality networks vary from organization to organization. They often contain teams that parallel the functional hierarchy as suggested in Figure 4-1. This quality network is made up of a quality council and quality improvement teams (QIT). The quality council is made up of the organization's top officers. It is intended to visibly show the organization's commitment to achieving the highest quality. The intensity of the quality program is based on the leadership in the quality council. Each department and unit QIT is responsible to this Quality Council.

This network parallels the functional hierarchy. The quality strategy is driven by this network. The quality council's priorities and power ensure that the quality strategy won't be lost to other strong interests. Thus a manager trying to meet a cost goal can't cut a QIT project. The manager is a member of the departmental QIT, but it is responsible to the Quality Council. The Council is responsible to the overall quality goals.

Unit QITs have some independence in investigating quality problems. Once an organization commits to a quality strategy, the idea of diminishing error, defects and variation becomes the focus. The idea of kaizen, or continual improvement, becomes the core of the organization culture. At this stage the Quality Network isn't threatened by the functional hierarchy. The planning process and consequent plans and objectives reflect the quality priority in business plans.

📧 Chapter 6 details the elements of a **kaizen** culture.

In Table 4-1 the old-design strategy to increase teamwork is likely to increase involvement. This strategy gives the company access to more of the intelligence of its employees, but doesn't touch the fundamental building blocks of the old-design company. The involvement strategy takes the organization from Block 3 to Block 2. A transformation is necessary to go from Block 3 to Block 1. This means full implementation of the key quality systems and culture make over. If an organization is intent on

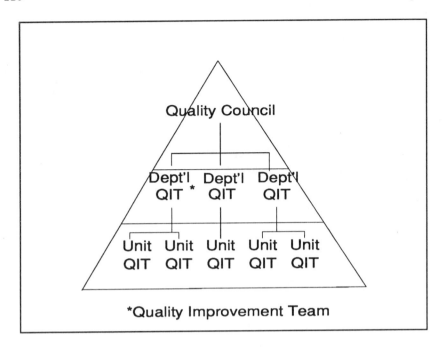

FIGURE 4-1
The Quality Hierarchy

going from the old design to the new design, the team network is one of the approaches that can help. The network gives the developing teams some cover from a still suspicious old-design organization. It creates a forum for quality leadership to emerge.

PROCESS MANAGEMENT TEAMS

When customers deal with the organization, they just know that their order, inquiry/phone call, or complaint mysteriously goes into a "black box" and disappears. The traditional customer complaint relates the number of times their phone call gets shuffled around an organization. The telephone transfers generally are different departments on the paper trail of the customer's order or warranty inquiry. Each department does their part of the transaction without really knowing what other units are involved or the time it takes to do the entire process. This is typical in the old-design organization.

In the customer-focused organization, the five or six departments in the previous example, are viewed as five or six steps in one process. These are cross-functional processes. In the new-design organization there still are functional departments, but they support customer requirements for the entire process instead of doing what is best for the function.

For example, an accounting unit might more efficiently use its personnel in checking credit on customer orders on Friday of each week. However, it lengthens the time the customer order is in the process by up to four days. With the priority of rapid response to customer needs, the accounting unit might have to hire additional personnel, or find some other way of organizing so that credit is checked daily.

The way an organization ensures that process objectives have priority is through managing the entire process. It does that through process ownership and process management teams (PMT). In the organization hierarchy the person that has authority over all the functional units is the process owner. For example, a senior vice president might be process owner of the customer service process. Part of that role is to make sure the customer response objectives are met. To ensure the continual improvement of that process, a process management team is assigned to find and solve problems.

Figure 4-2 illustrates this refinement. The PMT is illustrated as another part of the team network. Thus far, the network has departmental and unit QITs and now a PMT. The PMT is significant because it signals that the organization has a priority on the entire process. In addition, PMTs operate under the auspices of the process owner and the Network, but can be rather powerful. Figure 4-2 shows a PMT with two QITs. This illustrates a number of points about the potential of the network. The QITs were formed because the PMT was working on a complex process problem in several different units. The PMT forms two QITs to work on separate parts of a cross-functional project. For example, a major change in how an order is processed might be accomplished through this process.

Once the QITs have finished their part of the project, they are disbanded. When the project was done, the PMT might disband. This illustrates the power of the team network. It can expand or fold to meet the needs of the organization.

A process owner and process management team are structures that ensure the organization priority on cross-functional process effectiveness.

The team network creates many opportunities for the organization to become more effective. It is an invaluable resource for concentrating resources to deal with problems facing the firm. One of the key areas is in utilizing information about customers. This next section discusses the organization structure in response to customers' needs and satisfaction.

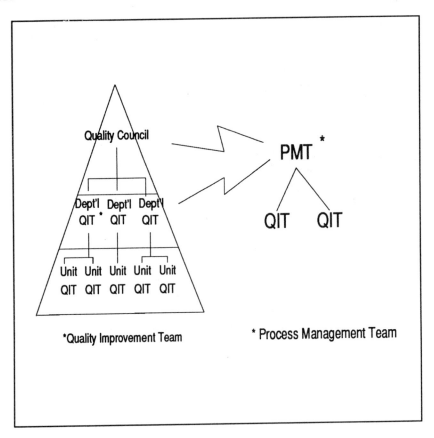

FIGURE 4-2
Process Management Teams

THE CUSTOMER RESPONSE STRUCTURE

The customer is center of decision-making, problem solving, and planning in the organization. Knowing precisely what the customer needs are and being able to translate that knowledge accurately into a product is important. How the integrated core technology is planned is dependent on knowledge of customers' needs, price expectations, and competitor strategies.

The organization builds units that span the organization's boundary to keep up with customer changes. These marketing units research customer needs, respond to customer service demands, and diagnose emerging trends and competitive efforts. Information from these areas is used to respond to immediate needs, feed into key quality systems, and provide base information for the planning system.

In this section, the role of these boundary-spanning units in supplying information to key quality systems is explored. The information has to be communicated, used, perused, and manipulated. The computer enhances this process and makes more comprehensive assessment possible. In a later section the importance of this information in the strategic planning system is explored.

CUSTOMER NEEDS

The product/process design system is important in both the old-design and new-design organization. The significant differences between the approaches are (1) the philosophy emphasizing customer priority, (2) the intensity of communication, and (3) the use of teams.

It isn't enough to have a product. It is important to have the right product, at the right time, at the right price. Adjustments or modifications in the design or manufacture of the product are not acceptable to the firm focused on being quality leader in the marketplace. Because of the intensity of competition, the time lost to miscalculation can be fatal. Concurrent engineering and the expert use of teams increase the translation of customer need information into product or service requirements.

Customer Information: Organizations build elaborate customer information systems to feed relevant information into the organization. Customer information is gathered and processed by special teams of engineers and marketers, or in marketing units. Because of the demands for quality excellence, increasing amounts of information yield new insights for product or service features that satisfy the customer even more. Information about potential customers and competitive information is also useful to the product/process design system.

These units gather data to initiate design of the product or service at the beginning of the cycle. At the end of the cycle, these units measure customer satisfaction. Information from the research increases the probability the product is going to satisfy the customer. Satisfaction information can be fed into the production units to change the existing product. It can also yield insights for product re-design. The following units gather customer and market data useful in product design.

♦ Customer service units rapidly respond to customers' actual or perceived problems. This unit increases or decreases in size depending on the warranty problems consumers have. The more quality designed into the product, the fewer warranty problems. To the extent that organizations intend to inspect, fix, and educate quality, the service unit is large.

Either way, the information collected in the service unit is useful. In the old design, information can be used to correct problems in the current product through building-in additional quality. Perhaps the information causes the organization to increase the inspection intensity, or establish an extensive service facility. As a last resort, this information can be fed to marketers to try to educate people that the product is better than what they think.

♦ Market research provides information on customers' present and future needs. It also investigates the needs of people who are buyers of the product or service, and potential customers of the firm. The investigation is often by a questionnaire that is administered to an appropriate sample of people. The information is analyzed using statistical tools. Follow-up interviews or focus groups might be part of the data collection. Conclusions about tastes, needs, and product characteristics can often be made from this effort. Table 4-2 illustrates the many ways the marketing unit can collect valid customer data.

Computerized data accumulated from sales or service units can be explored for any additional insights. A market research unit might explore this information to see what insights it yields about customer behaviors

TABLE 4-2
Examples of Customer Information Techniques

→ External Demographic Studies
→ Executive Phone Calls to Customers
→ Management/Employee Travels to Customers
→ Customer Seminars
→ Focus Groups
→ Customer Needs Surveys
→ Design Partnerships
→ Customer Beta Sites
→ Industry Association Participation
→ QFD* with customers
→ Sponsored Market Research

* QFD: Quality function deployment tool
ADAPTED from Zytec Application Summary, The Malcolm Baldrige National Quality Award, 19, 1992, p. 9.

and company responses or quality efforts.

In addition to the value of this research to the internal quality systems, it is useful to advertising. The insights into how the product is used yield additional input into what the quality organization tells its potential customers about the quality characteristics.

Field market research is conducted in a variety of way. Surveys, focus groups and interviews are some outside methods of gathering information. Often non-customer groups are targets for field research. Sales people contact customers every day. A large sales organization can quickly gather specific data that can answer a query from a production or design unit.

Observing how a product or service is actually used, versus how the company thinks it is being used might be one example of field research. Observing the product or service in use might result in an insight that a customer couldn't define in an interview or on a survey. Field research is a major source of competitive information. Researchers see competitor products in use. In addition, they hear the perceived benefits as objections to the sale of their own product.

New Product Ideas: Getting new product ideas is a major effort in organizations. Product cycles result in growth in revenue and market share. Being responsive has value to the customer and builds the company's image. The following list suggests ways the organizations gets new product ideas.

♦ Customer surveys can research for customer needs that are presently unfulfilled. This information yields new product ideas. Satisfaction surveys are designed to determine the reaction to an existing product or service. Careful analysis of this data suggests when the customer's needs are changing, or a competitor is meeting the needs better. Federal Express conducts a quarterly telephone survey of 2100 customers.[8] Customer surveys generate a response to present products and generate new product ideas. A professionally designed and administered survey suggests market niches, entirely new market needs, or new uses of an existing product. Deploying information into sales and design units can result in innovative changes being made.

♦ New Process Capabilities yield product ideas when an organization has pride in its technology. Pride is based on employees "psychological ownership" of the processes. Psychological ownership, coupled with a

---

[8]   American Management Association, *Blueprints for Service Quality*, (New York: Amacom, 1991), p. 61.

strong suggestion system, results in new product ideas.

♦ Benchmarking is a major source of new ideas in organizations. Benchmarking is one of the key quality systems in the organization. Briefly, teams of employees scan outside organizations for ideas on how to improve organization. Not only are they scanning how well other firms do their activities, but they also see new product ideas.

THE EASTMAN RESPONSE SYSTEM

Eastman Chemical Company (ECC), a 1993 Baldrige winner, developed a comprehensive customer response system. Figure 4-3 describes the system. Customer complaints/perceptions stimulate the internal system. The company involves customers in survey research or requests for partnerships in internal processes. Field research through customer contacts is another means of gathering information on perceptions. Listening to customer complaints is another function of the customer response system.

All this information is received and analyzed by the appropriate units. If there is any immediate resolution required, the firm does that. The other information is incorporated in the planning system. This changes the way an organization responds to the customer in a permanent way. The intermediate response is build-in to change by improving or changing the process/product. The long-term response is to make comprehensive innovation in process/product.

The Eastman model illustrates the complexity of an organization's response to the customer. Not only is there an active proactive interaction with the customer, but a reaction to complaints is important. This model is stronger because the team network in an organization is active in each of these categories. Key quality systems include partnership systems, product or service design (surveys, contacts), benchmarking, and core technology (all the changes affect it). The intermediate change and long-term response illustrates such concepts as kaizen, reengineering and transformational change. A highlight of the model is the feedback of this information into the planning system.

Chapters 6 and 7 details kaizen, reengineering, and change.

The next section in this chapter illustrates a comprehensive planning system for the organization. Planning is the system by which the organization focusses resources on the changing customer and competitive

FIGURE 4-3
Eastman Chemical's Customer Response System

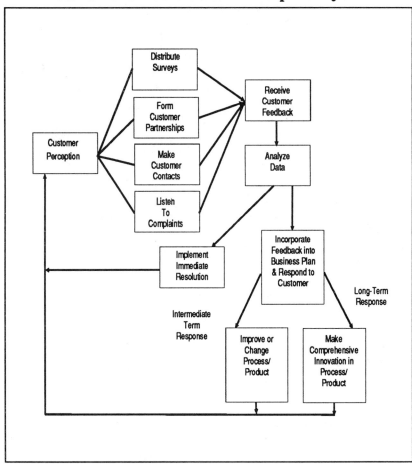

conditions in the marketplace.

ENTERPRISE PLANNING SYSTEM

The organization formally updates its strategies and objectives and sets the course of the organization for as far ahead as the information will support. Every organization is faced with a marketplace of unknown complexity. Trends change constantly and competitors are unpredictable. Internally, the intensity required to sustain any positive momentum is relentless.

Aligning organization resources to the dynamics in the external environment is called strategic fit.[9] To what extent does the planning process get an accurate "picture" of the dynamics of the external environment? Then, how effectively is that picture deployed to the organization in the form of strategies?

One model used for this activity is a SWOT analysis. The acronym SWOT stands for internal strengths and weaknesses (where is the organization now) and external environment opportunities and threats (where is it going). To be successful an organization's strengths have to give it marketplace victories. The quality of Japanese vehicles resulted in marketplace victories. Their strengths included continual improvement norms, strong human resource capabilities, and expert use of labor and suppliers in their manufacturing system.

Table 4-3 illustrates one use for a SWOT analysis. Strengths and weaknesses are arrayed against present opportunities and strengths and future opportunities and strengths. The table asks these questions:

1. What are the strengths and weaknesses of the organization in relation to a firm's current marketplace.

2. What are a firm's strengths and weaknesses in relation to future opportunities or threats?

The first challenge is to address weaknesses that limit success in today's marketplace. Survival is important. Another challenge comes when a strength turn out to be weaknesses in discussing how the firm would address a future opportunity. The strengths of the American organizations in the 1970s turned out to be major weaknesses as the environment changed dramatically in the 1980s and 1990s. Domination of management by finance/ accounting was a strength as long as the customer could buy only American products. The future opportunity was in addressing changing customer tastes with high quality items. With higher-quality alternatives, financial domination became a weakness. Most organizations had difficulty addressing this weakness.

For example, a company with strong distributors might suffer if a customer demands direct delivery and lower distribution costs. An opportunity in the environment can become a threat overnight. An extensive research and development program might be undertaken in

---

[9] Paul Lawrence, "Why Organization's Change", in Mohrmann, Allen, et al. *Large-Scale Organizational Change,* (San Francisco: Jossey-Bass, 1989), p. 51. Also, J. D. Thompson, *Organizations in Action,* (New York: McGraw-Hill Book Co, 1967).

	Current O & T*	Future O & T*
Strengths		
Weaknesses		

*SWOT- Strengths, Weaknesses, Opportunities, and Threats

TABLE 4-3
SWOT Analysis*

response to an opportunity. An innovation or invention by a competitor might make the R&D strategy redundant, and make the company's survival a question mark.

Massive amounts of information are potentially available to deal with this problem. What part of this information is applicable? How should it be organized so it is best implemented?

The success of the new-design organization is that the planning system acts like a lever in changing the organization. Once the formal planning period is over, the plan is deployed to adjust the direction of the firm. As the year goes on information is accumulated about each facet of the plan. These facts adjust the implementation of the plan, and provide small adjustments throughout the year, and the basis for the next year's formal planning events.

The essence of the plan is to develop information about the strengths and weaknesses of the organization in relation to the opportunities and threats in the environment (a SWOT analysis). Strategies are developed that describe how resources can be allocated to exploit opportunities, avoid threats strengths and fix weaknesses.

MANAGING BY PLAN

Managing by plan emphasizes the importance of implementation, or deployment of the plan. Without a planning system that develops sound strategies, implementation fails as well. The formal planning period is a "time-out" period. The organization holds planning events to comprehend everything that is happening. It integrates information already collected in the plan, asks additional questions, and updates the long-term forecast. The active day-by-day collection and analysis of data in the new-design organization results in constant updating of plans made. The Eastman model in Figure 4-3 illustrates the constant updating of customer information.

The process of planning is valued in a new-design organization. There is constant addition of information associated with correcting some weakness or exploiting some opportunity. Accumulating facts that are useful in the formal planning period is a continuous activity. "Catchball" negotiations occur up, down, and across the hierarchy. This interaction has established the issues and collected information by the time the formal planning period starts. The continuous has the effect of reinforcing the long-term context of the organization and disciplining decisions within this context.

Managing by plan recognizes the idea of logical incrementalism.[10] It "binds together the contributions of rational systematic analysis, political and power theories, and organization behavior concepts."[11] This is a recognition of the complexity of the organized world. Nothing is perfect. Many people with good will, working very hard, are going to understand only a small part of what is going to happen in the future. Recognizing this helps the organization develop systems that make it work all the time to get additional insights into the external environment.

> *Hoshin Kanri* is the Japanese name for managing by plan or policy deployment. These terms are used interchangeably. They mean *"pointing direction."* The purpose of *Hoshin* planning is to turn the entire organization in the same direction.
> See B. King, *Hoshin Planning: The Developmental Approach, (Menthuen, MA: GOAL/QPC, 1988).*

THE PLANNING SYSTEM

This complexity is why a firm's planning system anchors any success it has had in the past. Figure 4-4 is a schematic of a more complex planning system adapted from Marlow Industries, a 1991 Baldrige winner. Here is a thumbnail description of that schematic:

> Notice the opportunities and threats box on the left margin and the strengths and weaknesses box in the bottom center. This is the core of the SWOT analysis referred to earlier. This information is embellished with a competitive and portfolio analysis. Combined, this information is a combination of the questions

---

[10] James Brian Quinn, "Strategic Change: Logical Incrementalism," *Sloan Management Review*, (1978), pp. 6-21.

[11] Quinn, "Strategic Change: Logical Incrementalism", p. 18.

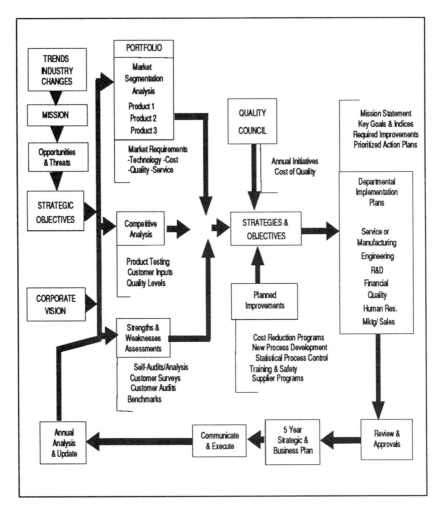

FIGURE 4-4
Integrated Planning

where do we want to go (opportunities and threats). and where
are we now (strengths and weaknesses and assessments of the
product portfolio and competitiveness). The major question
facing the firm is how do we get there. The strategies and
objectives box through the departmental implementation plans
box is the answer to that question. From the review box,
through the communicate box to the annual update box, is the
implementation cycle.

Beyond the overall understanding described above, here are some insights on other activities in the planning system.

In the managing by plan approach, the planning process goes on all the time. Data is being collected, projects worked on, and ideas generated, which all add to the database of information available when the formal planning period starts. Important contributions come from the key quality systems. The team network is a major source of information as it supports the norm of continual improvement. As an example, a firm might dedicate as much as six months, often starting in April or May and ending in September or October for a planning period. The previous year's plan and the new information become the basis for the planning discussions.

♦ Opportunities and threats, in the upper left of the figure, are defined through the lens of the organization's mission. The mission broadly describes how the organization fits into its industry, and meets customer needs.

MISSION

To market vehicles developed and manufactured in the United States that are world leaders in quality, cost, and customer satisfaction through the integration of people, technology, and business systems and to transfer knowledge, technology, and experience throughout General Motors.
Mission of the Saturn Division of G.M.

♦ The databases with information about the company's strengths and weaknesses, competitive analyses and financial analyses, take a long time to develop and are under continual review. Benchmark teams, market research, customer service, and functional and quality problem-solving teams contribute to these databases.

♦ Strategies and Objectives result from an arduous internal process of communications and negotiations in the "catchball" fashion. The confidence of an organization is evident in the challenging strategies and objectives that are set. "Stretch" objectives increase the response of the organization to customer needs.

♦ The Quality Council is representative of the elaborate team infrastructure devoted to pushing the organization to quality leadership. The team infrastructure in a large organization involves hundreds of teams and thousands of employees in problem solving, benchmarking, and partnership activities. They supply much of the input for the planning exercise.

Texas Instruments' Defense Systems and Electronics Group has over
1,900 Quality Improvement Teams. TI won the Baldrige in 1992.

♦ The priority issues box lists the core quality issues in the organization. The strategies targeting these issues have independent standing because they have a direct impact on the goal of exceeding customer requirements. They also are affected and gain importance when benchmarks or competitive analyses suggest these areas are competitive weaknesses.

The model illustrates the importance of quality in the planning process with the independence of the quality council and its concerns. It also exhibits the importance of competitive strategies through the SWOT analysis. Implicit in this analysis is the organization's strategic intent. This is another way of indicating its need to "win" in the marketplace. Komatsu showed its intent by saying they wanted to "surround Caterpillar." The need to win played out in product strategies and marketplace strategies.

QUALITY SYSTEMS INPUTS
This model directly addresses the issue of marketplace realities crowding out quality considerations. They are complementary concerns of the organization. The "cost of quality" results when an organization doesn't meet customer's needs. Costs can be high because of high rework or high warranty demands. High costs of quality results in organizational failure, irrespective of competitor moves. Quality strategies address these costs and thus are necessary for marketplace success.

Figure 4-5 highlights the quality planning subsystem that ensures that quality objectives are inserted into planning process. The quality network power is represented by the boxes "quality council" and "planned improvements." They have equal standing with other business issues in the "strategies and objectives" box.

The key quality systems that distinguish new-design organizations become key elements in the strategic planning process. These are the systems that focus the day-by-day work of the organization when given direction by the planning process. They provide the discipline for the organization to meet the objectives set in the planning process. Each system provides reinforcement for behaviors that support quality performance. As the content of plans change, the systems adjust quickly, and output reflects those changes.

These systems provide the infrastructure for developing objectives and supporting problem-solving efforts. Table 4-4 lists each of the key quality systems and shows how each one contributes to the planning process.

FIGURE 4-5
The Quality Council and Planning

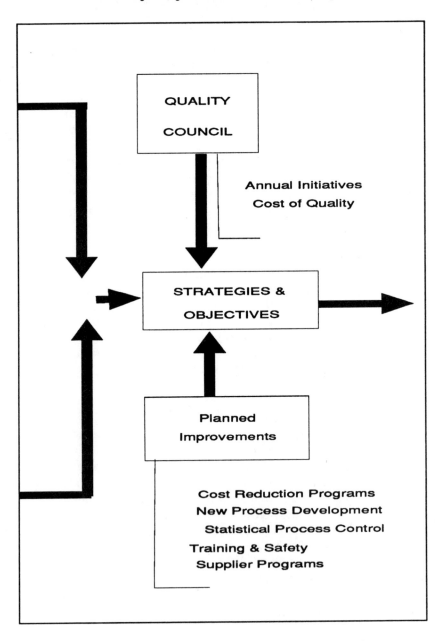

TABLE 4-4
Strategic Planning System Nodes
and Quality Systems

SOURCES OF INPUTS	INFORMATION CONTRIBUTED TO QUALITY PLAN
Partnership system	Teams associated with supplier and customer partnerships are the source of important external information. Audits, surveys, and observations are part of the regular activities of these teams. Information ends up in these databases in Figure 7A: strengths & weaknesses assessments, planned improvements, and departmental implementation plans.
Benchmarking systems	Benchmarking teams generate information on processes in every part of the organization. Information from benchmarking exercises can result in a) challenging objectives for internal units, or b) a challenge to completely reengineer a process. Information ends up in these databases in Figure 4-4: strengths and weaknesses assessments, competitive analysis, and planned improvements.
Product or service design system (R&D)	Teams of design and manufacturing engineers with suppliers and customers characterize the system. Data from market segmentation analysis, competitive analyses and benchmarks all feed this system. As teams progress through development, information is provided to these same databases. In addition, audits of the system are input to strengths and weaknesses. Information from product design teams are integrally involved in competitive analysis, market segmentation, and strengths & weakness assessment in Figure 4-4.
People Systems	The team infrastructure runs throughout the organization. Some teams undertake continual improvement activities within core units. Other teams undertake large-scale cross-functional strategies for the organization. Teams undertake surveys, benchmarks, testing, and segmentation analyses to add data to the portfolio, competitive and strength & weaknesses databases of Figure 4-4. Teams are an integral part of solving the on-going issues in the planned improvements box.
Integrated core technology	An increasingly flexible core technology results from closer integration of components due to partnerships, computer intelligence, and human integration. The effectiveness of all the systems is indicated by the product/ service success in satisfying customers.

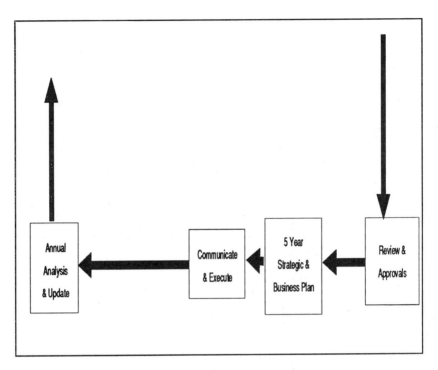

FIGURE 4-6
Managing by Plan

DEPLOYING/ IMPLEMENTING/ ALIGNING

While the formal planning development cycle depicted above is being undertaken, the organization is busy implementing the previous year's plan. Figure 4-6 highlights the implementation cycle. It progresses from the review and approval to inputs into the next formal planning period.

By the time the implementation arrives, reviews and approvals have implicitly, if not explicitly, been given for most actions. This is seldom a problem in new-design organizations. Catchball and negotiations go on constantly during the development of the plan. The Communicate and Execute box represents the tactical activity during the year. Communicating and executing the plan is a large part of the definition of managing by plan.

SUPPORTING SYSTEMS

All systems are interdependent in an organization. They function together to yield sustainable success. Important systems like the team network depend on systems that supply it with people and information. They also depend on systems that maintain their competency like training systems.

Figure 4-7 points out an important set of relationships. Information from the planning system guides the teams. Training and assessment are two subsystems that energize and guide the team infrastructure.

ASSESSMENT AND REWARD SYSTEMS

Assessment systems look at team/individual performance at regular intervals and reports the results to the team/individual and the organization. Reward systems are sometimes tied to this assessment system. The sequence is

1. Objectives are set through the planning system as plans are made. Both acceptable performance levels and timelines are detailed in this system.

2. The assessment system determines whether the individuals/teams/organization have met the intended performance levels within the timeline.

3. If the performance meets expectations then a reward is given.

Organizations have to meet certain performance levels in order to remain competitive. Profitability allows investment and provides the opportunity to accomplish many projects. The question is how to achieve profitability. An important method is to set objectives. Objectives are performance levels to be accomplished within a certain timeline.

Management by Objectives: Management by objectives (MBO) is a system that fits the requirements listed above. This system is used in the old-design organization to focus subordinate behavior toward acceptable results. There are unintended results with this system. The system is more appropriate to individuals and, thus, reinforce the simplified role and minimal communication. It discourages group/team activities because responsibility for performance isn't as easily determined. Pinpointing responsibilities to individuals is a key element of old-design management control philosophy. The MBO system cascades from the top down. With a little variation, subordinate performance levels are dictated by managers

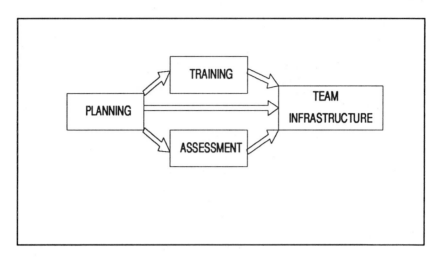

FIGURE 4-7
Supporting Systems

in the hierarchy.

In the new-design organization there is an equal emphasis on meeting objectives. The difference is that the participation level in major systems results in objectives set from below. In addition, when objectives aren't met, it is assumed that there was a system breakdown. The search is for problems in systems. The objectives aren't set to pinpoint individual responsibilities. A successful team network requires individual responsibilities.

♦ Hewlett-Packard (HP) learned its system from Yokagawa-HP, its Japanese subsidiary. It set business objectives for sales, finance, or process improvement through its business fundamentals planning. It reserves hoshin planning for breakthrough improvements. It sets objectives and conduct formal and informal reviews. It also focuses on problem solving during the reviews.[12]

Assessing performance varies between the new-design and old-design organization because of the different balance placed on individual versus team activity, and between quality and profit activities. Table 4-7 outlines the relative emphasis on these variables.

---

[12] American Telephone and Telegraph, *Batting 1000*, (Indianapolis: AT&T, 1992), pp. 77-78.

COMPONENTS	OLD-DESIGN ORGANIZATION	NEW-DESIGN ORGANIZATION
Individual performance	High emphasis	Moderately low emphasis
Team performance	Low emphasis	High emphasis
Overall quality performance	Moderately low emphasis	High emphasis
Overall profit-ability	High emphasis	Moderately Low emphasis

TABLE 4-4
Assessment Systems
Relative Emphasis

♦ Individual Performance: The high emphasis in the old-design reflects the underlying control philosophy. There are individual tasks in the new design, but the emphasis is on finding organizational and system errors that limit performance of teams or individuals.

♦ Team Performance: Teams don't flourish in the control environment. People don't have experience in them, and they don't function continually. Teams are part of everyday life for most people in the new-design organization. The goal-setting and assessment systems complement the teams and the empowered culture.

♦ Quality: Quality is a factor in both designs. It is a primary goal in the new-design organization and is secondary in importance to profitability goals in the old-design firm. The designs of the respective firms dictates the different potentials for achieving and rewarding high quality.

♦ Profitability: The old design's primary goal is profitability through assumption of cost leadership and market dominance.

New-design organizations control internal outcomes and follow marketplace rules to gain share. The new-design organization assumes that quality leads to both profitability and market dominance. The old-design organization assumes stability in the marketplace and the new-design organization assumes a demanding customer and constant change.

The logic in the new-design organization is that overall profitability derives from overall quality performance. Quality performance, in turn, is due to team and individual performances. Teams assume responsibility for accomplishing projects within budget according to the timeline specified in the plan. They are accountable through their functional unit and the quality network, or both.

Once every year Federal Express has its couriers and customer service agents use an interactive, PC-based, job-testing program. The program checks whether these employees have kept up with changes in their job requirements. More technical, or regulated roles are assessed more frequently.

◆ Novell is a leading technology company. It uses teams in most functions. Employees in customer support or technical services are graded as teams. They give a team "report card" as part of their assessment program.[13] Customers and suppliers are polled about team performance. This program is part of the company culture, described as "coopetition." This is a conduction of the words cooperation and competition. It means compete hard and then pull together.

◆ Federal Express, a new-design company, has a modified system.[14] Divisions set objectives within the constraint of the board approved strategic objectives. All objectives reflect the corporation's objectives in three categories: people, service, and profit (PSP). The priority objectives are people and service. Front-line employees are evaluated on performance of these objectives. Their accomplishments are turned into points. The points are then turned into cash based on how well the company does against PSP strategic objectives. If the company doesn't meet its PSP

---

[13] Karen Southwick, "Novell- an Enterprising Company," *Upside,* (May 12, 1993).

[14] American Management Association, *Blue Prints for Service Quality,* (New York: AMACON, 1989), pp. 31-35.

objectives then no one receives any bonuses, including the president. Hourly workers earn extra pay based on performance and improved skill.

Performance rewards are also received by quality action teams (QATs) which are in these forms:

♦ The Quality Success Story Awards are given quarterly to teams for process improvements.

♦ Bravo Zulu Awards are given spontaneously for jobs well done. They can be tickets to an event, meals, or quick cash (about $50). These awards are given about 2,000 times a month.

♦ The Golden Falcon award is given to nonmanagement employees for exceptional service to customers. It is triggered by a letter or phone call from a customer. The award includes 10 shares of stock and a visit from the Chief Operating Officer.

Objectives in the old-design organization: The formal assessment program in the old design is a variation of management by objectives (MBO). This system pins individual employees to specific, quantifiable objectives. Through a formal assessment period, each individual is rewarded based on meeting or exceeding those objectives. The individual is responsible for the results. Evaluations of individual performance against objectives were fundamental in determining promotion opportunities.

The objectives in the old-design organization are some result of the individual's job. The reward is based on meeting this end result. The problem is that people have many ways to meet objectives. Most of these ways enhance their reward at the expense of the unit and organization. Objectives often result in the individual suboptimizing and minimizing those behaviors that positively affect the team, unit and organization. These behaviors are difficult to quantify, and consequently aren't used in objectives systems.

Old-design managers think the objectives system is the only way to root out incompetence. Incompetence isn't excused in the new-design organization. Following Deming, employee failure is thought to be largely a result of inadequate systems or management. The culture, then, is a "no fault" culture. Failure generates problem-solving strategies instead of finger-pointing. Incompetence shows up in the inability to problem solve, communicate with team members, or keep up on the line. In most cases, these people aren't hired. If they are hired, it is difficult to hide, or to avoid pressure. They either leave voluntarily or are asked to leave.

The old-design organization assesses and rewards individuals no matter how much others contributed to that success. The new-design organization emphasizes the team over the individual, thus discriminating against the individual who might "carry" a team. Although this might be an inequity, it is likely that the talented individual can be singled out for promotion or extra reward. First, there are individual functional roles where performance can stand out. Second, a person with good group skills is often rewarded with group leadership. This results in an opportunity to stand out.

Rewards in the new-design organization: One way of giving monetary awards is to accumulate team rewards in individual accounts for quarterly distribution. There are several schemes that formalize the negotiation process for productivity based rewards in organizations. Gain sharing, The Scanlon Plan, and the Rucker Plan are all variations on the same theme. They establish productivity measures for baseline measures. Through an elaborate committee network they negotiate the monetary awards.[15]

Parties, rallies, and awards are part of the quality reward system. Singling out teams in public settings because of an accomplishment is a major feature of the team culture. More than 40% of Granite Rock employees (1992 Baldrige National Quality Award winner) received Incentive Recognition Awards during 1991. Novell has several far-flung operations. Their approach is to have a "Red Rally" week. Executives fly around to such festivities as a Mexican Fiesta in Texas, a beer party in California, and a rally in Utah.

It's unlikely the individualist personality, no matter how talented, could survive long in the new-design organization. A lot of time is spent in team settings. Successful team efforts result in engaged individuals who value their membership on the team. Those individuals who don't value the membership often leave the setting. Many firms spend a long time attracting and hiring people who have good group skills. Nissan's plant in Smyrna, Tennessee, for example, requires people to engage in group activities for weeks before being hired. The intent is to see how the applicants interact with others. The team culture at the plant would be disrupted if individualists who have problems interacting with others were hired.

Criteria for Pay: Market share is an important component of successful competition. However, it is not an end in itself. There are unanticipated problems for companies that reward executives for increasing market share. Protecting market share sometimes forces extraordinary advertising expenses and perhaps foolish capacity decisions. The focus on the

[15] Gary W. Florkowski, "Analyzing Group Incentive Plans," *HRMagazine*. (January, 1990), pp. 34-38.

competitive battle in the short run also causes organizations to miss market changes that should stimulate new product designs. It can result in pressure on the organization to produce quantity at the expense of producing quality.

Market share is important to the new-design firm just like other firms. High-quality product, appropriately priced and delivered correctly, will increase market share. Even at that, the old rules about having the largest market share and the biggest production runs to achieve the lowest cost are being questioned. For example, flexible batch manufacturing made possible by employee improvement, teams and partnering creates the opportunity for smaller runs with more variations. Market share isn't as important in this case.

Profitability is a key element of a successful organization. Unless the outcomes of quality strategies result in profit, they should be reconsidered. By definition, meeting customer needs results in increased satisfaction with follow-on sales. Even strategies parading under the quality banner can be wasteful. The key is quality strategies that result in marketplace success over a long time. Quality strategies don't respond to arbitrary deadlines.

A key question revolves around how to reward employees as the organization becomes profitable. The core of good programs is to reinforce quality projects, while rewarding profits. Recall that there are too many unintended ways to erode quality, by focusing on short-term profit. The trend in executive pay is to emphasize quality efforts.

TRAINING SYSTEMS

Training is the second major system. Training has a critical role in supplying the skills that are necessary to support reliable team decision making and problem solving. Training increases the discipline and increases the likelihood that the team will succeed in meeting their performance objectives. Because training is uniform in an organization it creates, it is, in AT&T Transmission Divisions words, "one from many."[16] This means that employees all speak the same words, use the same tools, and adopt similar performance norms. Because of these commonalities, the teams across and up the organization become aligned to respond to the customer.

Problem-solving tools, interpersonal skills, and functional skills are three levels of training required in the organization. The training intensity required to sustain a dynamic team infrastructure is high. Solectron, a Baldrige winner in 1991, averaged 75 hours of training per

---

[16] *Quest for Excellence Conference,* Washington D.C., (February 15-17, 1993).

year per employee. Its target for 1993 was to be more than 100 hours of training per year per employee.

FINANCE AND QUALITY

Traditionally, American business focused on financial outcomes.[17] For example, a firm might look to achieve an overall return on investment of 20% in five years. With this as an objective, it would set criteria for the allocation of capital to those efforts that promised the highest return. Such a firm would minimize costs, look to increase the marketing strength of the organization, undertake strategies to exploit niches, disrupt competitors, look for synergies and economies and produce for scale. These ideas dominated the planning process. All of these ideas are powerful concepts. It's just that, together, these strategies result in eventual failure in the marketplace. Neither the customer nor quality is featured in the financial model.

This issue is complex for the firm pressured by bankers, financial analysts, and others for bottom-line results. On the one hand, the financially dominated planning process is part of the reason business got themselves in trouble[18] during the post-war period. On the other hand, financial returns are necessary for survival.

The issue comes down to what is the most effective way to achieve a satisfactory bottom-line profit. Minimizing the cost of quality results in lower costs for the product. Higher- quality products or services attract people to buy from the company. This logic suggests that the bottom line takes care of itself. This new-design system can sustain profitability because the systems are present to support the continuing effort. The traditional focus on costs has no relation to customer needs or quality. Cost reduction is an end in itself. Eventually this firm loses.

This analysis is complicated by the fact that some organizations aren't very well managed. In this less than perfect world, many managements lose sight of their goals and get side-tracked. These organizations have continual problems and soon fall behind the competitors. If the organiza-

---

[17] Robert H. Hayes and Steven C. Wheelwright, *Restoring our Competitive Edge,* (New York: Wiley, 1982), p. 19.

[18] The nature of the Post World War II American marketplace led to financial and marketing logic dominating executives. Returns on capital criteria resulted in decisions being made for the shareholder instead of the customer. It resulted in entire marketplaces being abandoned because capital could be better utilized elsewhere. Disruption of competitors became a focus instead of improving quality and satisfying the customer. See James A. F. Stoner, and Frank Werner, *Remaking Corporate Finance,* (New York: McGraw-Hill, 1993).

tion has a tradition of mediocrity, it is difficult to refocus on sustaining success.

This situation exists in new-design as well as old-design organizations. More direct financial control is sometimes legitimate when an organization is faced with survival. These firms lose the confidence of most stakeholders like employees, bankers, suppliers, and investors. The perception of financial action and the results of direct financial control are temporarily required. Any organization, though, that succeeds, requires a combination of quality and business planning.

In the new-design organization, people from finance becomes a member of teams.[19] They help in hammering out the financing possibilities for larger projects. Available financing determines at what pace the organization moves to attain quality leadership. The goals don't change. Decisions are based on how fast quality strategies can be implemented. It's not a question of whether the strategies will be undertaken or not.

Horst Schulze, president of Baldrige winner Ritz-Carlton, illustrated the issue. In 1989, the country was in a recession, and the Ritz was being squeezed as guests stopped traveling. The Ritz-Carlton had an extensive quality program underway. It established a quality infrastructure with teams, extensive training, and an elaborate reward structure. Pressure came from the financial side to cut costs and conserve resources.

The knee-jerk response to decreasing revenues was to cut expenses. The momentum started to build to stop training, suspend the quality initiatives, minimize travel, lay off front-line people, and cut back where it was possible.

> *In the new-design* organization, the human resource function is very *important as a support for the team network. Teams, from benchmarking to product development, often contain people with different functional skills and widely varied backgrounds. Teamwork describes the interpersonal skills that support an effective team.*

Schulze told managers they could cut costs wherever they wanted as long as guest treatment didn't change. They could lay off anyone they wanted, including themselves, but they couldn't touch the human resource budget or the quality manager. The Ritz-Carlton not only survived the recession, but won the Baldrige in 1992, just as the economy started to get on its feet.[20]

---

[19] D. Berlant, R. Browing, and G. Foster, "How Hewlett-Packard Gets Numbers It Can Trust" *Harvard Business Review.* (January-February, 1990), pp.178-183.

SUMMARY

The new-design organization is built on the five key quality subsystems. These subsystems are integrated through an elaborate infrastructure. This chapter examined the infrastructure that supports the efficiency and effectiveness of these sub-systems. Three components of this infrastructure were highlighted in this chapter.

The first component is people systems. People systems are a number of subsystems that focus on directing the energy and talent of people on the organization's tasks. The means of getting the level of commitment required in the high quality organization is through empowerment. Empowering people requires a complex set of subsystems.

The team network is a complex subsystem that focuses energy on improving the organization. The framework of this network is the formation of teams at every level and in every unit to solve problems. They have some autonomy to solve problems as they come up. The separate network reporting to a quality council provides the authority and resources for this problem solving. These teams are called quality improvement teams (QITs).

Process management teams (PMTs), feature a strength in the new-design model. They highlight the importance of the horizontal process even if it crosses functions. If a customer process doesn't meet quality, timeliness, or cost requirements, PMTs are formed to solve the problems. Depending on the complexity of the challenge, they might form their own departmental QITs. These QITs could have experts to help with sub-projects.

The problem-solving teams focus on improving processes. The work of the organization is producing a product or delivering a service. These jobs were traditionally designed to simplify tasks and minimize human participation. Some production and service jobs are designed so that work teams are required to do the task. Every member knows multiple jobs, and successful performance requires teamwork. These teams are often largely self-managing.

The second component is customer information. The customer drives the action of the new-design organization. The new-design architecture complements the need for diagnosing customer needs and operating on

---

[20] Speech by Horst Schulze, *Quest for Excellence Conference*, Washington, D.C., (February 15-17, 1993).

that information. Information about the client is often obtained by a marketing research function in the organization. Through numerous techniques customer needs are determined and the information fed into product or service design systems, team networks, and into the planning system. These systems differ from the old-design in that the focus is on gathering information to improve product or service quality. It is not gotten to improve the marketing of the product.

The third component is the planning system. The planning system is the formal system for methodically collecting information about the organization's strengths and weaknesses and plotting them against environmental opportunities and threats, both current and future. Out of this analysis strategies to effectively win in the marketplace are evolved.

Managing by plan captures the planning system and emphasizes the implementation of the information. The point is that day by day the addition of information subtly adjusts the strategic plan. The system, then, emphasizes action and flexibility through constant implementation of these changes.

Business planning and quality planning are often at odds in organizations. Business planning traditionally has been denominated in costs and returns on investment models. Quality is denominated in the need to continually improve it. Quality is perceived as too expensive in the logic of the finance function. This traditional rivalry is discredited in most leading firms. Finance plays a team role in financing those strategies that help the organization achieve quality leadership in the marketplace. The planning model in the chapter illustrates the combination of business and quality planning.

◆◆◆

POINTS TO PONDER

1. If most everyone agrees that quality is important, why is vision so important in the quality process?

2. Why would self-managed teams have been so successful in the implementation of quality programs? Is there a message in this conclusion?

3. How have you seen infrastructure or organization help or hurt quality attempts? What could be done to make infrastructure more supportive of quality or other improvements?

Please see additional questions at the end of the reading.

◆◆◆

READING

Preston Trucking's Journey

"Becoming world class" is a journey for some firms, for others its only a dream while many others don't even think it. For those on the journey, the possibilities are exciting. Doing the right things and doing things right consistently is the reward. The successes are contagious. Not only is it fun to be on the journey, but winners attract winners.

The difficulty is that getting into the class of firms that are "on the journey" is difficult. People and organizations develop in uneven ways. They aren't always honest. They develop internal activities that look good and sound good, but they contribute more to the players doing them than to organization performance. Bottom-line there is a little too much finger pointing, a little too much ego, and a little too much authority/punishment to be on the journey.

Sometimes the charlatans know the language of the world-class organization. However, it doesn't take long to determine who is genuinely on the journey and who is a pretender. The difference is in the stories they tell, and the length of time they have been trying to achieve journey status. Stories don't lie. Stories about customers; stories about difficulties; stories about victories, and so on.

Will Potter is CEO of the Eastern Shore's Preston Trucking Co. Preston was on the journey to being world class. Potter says "...everyone knows the importance of being on that journey."

The journey's success in the last decade has been the result of a combination of strategies. The first was finding the right competitive strategy to help a small Eastern Shore carrier survive a massive change in a highly unionized industry as it went through deregulation. The second has been to build a good organization that could sustain success. This strategy is complex and involved several concomitant efforts. One strategy is building an organization characterized by high-performance systems. High-performance systems are those that involve people to improve quality.

Another critical strategy is building a culture to support a world-class transportation company. Culture is a function of beliefs, values, and expectations. The way organizations formalize these values is through powerfully establishing the organization vision, mission, philosophy, and commitment to excellence.

Potter powerfully uses vocabulary right out of business school leavened with the hard fought stories showing how the strategies were implemented. There was nothing more difficult than establishing a new culture at Preston. Dismantling an old reinforcement system and establishing a new one is the most difficult chore a management has. It takes lots of time and the victories are more akin to a "three yards and a cloud of dust" football strategy.

Running through the entire process is the notion of trust. It takes a long time to earn the trust of the employees. "Walk the talk" is the key. However, it is more than a cliche. "Trust is based on integrity, competency, and consistency in communications." The idea of "heart" is important at Preston. Potter says, "If it doesn't truly come from the heart, it doesn't mean a darn thing."

These are the "soft" concepts with which most managements have trouble. For these ideas to mean anything they must have an impact on the marketplace. The connection is the basic belief that "The respect that Preston earns from its customers depends on the actions and conversations of each associate."

"Associates" are what Preston calls its workers. Employees work for others, while associates work with each other. According to one associate, the difference is "an employee punches in and leaves his mind at the time clock. An associate punches in and brings his mind with him."

The organization's philosophy articulated a work environment where people have "respect, interesting work, and an opportunity to develop their skills and abilities. They want freedom on the job and recognition." Pre-1980 Preston supervisors motivated their employees through the use of negative reinforcement and punishment. This was a typically "tough" management they thought necessary to match the Teamster aggressiveness. Post-1980 supervisors were trained to communicate in a positive way and were supported by an increasingly sophisticated organizational reward system. Examples include an extensive system of group celebrations and individual recognitions.

The performance system was slowly integrated into the environment to become the Preston management process. Internally the improved relationships create the willingness to help the firm continually improve. For example, they get about 7,000 suggestions a year for improvement from their 6,000 employees. Over 75% of these suggestions get implemented.

Preston created an organization that can sustain winning market strategies. Developing a strong set of values and a philosophy that supports a strong employee base is a key component of their effort. A statement Potter made about leadership characterizes a major strength of Preston's: " Leaders care for their people. That means they have to listen, have to listen emphatically. They have to listen to understand... rather than to be understood."

4. Can you find evidence of all five key systems in the case?

5. What elements of the supportive infrastructure are evident from the reading and what elements can you infer?

◆◆◆

CHAPTER 5
THE SERVICE INDUSTRY AND QUALITY

◆◆

The objectives of this chapter are:
1. To compare and contrast the service and manufacturing models.

2. To illustrate the complexities of the service organization.

Key words introduced in this chapter:

QAT- Quality		Technology
Advisory Team	Value	Profit chain
Intangible	Delight	Internal service
Optimize	Service design	Employee
Tangible	Attitude	satisfaction
Facilitators		Customer retention

◆◆

INTRODUCTION

> *"That person buying the tickets is our bread and butter and we don't forget it."* Red Auerbach, GM of the Boston Celtics.

Service is a major sector in America's economy. Sixty million people work in an industry with about $3 trillion of the Gross National Product in the private sector. Government adds another 30% to the employment. The more complex the international economy, the more services are needed to address problem areas. Legal, accounting, and education are some of the professional service organizations that parallel retail stores, financial institutions, and not-for-profits. Service organizations add to the competitiveness of organizations and support a high standard of living. These organizations are similar because they don't manufacture a product.

Table 5-1 illustrates the difference between manufacturing and service organizations. One primary difference is that products are tangible, and services intangible[1]. Another is that the manufacturing system is relatively closed, and the service system relatively open. The message of the past two chapters was to use the key quality systems to open up the closed system of the old-design organization to increase its adaptability to rapid market place changes. The work of the service chapter is to use the quality subsystems to manage the boundaries of the service organization more closely. This is likely to increase the reliability and flexibility of the service firm.

TABLE 5-1
Comparing Manufacturing
and Service Companies

MANUFACTURING	SERVICE
Products are transformed from materials. They have physical dimensions and attributes, take up space in inventory, are depreciated, and often wear out. Products can be evaluated against specifications and criteria.	Services don't exist until they are provided at the call of the customer. They take up no space, can't be inventoried, and have no shelf life. Service quality is evaluated against satisfaction of the customer.

The challenge of business is to organize to deal effectively with customers. Customer standards are usually vague, transitory, and situational. Identifying and controlling the factors that govern standards is very difficult. The challenge of service is translating customer needs such as timeliness, cleanliness, and friendliness into service standards.

Historically, both manufacturing products and services were sold on benefits. Service was categorized as a variation of manufacturing. Many service organizations used the manufacturing model approach and profited by it. The fast food store epitomizes the service use of the manufacturing model. Make the hamburger efficiently, with low skill and minimum pay, and then market it heavily. Fast food outlets like McDonald's and Burger King concentrate on manufacturing meals. Sears used a similar philosophy in managing its stores during the 1970s and 1980s. A cost focus and

[1] Theodore Levitt, "Marketing intangible products and product intangibles," *Harvard Business Review,* (May-June,1981), pp. 94-102.

an attempt to optimize sales through the stores resulted in little growth in sales. Sears went from the #1 to the #3 retailer in the country. The factory focus resulted in a typical old-design strategy. Staffing in the stores declined from 70% full-time professional employees to 70% part-time employees in a decade. This paralleled Sears' decline in retailing.

Marketing in these old-design organizations is considered a communications challenge. Educate or manipulate the public's view to buy the product or service. The product or service in this case is a given. Marketing and operations don't talk to one another. They each have their own job to do. For example, advertising is considered a creative exercise, quite separate from the mundane organization world. Sales closes and gimmicks fill books. They aren't related to the quality of the service. Sales and marketing are an end in themselves.[2]

The service sector has been characterized as yielding primarily low-skill jobs. Many of the jobs in the service are not low skill. Further, even these low-skill positions are going through a radical change. According to Leonard Schlesinger, following the manufacturing model is no longer effective.[3] Modern service organizations realize that empowering front-line positions results in satisfied customers. The manufacturing model for service organizations no longer works well.

The quality revolution and a more sensitive customer are major reasons that the model is shifting. Even more subtly, the service organization is being studied and new ideas are emerging. The competitive advantage in the service organization is no longer as clearly the low-cost, high-volume organization. Instead, it lies in the organization that is the quality leader in the market place. How the service is delivered from the front-line person is the major issue. For example, modern medical clinics advertise the ability of patients to select, to talk with, and question their own doctor. This counters the problem of being visited by faceless individuals in medical factories, whom one gets to know through their bill.

> **"The most** important thing to know about intangible products is that the customers usually don't know what they're getting until they don't get it."
> Theodore Levitt. "Marketing intangible products and product intangibles". *Harvard Business Review*, (May-June, 1981), p. 100.

---

[2] Al Ries, and Jack Trout, *Positioning*, (New York: McGraw-Hill Book Company, 1981).

[3] Leonard Schlesinger, and James L. Heskett, "The Service-Driven Service Company." *Harvard Business Review*, (September-October, 1991), p. 71.

Another major factor is that competitors often offer the same products or services. In this day of instant communication, any innovative product or service will be copied quickly. To get a competitive advantage, firms look at the delivery of the product or service. The service component is the difference. New insurance products, new cleaning devices, an innovative menu, and a different way of pricing savings instruments will all be coopted by competitors rapidly. Feelings of satisfaction on getting a product with the right features, at the right time, and at the right price is what counts.

As a measure of how difficult it is to manage service excellence, Federal Express was the first company to win the Baldrige National Quality Award in the service category. This came in 1990, three years after the first award. The Ritz Carlton Hotel and AT&T Universal Card were named in 1992. In the Baldrige's five year history, no service company qualified in three of those years.

VALUE IN SERVICES

Like its manufacturing counterparts, newer service organizations have adopted a new model during the last decade or so. This one shifts the emphasis from financially optimizing assets to satisfying the customer. The emphasis has shifted from emulating old-design manufacturing to making the core technology flexible, highlighting the key role of the front-line employee and accentuating customer satisfaction.

Service standards are increasing because customers are increasingly sensitive to quality. The accent is now on meeting the customer's needs. The focus has shifted from efficiently manufacturing service items. It now depends on a more flexible model that focuses on responding to a more quality sensitive customer. The system has moved from the closed-system logic of the old-design organization to the open-system ideas of the new design.

All organizations have variations on customer service. At the base, they all are designed to satisfy their customers. Whether service or product, they have to ask their customer if the services met their needs, and they were satisfied. Davidow and Uttal define service to mean "all features, acts, and information that augment the customers' ability to realize the potential value of a core product or service."[4] Karl Albrecht[5]

---

[4] W. Davidow, and B. Uttal, *Total Customer Service*, (New York: Harper Perennial, 1986), p. 22.

[5] K. Albrecht, *At America's Service*, (Homewood, IL: Dow-Jones-Irwin, 1986).

defines quality this way. Quality is "a measure of the extent to which a thing or experience meets a need, solves a problem, or adds value for someone."

> *"Customer Delight"* is the term used by the Universal Card Division of AT&T to express its focus on the customer. Delight implies exceeding customer expectations.

Davidow and Uttal talk about augmenting the customer's perception of the value of the service. Albrecht's definition features the customer's need satisfaction. Together, they mean that the quality criterion is what the customer perceives, rather than what the provider offers. An advanced level of quality could provide capabilities the consumer had not thought to expect. This should speak of a perceived high level of satisfaction (such as exceeding the expected).

Much of the concept of quality has to do with value, the recognized worth of some attribute or object. The mission of any organization is concerned with creating or adding value for some customer. The technical core adds value by transforming or converting inputs into outputs. However, value only exists when it is recognized in the market place by customers; whether as buyers, diners, audience, or clients. Customers are the final arbiters of value. Value is being identified as a byword of the 1990's. Quality organizations are the adders and creators of value.

Quality processes are directly related to value. The value-added approach can be either explicit or implicit.

    1. Explicit value can be measured, converted to dollars and cents, and can be clearly defined or visible.

    2. Implicit value is not easily converted to currency and is related to perceived performance needs or image.

At the consumer level, there have been growing indications of dissatisfaction with the treatment of customers and clients in services, banking, transportation, and health-care, among other sectors. In fact, the Business Week cover story of November 11, 1991 stressed quality, service, and fair pricing as the keys to selling in the 90's, and hence, value.

QUALITY POINTS

The quality points were introduced in prior chapters. Table 5-2 lists the five places that an organization can put quality into its service. In the organization determined to meet/exceed customer needs, resources are

TABLE 5-2
Building Quality into Services

QUALITY POINTS	SERVICE ORGANIZATIONS
Design it in	Heavy emphasis in new-design to meet changing needs and constant revision in service items.
Build it in	This is the delivery of the service itself. The customer is part of this setting. The front-line person is a major player here. A dinner is served; advice is given.
Inspect it in	Inspection occurs during the delivery of the service. This function is minimized in the new-design setting. In the old-design, inspection was used in these ways: close supervision monitored behaviors and made routine decisions; telephones were monitored; or service delivery was videotaped.
Fix it in	In the new-design organization, the warranty is 100% satisfaction guaranteed. The service is replaced, no questions asked; a carpet is replaced; credit is given; a meal is cooked over.
Educate it in	Telling a customer about additional benefits to a satisfying experience is the new-design approach. The old-design approach is to convince a person that the service was great, no matter what their experience was.

allocated to designing the service carefully and the appropriate systems to deliver the service flawlessly. This strategy limits the need to allocate many resources to inspecting, fixing or educating.

Many organizations work hard to design quality in and think through delivery barriers. For example, the Ritz-Carlton Hotel builds-in its quality so they don't allocate major resources to supervision, fixing, and service recovery. Its particular customers won't come back if the Ritz makes errors or creates an uncomfortable atmosphere. Because of this approach, every front-line employee can cancel up to $2000 of a guest's bill on their own authority to solve a problem, no questions asked. The supervisor has the same authority up to $5000.[6] This is equivalent to the unconditional guarantee of some manufacturing firms.

This proactive system puts pressure on the company's ability to deliver the services its guests expect, flawlessly. They learned how to listen to the client and translate those needs into a close relationship between the front-line employee and the physical aspects of the hotel. "Bugs" Burger Bug Killers, or BBBK, has an unconditional guarantee that illustrates confidence in how it has designed and built quality into the core technology.[7] The four provisions of its guarantee are: 1. you own nothing until all pests have been eradicated; 2. if you are ever dissatisfied you'll receive a refund up to 1 year of the company's services and fees for another exterminator of your choice; 3. if a guest spots a pest BBBK will pay for the meal or hotel room, and second send a letter of apology, and pay for another meal or hotel room in the future. If authorities close the store due to roaches or rodents, BBBK will pay all fines, lost profits, plus $5000.

The famous catalog retailer L.L. Bean's guarantee is "100% satisfaction in every way." A customer gets a refund, a replacement or a credit upon return of the product, at their discretion.

KEY QUALITY SYSTEMS IN SERVICE SETTINGS

The key quality systems were introduced in Chapter 3. They are required to respond to the changing environment demand for more

[6] Presentation at the *Quest for Excellence Conference,* Washington D.C., (February 15-17, 1993).

[7] Christopher Hart, "The Power of Unconditional Service Guarantees," *Harvard Business Review,* (July/August, 1988).

flexibility. The new orientation is a communications-rich environment of teams, supplier, and customer partners that can rapidly adapt to changes. The open system logic increases the intensity of management.

The five systems apply to the core technology of a service or manufacturing firm. Production in manufacturing is comparable to delivering a service. There is one major difference. They can make, inspect, and fix the product before the customer takes delivery. A service is generally made and delivered right in front of the client. Feedback from the customer is immediate because they are participants in the making of the service.

The following list examines the immediacy of feedback in service situations.

♦ Was the haircut (service) good or bad?
♦ Did the consultant solve (service) the problem?
♦ Was the meal (service) good or bad?
♦ Did the loan officer deal with you fairly?
♦ Did the plumber fix the pipes and leave the area clean?

The immediacy of the customer to the delivery of the service (core technology) affects the interpretation of the five key quality systems. Table 5-3 defines each subsystem in the service context. Many of the systems are more active given the nature of services.

The next section expands the impact of each quality system on service quality.

BENCHMARKING

Benchmarking means compares all internal organizational processes with those of excellent organizations. Benchmarking entails highlighting key processes, searching for companies, within or outside the industry, that have world-class reputations, measuring performances, and improving the internal process. It is an objective, stable and dynamic process. The underlying process is a component of the continual improvement (or kaizen) process of the organization. From a systems perspective, it is another means of managing the boundary of an open system.

Many firms get ideas on how to improve from other firms. Often, though, it comes by chance from a story picked up in the press or from a street story heard by a sales person. Without a formal mechanism for measuring processes and determining the validity of data, this approach is unlikely to have a long-term effect on the firm's performance. Benchmarking is proactive, while this latter approach is reactive.

For example, the Ritz Carlton benchmarks product/ service quality,

KEY SYSTEMS	SERVICE ORGANIZATION EXAMPLES
Benchmarking	Benchmarking world-class processes becomes a major effort because of the constant competitive pressure in service operations.
Service or Product Design	Service firms face shorter and shorter life cycles of their service putting a pressure on the design unit to continually improve the support system quality and delivery of the service.
Supplier partnerships	In many service businesses, suppliers work as partners in developing proposals and delivering services.
People systems	People systems are important in service and manufacturing in the new-design organization. In service, the front-line person is the service. The level of competency in people systems becomes critical.
Integrated core technology	The service core needs to empower participants by providing resources on demand to the front-line employee, supplier partners, and customers.

TABLE 5-3
Key Quality Systems

customer satisfaction, supplier performance, and internal operations. AT&T Universal Card benchmarks three types of organizations: key competitors, best-in-class companies in industry, and world-class companies with similar processes.

Stew Leonard's is a famous grocery store in Connecticut. They own a bus. The reason for the bus is to take groups of twelve employees on

"One Idea Club" field trips. They'll drive as far as 400 miles and go to a competitor's store. The employees fan out to find one area of the store that outdoes Stew Leonard's. Suggestions are then made about how to do it better at Stew's.

SERVICE DESIGN

A service firm is, by definition, around customers all the time. The service process is conducted with customers. This immediate feedback is an invaluable source of new ideas for innovating existing services or developing new services. The service design system has to design quality in the service itself, with the internal support systems.

Michael Dell is the <u>wunderkind</u> pioneer of telephone microcomputer sales. Dell Computers grew dramatically during the 1980s and early 1990s. Its offers innovative products direct to the public. Naturally, he has imitators selling computers direct to the customer. Most of them achieve modest success and then fade away. Dell says his advantage is that he tracks the comments, requests, and complaints of the thousands of customers dealing with his firm every day. Analyzing customer comments and troubles results in constant innovation in his product line and service offerings. Dell's service design process is intimate with the actual delivery of the service.

The Ritz-Carlton offers its service in the hotel itself. The physical design of the hotel is critical to the final delivery of the service. Designers go through a rigorous planning exercise to make sure the hotel can please the guest and allow easy interaction between staff and guest. The Ritz's Hotel Opening System evaluation improved from a 2.1 to 3.9 (on a 1-5 scale) from 1989 to 1991.

The "10 foot rule" is taught as part of an associate's training at Wal-Mart. Greetings have to be given to associates or customers when they are within 10 feet.

SUPPLIER PARTNERSHIPS

Wal-Mart's service plays out in the store. Goods are stacked and readily available. Part of the design of the service product that Wal-Mart offers is the just-in-time purchasing program. It ties suppliers directly into Wal-Mart and supplier warehouses. The information network that connects the pieces of the quality/value chain is critical to its success. The company has just installed a high-speed, enterprisewide local-area network, which lets it communicate more volume and faster between suppliers, stores, and headquarters. Not only will this allow more store-to-supplier connections, but also applications like multimedia computers for training purposes.

Federal Express delivers packages overnight with an extensive, highly automated, air-land core technology. Customers sending packages are suppliers to the service business. Fedex gives about 10,000 of its biggest customers their Powership computer system. This system prints airbills and shipping labels, tracks and confirms package delivery, and receives invoices automatically.

Sometimes construction firms develop partnerships with key subcontractors to write a proposal for a construction project. The trust level has to be high because any information leaking outside would hurt their chances to win the contract. In another service situation, physicians will sometimes take a supplier (non-physician) of a key piece of operating equipment into the operating room with them to respond to technical emergencies. The supplier has key technical information and user experience that makes him or her a useful partner during the operation.

PEOPLE SYSTEMS

The success of a service organization depends on the effectiveness of the front-line employee in dealing with the customer. Supported by information and empowering physical supports, the front-line employee is likely to succeed in selling and delivering the service. The complexity of a real-time delivery system requires constant adjustment. The team infrastructure develops enough problem-solving power to solve the problems in balancing the delivery and improving it.

For example, the Ritz-Carlton places emphasis on the extensive orientation, training certification, and daily line-up meetings in addition to a quality improvement teams network. Repair people and bus drivers work largely by themselves. The continual pressure for ways to increase the organization's competency and improve its problem-solving capability is high. Though employees aren't in natural work teams, they can form quality improvement teams for certain projects. Suggestion systems and reward systems (e.g. employee of the month) can focus the energy of these front-line employees on quality improvement.

The team infrastructure at Federal Express is extensive.[8] Federal Express has a quality assurance department at the executive level. Each business unit has its own quality administrator. The Executive Quality Board groups key executives, while the Quality Advisory Board includes business level people. This integrates the quality effort horizontally. Quality Action Teams (QAT) are work level teams formed to improve process. Corporate QATs are permanent and are assigned to each

[8] American Management Association, *Blueprints for Service Quality*, (New York: American Management Association, 1991), pp. 65-70.

indicator of quality. Other QATs are under the guidance of the quality administrator or facilitators.

One of the significant elements in service quality is education and training. Once strategies have been put in place, the execution of those strategies requires the orientation of personnel to the new culture. One of the top organizations in training is Motorola Corporation, the 1989 Baldrige winner.[9]   Motorola University teaches many courses, from orientation to basic robotics. They taught the equivalent of 102,000 class days to employees, suppliers and customers. In modern, computer-equipped classrooms, instructors use cases, simulations, and experientials as their primary teaching tools. They calculate that $1 in training yields $30 in productivity.

Learning can take place in many locations and in classroom settings supported by a wide range of electronics. Using PCs and interactive multimedia programs, companies can make a realistic and effective learning experience right at a person's desk. An interactive computer program asks for constant feedback which engages people and increases learning. Multimedia approaches increase the stimuli through a combination of verbal, pictorial, and graphic media. Together, interactive pedagogy and multimedia approaches together results in an intensive learning period for a trainee. Andersen Consulting uses such a program to teach part of a demanding course on consulting skills. They still use the non hitech teacher in a classroom for a portion of that effort.

*"...**The accessory** departments do an average of 25% of their total yearly volume just in the two months of November and December... Proper staffing and having a crew of service oriented, excited, intelligent, knowledgeable, volume-driven salespeople, will ultimately determine your success."*
Nordstrom, *Holiday Planning Guide,* 1991.

Table 5-4 illustrates the view of Zeithaml, Parasuraman, and Berry about the attitude shift required for improving service quality.[10] These represent the core components of some of the courses on customer service offered by companies. The column on the right describes a rather traditional set of attitudes of a rather defensive person with moderate expectations. Shifting their attitudes to those expressed in the left column

---

[9] Ronald Henkoff, "Companies that Train Best," *Fortune,* (March 22, 1993), p. 62.

[10] V. Zeithaml, S. Parasuraman, and L. Berry, *Delivering Quality Service: Balancing Customer Perceptions and Expectations,* (New York: Free Press, 1990), p. 16.

TO	FROM
Being excellent	Being good enough
All employees have customers	Some employees have customers
Quality in everything	Quality of products
Right every time	Mistakes are inevitable
Quality is my concern	Quality is someone else's concern
Continuous improvement	Quality improvement
Management involvement	Management support
Team energy	Functional isolationism
Recovery- opportunity	Recovery as a problem
Service system design	Service is shapeless

Adapted from Zeithaml, Parasuraman, and Berry, *Delivering Quality Service...*

TABLE 5-4
Attitude Shifts in Service Training

requires intense training and consistent supervision, teams, and leadership.

INTEGRATED CORE TECHNOLOGY

In a manufacturing system, a product can be fixed until it is delivered to the customer. When the service product is made, it often takes place in front of the customer. It is showtime and customers are immediately unhappy if the show is a flop. When the consumer comes to the hotel, or restaurant, or bank, or auto agency, there's no time for practice. The medical operation has to be done right every time. Sometimes the product is a presentation and sale of an intangible item in the customer's home or over the phone. The delivery area can be in those or a number of different locations.

Information technology supports the flexibility built into the physical components like inventories, machines, personnel, and customer service records. It allows decision making based on current information. This, in turn, optimizes processes governing the components. Information supports front-line employees by giving rapid response to information requests. The design of the stage complements the needs of customers. It is also designed to enhance employee service.

With a complementary physical setting, the Ritz-Carlton centers all its employee activity around the customer relationship. The company trains its employees around the theme of "Ladies and Gentlemen serving Ladies and Gentlemen." The successful delivery of the service assumes the design of the core technology is precise: rooms are made up right, meals are world class, security is tight, supplies are available when needed, supervisors are supportive. This is an example of designing-in and building-in quality. It means having to say "I'm sorry" very few times.

The 24 hour access to hotel personnel available from each hotel room has heavy information system support. The Ritz approach requires highly personalized, face-to-face and telephone contact with the customer. Cooperation between units like housekeeping, front desk, security, and the concierge is assessed regularly and improved continuously. The information system connects past requests a guest has made for towels, room temperature, extra facilities, wake-up times, etc. to the present reservation so all those have been taken care of when the guest arrives.

Nordstrom is a world class retailer of women's clothes.[11] It has an attractive physical store layout. The inventory is large but continually adapting to the sales and preferences of the community. The inventory system is computerized and allows flexible adjustment of the inventory with supplier partners. Moreover, the design complements the entrepreneurial boutique environment where individual buyers and managers feel they have their own store within the store. The underlying design element is to empower the managers and sales associates so they respond confidently to each customer.

At the core of its strategy is a respect for the customer. The steps leading to the sale are managed intensely to ensure customer satisfaction. Nordstrom feels its service is a value-added part of the business. By focusing on excellent service, it maintains margins. People will pay a premium over what a discount store might charge because Nordstrom offers service through quality personnel and large selection.

The reward subsystem of Nordstrom's people system supports its sales intensity. Sales quotas, sales contests, and competitions between stores focus the energy. In addition to pay and incentives, top salespeople get monthly recognition as All-Stars. Continuous high sales results in acceptance into the elite Pace-Setters. Promotions to supervisor and manager positions only come from within the store. These actions contribute to the prestige of the front-line position in the store.

Training is a standout feature. The University of Nordstrom in Southern California emphasizes the Nordstrom philosophy of selling and

---

[11] Susan C. Faludi, "At Nordstrom Stores, Service Comes First-- But at a Big Price," *Wall Street Journal,* (February 20, 1990), pp. A1, A16.

supervision. There are in-store training programs as well. Nordstrom has courses on softer behavioral areas that focus on the employee's self-image. This includes writing self-affirmations on how proud they are to be Pace-Setters. The Nordstrom employee is intensively trained at the skill, cognitive, and behavioral level.

Nordstrom employees take full charge of their clients. The culture has an entrepreneurial cast to it. They write thank you notes to customers. They deliver products to customer's homes, travel to other stores to get sizes or colors, and help determine inventory needs. This makes each sales-person appear like they are in-charge of their own business.

The constant emphasis on the service and customer satisfaction goals conditions this sales system and is the key to minimizing the problems usually associated with intense selling systems.

> "...*So what's* our challenge? Customer service, that's right. Are you thinking about doing those extra little things?... You know, you're the real reason for Wal-Mart's success..."
> From Sam Walton's pep talk at Memphis store #950. John Huey, "America's Most Successful Merchant," *Fortune,* September 23, 1991, p. 54.

JOB-EXPANDING TECHNOLOGY

In modern service situations computer technology is an important enabler of excellent service. As the computer becomes more pervasive in homes and organizations, its impact on how tasks are accomplished has increased. The PC originally gave individuals power on the desk top because productivity tools like spreadsheets and word processors were useful. Now computers can be connected by local area networks (LANs) and telecommunications to people world-wide. The amount of information at the frontline is staggering. These networks and supporting software increase the capacity of organizations to collect and analyze data and communicate it for decision making and problem solving purposes.

The organization structure required to meet the needs of the changing environment is very complex. Along with other new-design features, it is communications intense. Communication links among individuals, units, and teams anchor the management-by-plan, the problem-solving teams, and the delivery of the service. Communication links are an integral part of any empowerment strategies. Different time and place limitations are no longer problems. A person in a different place can be part of meeting or respond to a memo at a later time. If everyone is in the same place at the same time, a traditional meeting can be held.

Technology is used in organizations in a variety of ways to enhance the communications and problem solving necessary to meet customer needs. Here are some examples.

♦ E-Mail is simply the ability to type a message and send it to anyone connected to the local area network. It is used in companies to ensure that messages are delivered and to provide a record of the attempt.

♦ Groupware is software that supports group problem solving. People in different locations, at different times, can work on a single project using spreadsheets, word processors, and other productivity tools. The software keeps tabs on who contributes what at what times. It can undo mistakes automatically. Team projects, then, are available for work at a person's desk, at home, or for conference room meetings.

♦ Scanners in grocery stores develop databases that yield information on customer buying habits, tally up inventory requirements, and free the clerk to be friendly with customers. Connecting the store computer with the supplier's computer to transmit information is called EDI (electronic data interchange). Sales scanned at the register can result in electronic orders for replacement stock.

♦ ATMs (automated teller machines) automate routine bank transactions. This leaves the branch available for higher-value-added financial transactions.

♦ The Ritz-Carlton has an automated, repeat guest program named COVIA. The reservation comes in from a travel agent. It logs into the COVIA program to see if it is a repeat guest and becomes part of the hotel's reservation records. This guest is sorted out on a Daily Guest Arrivals Report that goes to the Hotel's Recognition Coordinator. The Recognition Report is given to employees at the line-up prior to each shift. When the guest arrives, employees will recognize him or her by name.

♦ AT&T Universal Card has an extensive customer information system called U-WIN. Through their own terminals, employees can query for any customer record. There are three databases in the system: for prospective applicants, for card member accounts, and for calling card accounts. AT&T Universal Cards has a customer services data access system that taps these databases. When employees are servicing a customer or selling a service they have complete access to whatever information they need to complete their task.

♦ Another card service builds expenditure profiles of customers. Uncharacteristic purchases might mean a stolen card. A broken pattern might suggest replacement of this customer's card.

♦ Smith & Hawken's is a direct-sales garden equipment company. It has grown dramatically. Its representatives are experts on the equipment. They are trained to be enthusiastic and colorful on the phone. When a customer calls and makes a comment, the representative can insert that comment right on the account screen. Every week these comments are collected, put into a report and given to each employee.

♦ Many businesses' core service is an information utility. Compuserve is a bulletin board for microcomputer owners. Dun & Bradstreet sells credit information electronically or in hard copy to millions of customers. PHH's automobile leasing business is an information utility service. Information is infinitely expandable, sharable, and substitutable.

THE PROFIT CHAIN

Table 5-5 is a model of the profit chain. The first column lists the key variables that result in profit for the company. Simply reading down the list of variables is a good picture of the causes of a profitable organization. The second column describes the relationships between variables. The following discussion illustrates how this model describes a successful service organization:

> Good internal service support (IS) is a major factor satisfying employees (SE). Satisfied employees stay loyal longer (ER). With a stable, satisfied, front-line employee it is likely that a service will be reliable and professional (SQ). If the service quality is high then the customer is likely to be satisfied (CS). Satisfied customers are likely to be loyal customers (CR). With a large group of steady and reliable customers (CR), the expenses associated with attracting with replacing dissatisfied customers are minimized. The result is that marketing expenses are focused on growth of the customer base. All this means that profit (P) is higher.

Of course, not all firms do everything right like the previous description suggests. Some organizations, for example, haven't designed quality into the service very well. This translates into poor IS and SQ. When IS is low, the ES will not be high, and employees won't be loyal (ER). Even more insidious, the service itself will just meet minimum customer needs. This has a damaging impact on CS and the possibilities of getting the customer to buy this service again (ER). Because of the expense of having to market more heavily to make up for low CR, P is always low.

INTERNAL SERVICE SUPPORT/SERVICE QUALITY

The IS and SQ variables make up the core technology of the organization. They result from a service R&D effort. Table 5-2 discusses the designing-in and building-in quality (Table 5-2) processes in the organization. A well designed internal support service, IS, refers to

♦ the design of the core technology with technology that empowers the front-line employee and

♦ the development of powerful people subsystems like teams, selection, rewards, and training.

Profit Chain	Relationships
Internal service-(IS) support services	If IS is designed well the impact on ES is positive.
Employee satisfaction-(ES)	With empowering IS, ES increases, positively reinforcing IS and improving ER.
Employee retention-(ER)	ER is positively correlated with both SQ and CS.
Service quality- (SQ)	SQ is the service act and results in CS.
Customer satisfaction-(CS)	If CS is high then CR is likely.
Customer retention-(CR)	CR is key to increasing organization profit.
Profit-(P)	Results from ER, SQ, CS, and CR. It has a positive impact on ES.

Adapted from L. Schlesinger & J. L. Heskett, "The Service-Driven Service Company," *Harvard Business Review*, (September-October, 1991), p. 149.

TABLE 5-5
Service Profit Chain

Service Quality, SQ, is the service itself. The quality of the service depends on a stable employee base. Employee satisfaction and good internal support services support employee stability. The quality of the service elicits two results:

♦ customer satisfaction or dissatisfaction which determines whether the customer returns, and

♦ information on customer needs which provides feedback for organization changes.

Customer satisfaction is a major issue in organizations. Even the best organizations have difficulty sustaining CS. The degree of satisfaction is subject to the perception of the customer. Customers are the final arbiter, and perceptions are based on a changing base.

> *"If you're not serving the customer, you'd better be serving someone who is." This quote captures the focus on the customer in leading service organizations.*
> Karl Albrecht, *Service America*, (Homewood: R.D. Irwin, 1985), p. 106.

In diagnosing falling sales a company has to determine the source of the problem. It's possible to do most things right and still miss the sales. Some examples include: a good service promoted poorly; a TV show scheduled on the wrong night, or with the wrong lead-in; a good retail store in the wrong mall. These conclusions are difficult to derive without information from the customer.

Customer information results from data collected from the interaction around the sale of the product or service. Information from the customer about satisfaction with the product or service determines refinements in existing operations and improvements in future designs. It can pinpoint specific limitations from features in the product or service to mastery of delivery details.

Product and service offerings can be copied easily by competitors. A firm offers a unique bank product, life insurance policy, new meal offering, or training program, and some competitor will soon have a similar offering. What can't be emulated easily is service. Wal-Mart, Home Depot, and Nordstrom's are three retailers that have had unparalleled success since the 1970s. They learned early about the importance of front-line personnel and making continual improvements. Other companies try to copy the physical design of the leader's stores and copied their policies and still failed to attain the success. Front-line service is difficult to copy. Like Michael Dell's successs story, the leading stores learned to take customer information and adjust their service and product offerings continually.

EMPLOYEE SATISFACTION/ RETENTION

Services are delivered by front-line people. Research shows a strong correlation between customer satisfaction and retention of front-line employees.[12] A stable group of employees delivers the service more confidently. A Sears study suggested that stores with low turnover of front-line personnel had higher customer satisfaction than stores with higher turnover. In a successful organization, the front-line employees are satisfied and confident. Customers notice and come back for more service because of this fact. James L. Heskett said that in successful organizations "... management shows it's aware that the health of the enterprise depends on the degree to which core groups of employees subscribe to, and share, a common set of values and are served by the company's activities."[13]

Besides the costs in customer satisfaction and retention, replacing front-line employees is expensive. Merck & Co. estimates turnover costs them 1.5 times the salary of the position. In 1989, Sears Merchandise Group had 119,000 sales jobs turned over. At $900 per position in recruiting and training costs, the total tab came to $110 million off the bottom line.

Mickey Mouse marketing is a tongue-in-cheek comment on the excellent marketing of the Disney Corporation.[14] Marketing at Disney is part of everyone's responsibility. It is an example of the fact that every role in the organization has responsibility for customer attraction and retention. They have a traditional marketing department. It has certain technical skills for addressing part of the marketing function. Like Karl Albrecht's quote, every person from the janitor to the behind-the-scene technician serves a final customer or serves someone who does serve that customer.

When an employee signs on at Disneyland or Disneyworld, they are cast members in the 'show'. Disney portrays customer service as a show (quality of service, QS). For example, policemen are Security Hosts and monorail drivers are Transportation Hosts. Both on-stage and back-stage employees are well trained (at Disney U.). Whether back-stage or on-stage, their job, every minute, is to help the guests enjoy the park. This is an example of support services (ES).

Support systems include constant communication. Disney writes to

---

[12] Schlesinger and Heskett, "The Service-Driven Service Company," p. 76.

[13] James Heskett, "Lessons in the Service Sector," *Harvard Business Review,* (April-May, 1987), p. 120.

[14] N. W. Pope, "Mickey Mouse Marketing," *American Banker,* (July 25, 1979).

its employees all the time. A professional newsletter includes bulletins and promotions. There is an extensive exit survey for all employees, including summer employees. This is one part of their strategy to retain employees (ER). White-collar managers all spend a week on the grounds selling popcorn, cleaning up, or selling tickets in a program called cross-utilization. This is designed to keep managers in touch with the customer. Disney has achieved unparalleled employee satisfaction and consequently retention (ES and ER).

SERVICE QUALITY

In the airline business, one seat on an airplane is much like any other. It is passenger service quality that makes the big difference in the treatment by front-line personnel. This includes situations on board the aircraft, at the ticket counter, and at the baggage area. The international airlines's challenge is complex. That seat is traveling at 500 mph, at 33,000 feet in the air. The passenger is likely to be in that chair for most of about 13 hours. What has to be done to ensure the traveler's complete satisfaction with the experience?

Jan Carlzon, President of Scandinavian Air System (SAS), coined the term "moments of truth" to describe every time an employee interacted with a customer[15]. He estimated that some 50,000 moments of truth occur daily as SAS personnel interact face to face with customers. Carlzon said, SAS is not the airplane, or the airport gate, or the overhaul station. It is the contact between the employee and the passenger.

The "moments of truth" occur when the customer, consciously or unconsciously, has a need and looks to an employee or the physical facilities for a solution. The moment of truth is successful if either the design of the physical facilities anticipated those needs, or the service plan provides anticipatory human intervention.

Dedication to customer service may take many forms. The notable organizations try to give the customer something extra. This means exceeding the expectations of customers. For example, at Stew Leonard's celebrated food store in Connecticut, the WOW factor is used to make the shopping experience fun for the shopper. Leonards uses live bands, overstaffed checkout stands, food samples, and friendly robots to provide the extra experience of satisfaction.

A carved inscription on a three ton rock in front of the Leonard store says it all:

Rule 1: The Customer is always right!

---

[15] Jan Carlzon, *Moments of Truth*, (New York: Harper & Row, 1987).

Rule 2: If the Customer is ever wrong, re-read Rule 1.

Incidentally, the sales volume per square foot for this store is ten times the average for stores of this type. Customer service does pay off.

CUSTOMER SATISFACTION & RETENTION

Zeithaml, Parasuraman, and Berry describe the problem as "the extent of discrepancy between customers' expectations or desires, and their perceptions"[16] of the quality of the service. The customer expects certain things and if the organization doesn't meet those expectations then the customer is dissatisfied. Given the range of expectations, the challenge for the organization is to perform at a level that meets all expectations.

The means by which customer expectations are generated include some factors familiar to all of us. Zeithaml, Parasuraman, and Berry[17] researched those key factors to be: word-of-mouth communication, personal needs, experience, and external communications that influence customers' expectations. Friends, consumer groups, and governments help shape service expectations. These play out in visits to stores where service standards are designed to meet such expectations.

When the discrepancy between customers expectations and their perceptions of the service is high, customers act on their dissatisfaction. LeBoeuf[18] cited a study on why customers quit that found:

> 3 percent move away,
> 5 percent develop other friendships,
> 9 percent leave for competitive reasons,
> 14 percent are dissatisfied with the product,
> 68 percent quit because of an attitude of indifference toward the customer by the owner, manager, or some employee.

LeBoeuf claimed that businesses spend six times more to get new customers than to keep old customers. Also, customer loyalty is worth ten times the price of a single purchase, in the average case. These problems add to the credence of headlines like the Time cover that had the customer

---

[16] V. Zeithaml, S. Parasuraman, and L. Berry, *Delivering Quality Service...* p. 16.

[17] Zeithaml, Parasuraman, and Berry, *Delivering Quality Service*, p. 19.

[18] M. Le Boeuf, *How To Win Customers and Keep Them for Life,* (Berkeley, CA: Berkeley Press, 1987).

saying, "Pul-eeze! Will Somebody Help Me?"[19]

There is an old saying in service industries that if customers like the service, they will tell three people. If they don't like the service, they will tell eleven people. So, in the service ball-game, it's three-to-eleven, you win. Failing at serving a meal, or meeting a hotel guest's standards for cleanliness, results in a dissatisfied customer. About half of those customers will tell the service firm about their dissatisfaction. There is an opportunity for service recovery, if the firm is listening. About half of the dissatisfied customers just go away.[20] Disney is effective in bringing people back to its parks. Red Pope says "When a company's customers are happy with the service and product, and find enthusiastic and knowledgeable personnel who are anxious to help, chances are that company will continue to enjoy the lucrative patronage of those customers for a long, long time."[21]

A firm that is doing a bad job with customers might lose 20% of its annual revenue. These customers don't come back. Any increase in revenue the next year has to be built on the 80% of customers who come back. The firm has to woo 25% more customers the next year to break even before an increase.

SUMMARY

This chapter illustrates the distinctive characteristics of the service organization. Organizing for a high-quality service output has some similarities to manufacturing, but differs in many respects. A service is intangible and manufacturing produces a tangible product. Both types of organizations try to design-in and build-in quality versus inspecting-, fixing-, or educating-in quality. Like the manufacturing organization , the leading service organization emphasizes efforts to design-in and build-in quality.

The delivery of the service is in the presence of the customer. There is immediate feedback to any mistakes. Innovations in service delivery are

---

[19] *Time* cover, (February 2, 1987).

[20] Technical Assistance Research Programs, "Measuring and Quantifying the Market Payoff of Improved Quality an Service," Presentation at the Quest for Excellence Conference, Washington D.C., (February, 1991), p. 3.

[21] N. W. Pope, "More Mickey Mouse Marketing," *American Banker,* (September 12, 1979).

likely to be copied by competitors quickly. Any competitor can copy the superficial aspects of a service by just shopping the store or buying the service. Organizing to meet these dynamics is difficult. These facts put a premium on the organization's continual improvement of the existing delivery. In addition, with all the information from customers and benchmarking efforts, the design system is highlighted. New ways of delivering service not only meet higher levels of customer expectations, but confuse competitors.

Satisfaction of front-line employees is correlated with the satisfaction of the customer in high-contact organizations. People systems play a key role in ensuring the satisfaction of employees. They become part of the internal support system variable in the profit chain. The team infrastructure is supported by key subsystems like selecting, training, and assessing.

The integrated core technology is mandatory in service organizations. Being able to respond quickly depends on a confident front-line employee. Confidence comes from training, selection, authority, and information. The core technology's design in leading service companies results in the empowerment of the front-line employee.

Information technology is a key system in empowering front-line employees. The design is only valid if it empowers the employee to deliver a service that satisfies the customer. If the employee doesn't feel a degree of ownership, then the service delivery isn't likely to please the customer.

The service organization is complex and fast-paced. Service delivery timed to meet the vagaries of customer expectations and perceptions is the challenge. The pressure point is the front-line employee. Authority and information are inherent in the front-line position. This gives the organization the flexibility and reliability to be successful. Designing-in and building-in quality results in employee satisfaction, successful delivery of the service, and a satisfied customer. Satisfied customers come back. If the firm's strategies are on target, the profit will be high as well.

♦♦♦

POINTS TO PONDER

1. Why do you think the quality movement has made more visible progress in manufacturing than in service organizations?

2. What is the best way to verify what customers think of the quality they get? Or what quality is to customers?

3. Do you agree with the statement that every person is a customer to someone else? Does this affect a service quality concept?

See additional questions at the end of the reading.

♦♦♦

READING

Thinking Ahead At Marriott

Marriott Corporation is an $8 billion company. It has over 451 hotels addressing four consumer segments: Marriott, Residence Inn, Courtyard, and Fairfield Inn. They have a premier reputation for customer service in all their efforts. In a corporate restructuring, they have been selling most of their large restaurant division over the last couple of years. In addition, they formed a corporation that holds most of their $2.7 billion corporate debt. They appear to be cleaning up the balance sheet for future growth in the service sector.

Marriott, like any major corporation in the 1990s, faces many organization issues. Increasing the reliability of an entrepreneurial culture is one issue. This strategy means making independent units more conscious of corporate issues. Simultaneously, they face the issue of delegating more responsibility to the front-line. This last strategy responds to increasing demands of customers for faster front-line decision-making. They are simultaneously centralizing at the strategic business unit level and decentralizing within the strategic business units.

Decentralizing at the business unit to the front-line has raised a number of human resource issues. The quality of personnel and the skills they have to deal with increased responsibility are two issues. An underlying strategy is to take advantage of current technology to deal with these and other customer service problems.

Marriott has always been competent in its use of information technology. But they have never been close to cutting edge in the use of technology either. Like many companies, the operating side hadn't learned to fully use information technology as a competitive weapon. Bill Marriott has always asked what he was getting for the investment in computers. This CEO cost concern evolved to the current question, "what is the role of information technology in Marriott's goal to be the premier hotel chain?" The challenge is taking a company with an entrepreneurial atmosphere and a moderate value on the role of information technology to the cutting edge or maybe leaping the cutting edge in information technology. Survival might depend on it.

As this issue plays out, according to Ed Kraus, then head of Marriott's Management Information Systems (MIS) unit, there are some organizational problems that have to be faced. One such issue addresses planning in the organization. The planning threshold for most business strategies is about three years out. Introducing new technology requires an understanding of what the corporation is going to do in five to seven years. The lead time is required because of the high cost and complexity of information technology.

Today's emerging technologies might be the standard in another decade. The investment in computers, telecommunications equipment, software and people can, on the one hand, increase the firm's competitiveness at a point in time. On the other hand, if the kind and level of information technology adopted by the firm is leap-frogged by competitors, the firm could be in serious trouble. This is one reason why the five to seven year technology question is so important. Kraus says, "If Marriott, or any corporation, is going to be preeminent they have to be planning for technology investment that far ahead".

The needs and wants of customers in hotels are constant and satisfaction has to be immediate. Customer contact is what Jan Carlzon of SAS airline calls "moments of truth." Whether a passenger in an airline or a hotel customer, there are thousands of moments of truth where the company has to respond or risk losing a customer. The leading companies meet most of these moments of truth with competent and attentive personnel and an elaborate infrastructure. During the 1990s this infrastructure is characterized by advanced information technology. The ability to get information to the frontline through networks of personal computers is unparalleled. Multimedia training facilities increase the comprehensiveness and flexibility of the training available.

In an established organization like Marriott, the problem is beyond the vision of responding to more customer needs in a more timely way. It includes changing present ways of behaving to new ways of behaving. It means changing internal processes and upgrading people skills, literacy, and language.

An example of the challenge internally is Kraus's own information system unit. It is a major service unit inside the company. Its customers are the business units. However, Kraus's unit, like most MIS units, were developed in the old centralized bureaucracy managing the corporate mainframe. This history stands in the way of adopting the new distributed personal-computer based information processing. The common name is client/server processing. Further complicating the MIS transition, strategic business units are taking the lead on the development of needs for this new technology.

The MIS unit finds it needs new skills. Kraus's view is that employees in units like his have to be business people first, and technicians second, in order to be effective. This makes it more likely that information technology will enable business processes to support competitive successes.

The increased standards of service in the 1990s are placing extreme pressure on companies like Marriott. They find they have to respond to increasingly complex service situations with a far more complex infrastructure. At the center of the solution to the response are employees and internal support units like MIS.

4. Apply the service profit chain model from the chapter (Table 5-5) to Marriott. Some of the points are addressed explicitly, and others implicitly. If Marriott is unable to adjust to the need for new frontline empowerment, what is the likely impact on each of the variables in the model?

5. How significant was the evolution of the CEO's concern about the cost of computers to the question about how to use computers for competitive advantage?

6. What aspects of the Marriott case are equally applicable to a manufacturing company?

◆◆◆

CHAPTER 6
PROCESS STABILIZATION, IMPROVEMENT, AND INNOVATION

♦♦♦

The objectives of this chapter are:

1. To understand the role of the problem-solving process and the use of tools in the continually improving firm.

2. To gain an appreciation of the major strategies used by leading organizations to sustain quality products and services.

Key Words introduced in this chapter:

Brainstorming	Information	Subprocess
Change	technology	Activities
Conformance	Innovation	Tasks
Countermeasures	Kaizen	Reengineering
Facilitating	Maintenance	Quality Improve-
Fishbone diagram	Pareto chart	ment Storyboard
Gantt chart	Plan-do-check-act	Upstream problem
Histogram	Process thinking	solving
Infrastructure	Macro	Variance
	Nested	Workflow

♦♦♦

INTRODUCTION

. . . .

Competing at the top levels of the National Basketball Association is very difficult. During the 1980s, the Los Angeles Lakers built a dynasty. They had a number of fine ball players, but two stand out: Kareem Abdul-Jabbar and Magic Johnson. The team became a dynasty in the 1980s, winning several championships and being in contention nearly every year. In order to sustain the dynasty it developed a system of continuous improvement called Career Best Effort. This was a detailed record keeping system that had been refined over the years. They tracked every player's records back through high school. It was called "taking their number." The Lakers used these numbers to judge what the player could do.

Career Best Effort ranked the players in their role against every player that shared that role in the conference. They tried to leverage "subtle improvements versus other high level competitors." They also compared performances historically. Month-to-month and year-to-year comparisons sharpened their understanding of the players' performance. Five trigger points defined the basketball essence of each role on the team. Each player was challenged to improve each of the five trigger points by at least one percentage point. The Lakers hoped that gradual improvement would raise team play another level above their competitors. According to Coach Pat Riley: "We made stretching beyond present levels of success both a habit and a system."

. . . .

The core technology in this example is playing the game of basketball. Winning or losing ball games are performance measures that result from twelve ballplayers working in various combinations of five players who combine to try to score more points than competitors during the ball game. Championships result from winning divisional and conference contests. The Lakers won the championship five times during the 1980s.

The Lakers are a world-champion team that uses measurement to sustain their domination of the league. Companies use the same approach. For example, Motorola is a world-class manufacturer of electronics. It uses the six sigma level of variance, or less than one error per million, as its standard of excellence. To attain these levels, Motorola measures variance in their processes and constantly problem solves to reduce variance error. The Lakers' Career Best Effort and Motorola's Six Sigma are quality programs that enforce continual improvement through measurement.

Continual improvement, or <u>kaizen,</u> is a major program in leading organizations. In Japanese organizations it goes beyond a program and becomes a philosophy that applies to personal improvement as well as organization improvement.

<u>Kaizen</u> is just one of the organization's strategies to improve. Maintaining the existing core technology is another strategy. Everything deteriorates with use. Maintenance programs check the inevitable decline, but don't improve processes. Innovation is another strategy. Innovation of a process results in a major improvement in performance. Innovation comes from major changes in processes.

These strategies all are focused on processes. Processes run throughout the organization and represent a major change in thinking about organizations. A major criticism of old-design organizations is that emphasis on results often came at the expense of maintenance, improvement, and innovation strategies. It was more important to increase today's output and meet cost and immediate profit objects than to expend resources on improvement or innovation. These strategies turned out to be short sighted.

PROCESS THINKING

This next section elaborates this notion of process thinking. Two elements of processes are highlighted. The first is the idea that everyone has either an internal or external customer. The second is that problems are solved upstream.

> Processes are used to refer to any sequence of activities that has a result. Processes can be macro as in a production process, or micro as in filing procedures. Process is also used to refer to more intangible organization features like a communication or problem-solving process. The term systems sometimes has the same meaning as processes.

CUSTOMER OF CUSTOMERS

This saying means that everyone has a customer and has a responsibility to serve them. Discussion in this section adds depth to the discussion in Chapter 5 about internal customer and quality of service. Normally customer means the final person or business that buys the company's output. However, in process thinking there are a number of customers. One very important customer is the external or final customer. The other important customers are those employees who receive product or paper from other employees. These are called internal customers. The way to look at the organization is that output of a subprocess serves the next customer. That customer has to be satisfied that the input meets the quality requirements of that part of the process. If all the internal customers are served, then the external customer will be satisfied.

The external customer is the primary stimulus for change in the company.[1] These customers want

---

[1] Augustus Donnell and Margaret Dellinger, *Analyzing Business Process Data: The Looking Glass,* (Indianapolis: AT&T Quality Steering Committee, 1990), p. 14.

♦ quality. Does the product or service meet the customer's needs?

♦ reasonable cost. Is the product or service worth what is being charged? Is the price competitive?

♦ timeliness. Was the product or service ready when customer was ready to buy?

Information about customer perceptions of quality, cost, and timeliness is the basis for improvement in the organization. If the external customer is not satisfied, then problem-solving is focused on finding problem areas. The ultimate goal is to meet those customer expectations and improve satisfaction. Each activity in the organization's process is supplier to the next activity in the process, its customer.

In the organization, horizontal emphasis means that every activity is a previous activity's customer. Every subprocess' output goes to an internal or external customer. For example, the inventory unit is the customer of the supplier. The customer of the inventory unit is the production unit, and so on. Each is a customer.

Horizontal versus vertical results: Figure 6-1 describes the situation most organizations face. The normal organization structure is functional organization. The vertical lines represent functional units like manufacturing, finance, and marketing. The vertical lines represent units that are responsible for its own performance objectives. This is represented by the functional objectives at the bottom of the figure.

On the same figure are horizontal lines representing billing, product development, and distribution processes. These processes have objectives listed on the right side of the figure. Process objectives are aimed at satisfying customers.

Imagine two situations:

Situation 1: the horizontal process is cut up into parts that are managed by each functional unit. Each functional unit has the authority to change their part of the process to meet their cost and performance objectives.

Situation 2: There is a process owner that is responsible for the process results. Process management teams use information gathered from the customer and at various points to ensure that

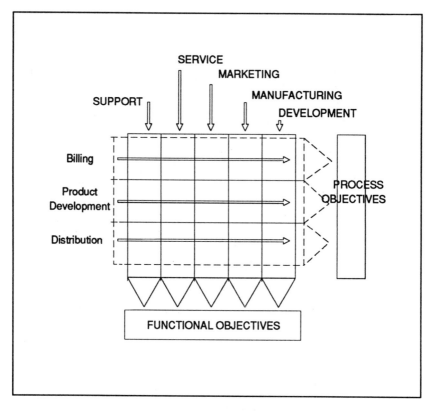

FIGURE 6-1
Process versus Functional Objectives

all subprocesses and activities work to optimize the process performance results.

Situation 1 causes each functional unit to try to do its best to achieve its own objectives. This is what it is rewarded to do. Functional objectives take precedence over process objectives. Indeed, process objectives might not exist. Thus, units might be rewarded for doing a great job and the customer might be dissatisfied. Customer dissatisfaction doesn't come up in the assessment process. Situation 2 emphasizes process results. Process results means serving a customer. Therefore, if the process results in customer satisfaction then employees are rewarded. Functional objectives are of secondary importance, if they exist.

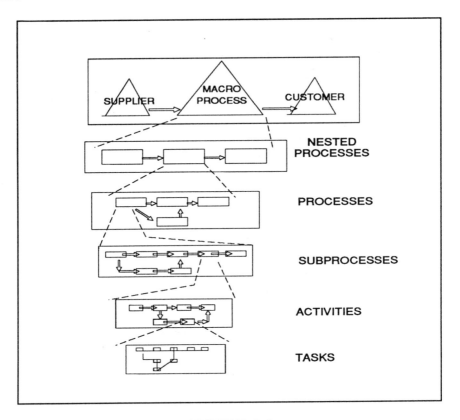

FIGURE 6-2
Hierarchy of Processes

<u>Mapping Processes</u>: Figure 6-2 shows the hierarchy of processes in the organization. The broadest process is called the macro process. It can be exploded into several nested processes. Nested processes are exploded into subprocesses which can be further exploded into a series of activities. Activities can be broken into a series of tasks and further into steps and elements.

From this perspective, the organization becomes very complex. There are several nested processes, each of which can be exploded into subprocesses, activities, steps and elements. In order to methodically deal with this complexity, the organization needs a disciplined approach. The next section talks about the problem-solving approach that supports mapping. The previous section on customer needs for quality, cost, and timeliness is the stimulus that directs the problem-solving.

Figure 6-3 maps a simple organization process. It shows a series of activities resulting in a product or service at the end. There are decisions, databases, and activities.

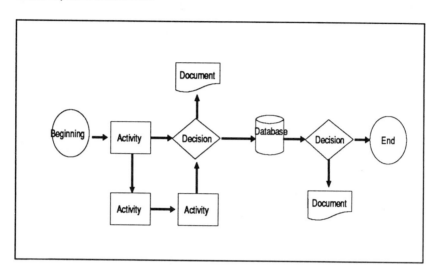

FIGURE 6-3
A Process Flowchart

The process in Figure 6-3 could represent any process in an organization. For example, it could represent an operations process (e.g., assembling a heater; servicing an insurance policy), a marketing process (e.g., steps in assembling an advertisement; responding to customer service), or a financial process (e.g., capital budgeting).

Organizational Processes: Looking at the organization as intertwining processes is the basis for improving the organization. IBM once had a list of nearly 200 processes they thought were core to a leading organization. This list was extreme and IBM narrowed the list which wasn't a useful way of seeing how the organization functions. At the other extreme, a set of four core processes, like designing a product, making the product, delivering the product, and managing customer relationships is clear. This list might be overly broad, however.

British Telecom, a large, international telecommunications company that manages networks, devised a list of fifteen core processes that enables

Four Generic Processes	British Telecom Core Processes
o Designing Products o Building Products o Delivering Products o Managing Customer Relationships	o Direct Business o Plan business o Develop processes o Manage process operation o Provide personnel support o Market products and services o Provide customer service o Manage products and services o Provide consultancy services o Plan the communications network o Operate the network o Provide support services o Manage information resource o Manage finance o Provide technical R&D

TABLE 6-1
Core Organizational Processes

managers to understand the dynamics of their company.[2] Table 6-1 lists both the four broad core processes and the fifteen Telecom processes. The Telecom processes are narrower. They appear, however, to focus on manageable processes and are an aid in focusing attention on the right activity.

PROBLEM-SOLVE ACTIVITIES UPSTREAM

Complex processes are imperfect and need constant maintenance. Assume there is a problem in the output of a process, a--> b--> c--> output. It makes sense to problem-solve activity "c" first, then activity "b", and then activity "a" until the source of the problem is found. This is problem-

[2] Thomas H. Davenport, *Process Improvement*. (Boston: Harvard Business School, 1993), p. 28.

solving upstream. Activity "b" is a likely source for low performance in activity "c".

In a process oriented business, the final customer is the major driver of upstream change. If customers' needs aren't being met, then that information is transmitted upstream into the internal processes of the organization. The problem is identified and solved, no matter how far into the organization the problem-solving goes. The solution to the problem improves process results so the products produced or services delivered are more likely to satisfy customer needs.

The significance of upstream problem-solving is that it reinforces the importance of horizontal processes. The source of the problem can be problem solved without concern for other organization factors like departmental authority, cultural taboos, or personal preferences.

Table 6-2 identifies several divisional subprocesses at Ford Motor Company. It includes examples from the manufacturing, finance, and engineering divisions. For each division a core process is identified along with the measures used to check its performance and the customer(s) of the process. Here are explanations of the processes in Table 6-2.

♦ The power train and chassis are basic parts on an automobile. They manage a large supply chain. In today's manufacturing environment suppliers are expected to be able to send more shipments of parts, just-in-time for their use on the manufacturing line. The pressure to send high quality parts is also important. In this case, the supplier process is in question and Ford is the customer. Ford measures the supplier based on exceptions. How many times did the supplier not send parts on time and not notify Ford in a timely way? How many parts failed during the month? These measures quickly uncover suppliers whose product and manufacturing process have defects.

♦ The accounting office processes travel expenses for its customer, the employee traveler. Employees are reimbursed for the funds they spent on the company trip. It is important to repay this money quickly. The length of time to process the expenses, then, is the measure which can be improved.

♦ The comptroller's office at Ford deals with thousands of invoices. The process has the potential for many errors. In some cases the process is still paper-based. Invoices are double-checked and verified by several people. The company's policy is to pay vendors on time. In addition, it is a key support to the company's preferred supplier program. The measure of effective-

DIVISION	PROCESS	MEASURES	CUSTOMER
Power train and chassis engineering	Supplier sends parts to company	o Time taken to notify of failure to send o Number of failures per month	Company
Accounting	Process travel expense	o Time to process	Employee travelers
Comptroller's office	Accounts payable-paying suppliers	o Errors that result in late payment to vendors	Vendors
Transmission and chassis division	Shipment of components to divisions	o Errors (quantity, wrong parts, wrong location)	Divisions

Adapted from Howard Gitlow et al., *Tools and methods for the Improvement of Quality,* (Homewood, IL: Irwin, 1989), p. 26.

TABLE 6-2
Examples of Processes at Ford

ness of the accounts payable process is simply the number of late payments.

♦ The Transmission and Chassis division is a supplier to its customers, the manufacturing divisions downstream. Because of the just-in-time nature of manufacturing, the demands on internal suppliers for high quality is as high as it is on outside suppliers. Ford's internal effectiveness measurement is the number of errors made.

The measures that determine the effectiveness of these processes provides the information that teams use for their <u>kaizen</u> efforts. Each of these processes contain many activities and the activities contain many steps. Teams analyze the activities and steps until they can improve the results.

STRATEGIES TO IMPROVE QUALITY

Maintenance, kaizen, and innovation are three internal improvement strategies of leading organizations. Understanding them and providing focus and intensity is very difficult. Maintenance is a traditional strategy. Kaizen is the continual improvement strategy discussed throughout the book. Innovation is a positive jump in improvement.

DESCRIPTIONS OF STRATEGIES

Figure 6-4 pictures these three strategies. There are four separate cases illustrated in the figure. They include

Case A: The dotted line showing a declining performance level, on the first stairstep, is a natural state of affairs in an organization. Anything that is used begins to wear down and performance declines. This happens in organizations when people get tired, careless and distracted. Machines get worn and out of balance with other machines. When they are not repaired, performance declines.

Case B: The extension of the horizontal line shows the performance of the organization that exhibits diligent maintenance of machines with scheduled maintenance and timely repairs. Service delivery systems are renewed with meetings, training, and updates. Recording data to track breakdowns is the basis for improvement. This corrective behavior is the minimal action required to sustain performance, but is not designed to improve it.

Case C: The line rising gradually over the flat maintenance line is the performance increase due to kaizen, or continual improvement systems. This gradual increase results from activities like reducing variation, decreasing error or defect rates, and finding improved logistics and activities. The new-design system is set up to create the culture that supports continual improvement.

Case D: The stairstep increase in performance comes from innovations in how organizations do their work. It represents a new way of organizing a process such that more can be done

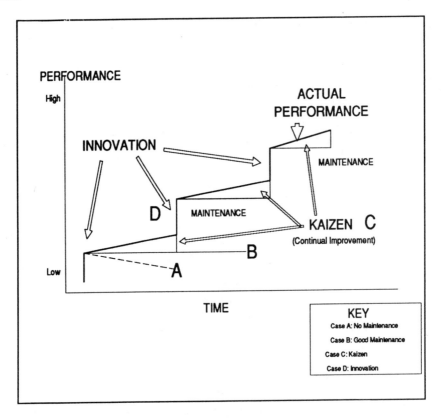

FIGURE 6-4
Strategies for Performance Gain

with less effort, or fewer resources. Reengineering, or process innovation, is one such technique used to innovate a process.

CASE A & B: STABILIZING THE CORE TECHNOLOGY

Maintenance is a critical aspect of any organization. Whether it is Wal-Mart's retailing consistency, John Deere's manufacturing excellence, or Daimler Benz's manufacturing reputation, quality depends on the stability and reliability of existing processes. Maintenance requires an internal intensity to apply resources to sustain the level of performance of all elements of the core technology. Examples of maintenance includes upkeep on machines, computers, and employee training in manufacturing. Also necessary are support of facilities, inventory, sales infrastructure, and people in service organizations.

Maintenance of standards is a functional or a unit responsibility. It becomes part of the individual worker's everyday role. Standards are set by the organization and responsibility assumed in the unit. The focus of maintenance is on sustaining organization standards. As the standards change because the process has been improved, the new standards become the focus of the employee's efforts.

Most organizations with large supply chains are very concerned about the stability of their suppliers. A major means of ensuring supplier stability is the audit of the supplier process. A more general method of ensuring a reliable supplier is through certification. Associations and governments are some of the agencies that audit and certify that a company's product or its operations attain a certain set of standards.

For example, in the United States, the Federal Drug Agency (FDA) requires an intense record and inspection efforts. This assures the public that drugs are produced reliably. The Nuclear Regulatory Agency (NRA) has stringent record-keeping, training, and inspection requirements to assure stability and reliability. The European Community adopted the International Organization of Standards ISO 9000 standards for certain dangerous chemicals and pharmaceuticals. The processes are certified.

☞There is more on ISO 9000 certification in Chapter 9.

Many organizations have extensive quality assurance (QA) units. Those firms with government certifications often have extensive QA units because continuing government certification requires daily records to insure quality. Governments use inspectors to insure a certain level of quality. Inspecting-in quality is the primary mode of insuring the public's safety.

The QA unit takes different forms depending on the firm's basic architecture. Some functions of the QA unit include:

Enforcement: Enforcement of quality in the organization falls heavily on QA units in old-design organizations and those regulated by certifying bodies. This occurs through inspecting goods or chemicals in-process and end-product. In new-design organizations with inspection requirements, the routine quality assurance is achieved by quality improvement teams, with additional support from QA units.

Failure analysis and problem-solving: In the old-design case, the problem-solving is largely the responsibility of the inspectors. In the new-design case, problem solving is largely the responsibility of the teams. The QA unit supports that responsibility by tackling difficult experiments or consulting in unusual problems.

Facilitation: Facilitating team problem solving is largely a function within the transitioning organization. Facilitators become part of the team structure to help the groups grapple with group, organizational, and technical problems.

Education and championing: A QA unit's role in a new-design organization becomes more focused on education and leadership. Teams are in continual need of supportive training. Championing the role of quality leadership through technical competence is another role for QA.

CASE C: KAIZEN-- CONTINUOUS IMPROVEMENT

The infrastructure to support a consistent problem-solving approach includes the team network and such ideas as customer of customers links and problem-solving competence. This infrastructure sustains kaizen. By following a structured problem-solving system, the organization insures a uniformity of good problem-solving efforts. The information that comes from problem solving fuels additional problem solving. As this never-ending problem solving delves deeper into the process, variation decreases, increasing the quality of the output.

At its most elementary level, problem solving consists of the steps of the PDCA cycle- plan, do, check, act. This cycle becomes the framework within which more sophisticated analysis occurs in the organization.

Problem-solving process: Tools are used in the context of a disciplined problem-solving process. PDCA is an acronym representing a problem-solving strategy that drives the continual improvement of processes. The acronym stands for plan, do, check, act. The sequence is:

♦ Plan-- data is collected, problem is identified, and an improvement is planned.

♦ Do-- a pilot project is done, or implemented.

♦ Check-- The results of the effort are checked or evaluated against the plan.

♦ Act-- Then acted on, or deployed, throughout the organization. At this stage the cycle starts again with planning an improvement.

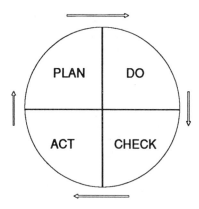

FIGURE 6-5
PDCA Cycle for Problem Solving

Figure 6-5 shows PDCA as a continuous process. It recognizes that problems are never-ending. A solution to one problem simply sets up the planning for the next PDCA cycle. This idea is a principal component of continuous improvement in the organization.

> The PDCA cycle is also called the Deming or the Shewhart Cycle.

A work force disciplined in problem solving is a competitive advantage for a firm. The Japanese took great pride in the competency of their employees. They refined their understanding of the problem-solving process. Using PDCA as a base, the Quality Improvement Storyboard was developed.

The Quality Improvement Storyboard (QIS): The storyboard is an elaborate problem-solving process. Japanese firms originated this comprehensive approach. Since then, many firms in Japan and America have initiated variations on this process. The intent is to insure that problems are fully investigated, solved, and implemented. One sure way of attaining a high level of complete problem solving is to have a work force trained and experienced in a comprehensive approach.

Kaizen pressures result in constant diagnosis which, in turn, results in many problems to address. Establishing priorities, selecting candidates, and determining problem-solving approaches are decisions to be made.

Counter measures to problems are proposed that result in minimizing sources of variation. Permanent changes are proposed and implemented when solutions are successful. The evaluation phase determines what problem area to take up next. The steps automatically support the firm's commitment to continuing improvement.

The QI storyboard originated with the Komatsu Company, a winner of the Deming Prize during the 1970s. Mr. Nogawa, president of Komatsu, named the process QI, for quality improvement. Florida Power & Light adapted the QI storyboard as the basis for their continuing improvement effort.

PDCA Cycle	Plan	Do	Check	Act
Quality improvement storyboard QIS	1. Diagnose 2. Select problem 3. Analysis 4. Propose Counter- measures	5. Results	6. Standard- ization	7. Evalu- ation

TABLE 6-3
Keying PDCA to the Seven Step QIS

PDCA is the generic problem-solving process that underlies the QIS. Table 6-3 portrays the PDCA cycle with the seven problem solving steps of the QIS. This problem-solving process is sufficiently robust to deal with most problems faced in an organization. It will guide the general problem-solving orientation of everyone in the organization. If all employees follow the problem-solving steps, the depth of, and reliability of, problem-solving in the organization will be good.

Table 6-4 elaborates the QIS. For each step the objective and key activities are listed. Using this approach has these advantages:

1) It results in a disciplined problem-solving effort.

2) It is a comprehensive process that has high validity.

3) It is an organization-wide approach to a widely varied set of problems.

Problem-Solving Tools: PDCA and the QIS set the base for the problem-solving capabilities of the firm. This is the disciplined procedure that the team network is encouraged to follow. Along with process thinking, the problem-solving capabilities of the firm set the scene for <u>kaizen</u>.

The final addition to the problem-solving process is a set of tools to support the evaluation and analysis of data. Together with the QIS, the process positively influences the reliability of decision making, problem solving and communication. With these tools, the organization is assured that the employees and teams know how to use data and logic to solve problems.

Tools are used to identify problems, analyze them, and report them. This section briefly describes some primary tools and how they are used in the problem-solving process.[3]

<u>Flowchart</u>. Refer back to Figure 6-3 to an example of a flowchart. It outlines the steps from the beginning to the end of the process. By studying this chart and increasing its detail, loopholes in the process can be spotted which are potential sources of problems. This makes flowcharting a general problem-solving tool for applications from accounting to manufacturing processes.

Flowcharts are used to identify problems through this approach. Managers are brought together to address a process problem. The first step is to draw a flowchart reflecting the way the process actually works. After a consensus on this task, the managers are asked to write a flowchart on how the process should work ideally. The difference between the two charts represents the problems to be solved.

> "The skill with which a company collects and uses data can make the difference between success and failure." Imai Masaaki, *Kaizen*, p. 64

---

[3] For a more comprehensive discussion about tools see Goal/QPC, *The Memory Jogger*, (Methuen, MA: Goal/QPC, 1988), Peter R. Scholtes. *The Team Handbook*, (Madison WI: Joiner, 1991), and, James Evans and William Lindsey, The Management and Control of Quality, (Minneapolis: West Publishing Co., 1993).

TABLE 6-4
Quality Improvement Storyboard (QIS)

STEP	OBJECTIVE	KEY ACTIVITIES
1. Diagnosis	Identify a problem area and reason for working on it	1. Scan for information pointing to limitations in products or processes 2. Collect data to track problem area 3. Look at problem area from many standpoints
2. Selection	Select a problem and set a target for improvement	4. Select problems and identify customer requirements 5. Show impact of problem area using appropriate tools 6. Write a clear problem statement 7. Utilize the data to establish the target 8. Schedule QI story activities
3. Analysis	Identify and verify root causes	9. Perform cause/effect analysis 10. Continue analysis to root causes 11. Select highest impact root causes 12. Verify selected root causes with data
4. Countermeasures	Plan and implement countermeasures	Countermeasures should: 13. attack root causes 14. meet customer requirements 15. prove to be cost beneficial Plans should 16. be complete (who, what, where, when) 17. reflect barriers and aids needed
5. Results	Confirm that the problem and root causes have decreased	18. Confirm effects of countermeasures 19. Compare problem before and after with same indicator 20. Compare results to objective

STEP	OBJECTIVE	KEY ACTIVITIES
6. Standard- ization	Prevent problem and root causes from recurring	21. Assure countermeasures implemented properly- process- es/ standards revisions and training 22. Establish periodic checks 23. Consider areas for replica- tion
7. Evaluation	Plan what to do about remaining problems	24. Analyze and evaluate any remaining problems 25. Review lessons learned

Adapted from Andrea Gabor, *The Man Who Invented Quality* (New York, 1988), pp. 170-1. and Annabeth L. Propst. "A Seven Step Process for Quality Improvement". p. 37-43. and Don White and H. William Vroman, *Action in Organizations,* (Boston, Allyn and Bacon, 1952).

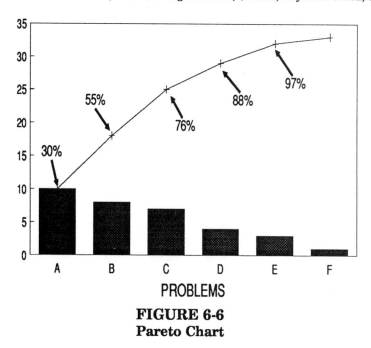

FIGURE 6-6
Pareto Chart

Pareto charts: Figure 6-6 is a Pareto chart. It is a bar graph and a line chart. The bar graph lists in descending order the problems affecting a process. These problems were collected by counting. For example, the problems, instead of being A, B, etc., might include shipping damage, workmanship, set-up, clerical error, etc. The line chart overhead accumulates the percentage of the total number of errors for each problem area.

Identifying the most frequent problems, the chart helps an organization prioritize projects. The figure suggests that the organization can deal with 75% of the complaint reports by addressing three major problems. More analysis can be done with the information from the chart. The cost of solving each problem area can be weighed against other problems in this project and against other organization problems.

Cause-and-effect diagram: The diagram in Figure 6-7 is also called a fishbone diagram because of its appearance. The effect is the problem to be solved. The causes are possible reasons for the problem. The causes are categorized. In this way all the causes of the problems are organized for additional analysis.

The category of causes listed in the figure are generic categories. Instead of the word "category" in Figure 6-7 substitute method, management, material and machinery. Most causes of problems in a manufacturing setting can be related to on these branches. Thus if the company had

FIGURE 6-7
Cause-and-Effect Diagram

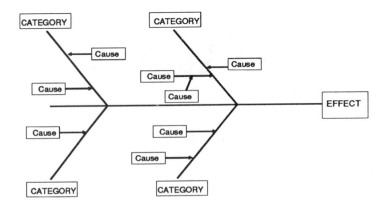

a problem with too many product defects, the causes of these defects would likely be either related to methods, management, materials or machinery. Another set of categories for a laboratory are equipment, policies, procedures, and people.

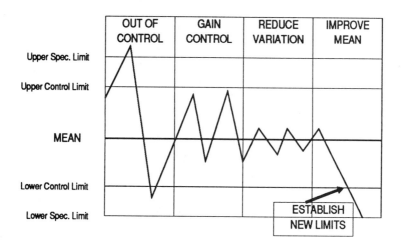

FIGURE 6-8
Control Chart
Under Varying conditions

Control chart: There are a number of ways to identify problems by simply counting what happens in a process. A control chart is pictured in Figure 6-8.   It is a time plot that shows the amount of variation in a system. The mean is the average number of errors.

Figure 6-8 depicts an entire problem solving effort. It shows the plot when the process is out of control.   The problem was identified and corrected and the process brought back into control.   Further analysis, perhaps a Pareto analysis, resulted in reducing the variation.   Further work resulted in lowering the mean number of errors in the process.

The UCL and LCL are upper and lower control limits. They indicate what the process is capable of doing. The variation around the mean is expected and comes from what Deming called "common" causes.   The spikes above the UCL or LCL indicate "special" causes of variation and can be corrected. The reduction in variation comes from making fundamental changes in methods, machines, or materials.

Checksheets, scatter diagrams, and plots of various kinds are ways of collecting information for later analysis.

Nominal Group Technique: This is a technique for increasing contributions from individuals in a group setting.   It is designed to overcome social and interpersonal barriers between people from different levels, social status, or competencies who are trying to solve a common problem.   It is structured so that people generate a list of solutions to a problem individually.   For example, a question might be "What are the limiting factors to this company delivering a product on time?"   Each participant would write his/her own list of limitations.   Each individual's list of limitations is collected and made public without comment and criticism.   This exercise is completed before anyone talks.   Thus, there are no inhibiting factors to a person putting down all the limiting factors they know.   The process shares this characteristic with brainstorming.

After a period of discussion to clarify limitations and to omit duplications, a vote is taken to prioritize the limitations left on the list. The priority list is then the basis for further problem solving.

Discussion: These tools are designed to provide a basis for diagnosing and selecting problems to pursue.   They are equally applicable to manufacturing and service organizations.   Where data is collected and a process is run continually, the problem solving reduces variation.   The process is said to be under statistical control.

CASE D: PROCESS INNOVATION

Innovation is a break with the past. It represents a fundamental change in a process.   Innovation has historically been an American strength and a Japanese weakness. Traditionally, the Japanese have been good at continuous improvement, and the Americans poor. This leaves American management less effective than the Japanese and trusting to innovations to achieve market leadership.

One of the organizational problems is that kaizen and innovation result from different management approaches. Continuous improvement accepts the reality of the present in order to improve it. Innovation rejects the sanctity of the present (considers improving the present situation a waste of time) because there are always visions of new ways of organizing a process. In reality, it becomes difficult to work on both kaizen improvement and innovation.   Some firms form process management teams (PMTs) which only have the goal of innovating processes. These PMTs don't have kaizen responsibilities. They focus on core processes that aren't meeting key measurements or competitive comparisons.   Continuous improvement can go on simultaneously with these innovative efforts, but with different teams.

Work-Out: The term Work-Out captures the full spirit of General Electric's culture which results in both continual improvement and innovation.[4]   The program tries to make better use of time through making work simpler by using both individual and collaborative effort. It not only focus on the work processes to make them more effective, but highlight candor, trust and honesty as necessary conditions for its success.

GE emphasizes 3 basic sets of practices.

1. Climate/culture change--the values and norms of the culture set the context for problem-solving.   Are employees empowered?   Is the organization customer focused?   Is process thinking standard in the organization?

2. Facilitative tools--does the organization have powerful tools to translate customer needs into process features and process control requirements?   Do the employees and teams have the tools to map processes for data collection and problem-solving purposes?

3. Execution tools--these are specific tools for identifying problems and for analyzing problems.   In order to diagnose complex problems, information needs to be collected and analyzed before decision making. The tools are frameworks and models that help teams collect the right data and suggest methods of analysis.

GE's Work-Out infrastructure includes a combination of activities. It uses town meetings to initiate change activities. Functional meetings provide opportunities to discuss general problems facing the unit. Natural teams provide a forum for continuous improvement of processes. And finally, the Business Best Practices benchmarking program inserts external perspectives into the system.

Reengineering: One approach to innovation is called reengineering. Reengineering means completely rethinking key processes in organizations. It is "The radical change and integration of the essential business processes in the customer value chain to achieve and sustain competitive

---

[4] Richard Kelbaugh, "Process Mapping", a presentation at the Association for Quality and Participation, April 1991.

advantage."[5] John Scully of Apple Computer said "this reorganization of work could prove to be as massive and wrenching as the Industrial Revolution."[6]

Some implications of reengineering include thinking across the organization instead of being constrained to the functional units. This is distinguished from innovations of existing systems, or continuous improvement of tasks. Single-function streamlining activities are process redesigns and not reengineering.[7] When the change is to match or create "best practices" in core processes like operations or delivery systems, the effort is named business reengineering. The complexity of the task requires skill and confidence on the part of the organization. The complexity of the projects and the unique skill requirements result in many reengineering projects not achieving their potential.[8]

The key to a successful reengineering effort is to be free of the restraints of current practices. "Thinking out of the box," paradigm shifts, and creative thinking are some of the ways to describe ways to think creatively about existing processes. Hammer and Champy suggest one way of designing a reengineering project is to think inductively. The method starts with a solution and works back to the problems it might solve. "How can we do things we aren't doing presently?" This is just the reverse of the normal deductive logic people are comfortable following.

Deductive logic starts with a problem, generates alternatives, and yields a decision. Deductive logic constrains the problem identification to one within the existing system. Inductive thinking creates problems companies didn't know they had. Information technology plays a critical role in this situation because it provides opportunities for dramatic change. There are many business possibilities that lie latent in the technology. It can break old rules and enable new ways of working together.

Hammer and Champy suggested rule-breaking as a major factor in a successful reengineering project. Table 6-4 captures some of the common problems organizations find themselves in and some solutions. The column on the left are the rules that govern most organizations and limit their creativity. In the right column are solutions to those old rules that

---

[5] Sandy Pudifin, "Reengineering at PHH," Presentation to the Mid-Atlantic Planning Association, March 11, 1993.

[6] Quoted in Al Ehrbar, "Reengineering Gives Firms New Efficiency, Workers the Pink Slip", *Wall Street Journal,* (March 16, 1993) p. A1.

[7] Rosemary Cafasso, "Rethinking Reengineering," *Computerworld,* March 15, 1993, p. 105.

[8] Rosemary Cafasso, "Rethinking Reengineering," p. 102.

are possible because of intervening technology. Technology enables the innovative solutions in the right column.

Information Technology (IT): IT made amazing advances over the last forty years. The early advances came in mainframe computers which handled transactions for companies. It made the giant corporation possible. Most applications were computerized. Over the years software and its interface to the user were refined regularly. No application is ever finished when implemented. There are always "bugs" and refinements are required. "Workflow design is rarely ever finished. Rather, it's a continuous process," according to Richard Pastore.[9] Years of investment into an application made it very reliable and very costly to replace.

The reason to replace this software is the perspective of the systems analysts and programmers that created the software. The traditional approach to this task complemented the centralized bureaucratic organization. Software was designed to control the options available to users. The mainframe computer controlled all processing centrally.

Over the last decade information technology made tremendous advances. One advance is powerful networked computers that made leading companies network centric instead of mainframe-centric. Personal computers connected with one another through networks give individuals power. Now they can collect data, analyze it, and report information right at the desktop. They have options at the desktop. With the mainframe, the central information systems unit had the options and acted as gatekeeper on information.

Michael Hammer and James Champy think IT is a necessary part of any reengineering project.[10] IT is an essential enabler that allows organizations to reengineer business processes. It allows much more flexibility because there are so many options available. The enabling technology in Table 6-4 is based on recent IT advances.

Most reengineering projects in large organization include going from a mainframe technology to a client-server (connected personal computers) technology. Client-server is a less mature technology than mainframe technology. This means that along with reengineering the process, the technology requires some breakthrough thinking. Elaine Bond of Chase

---

[9] Richard Pastore, "Paths of Least Resistance," *CIO,* (April 1, 1993), p. 38.

[10] Michael Hammer and James Champy, "Explosive Thinking," *Computerworld* May 3, 1993, p. 123.

Bank says "It's far more difficult to implement an application the second time around--especially on a different and less mature platform."[11]

Using information technology as the enabler suggests creative ways to increase the quality, decrease the cost, and increase the timeliness of the process. This suggests new processes and different structure.

> *"**What has** to happen is that the process is embraced by the entire organization. All three elements--technology, human resources, operations--work together in partnership to achieve an organized vision supported by top management. I'm playing the role of a partner, providing technical capabilities to satisfy the business requirements generated by business people. It's no longer me running point."*
> From Hank Philcox, CIO of the Internal Revenue Service, in "Reengineering," *Financial World*, (November 9, 1993), p. 45.

Barriers: A reengineering project might take several years to implement. In the meantime, the original process has to be maintained so the customer is served. This process is complex and expensive. Elaine Bond of Chase Manhattan says "For one thing, we [information systems people] don't have the skill base... We had decades to build up the personnel skills to keep our host systems up and running. We're just beginning the process in the distributed world."[12] Information systems units were expert at mainframe, or host, systems. The distributed, network-centric world requires different skills. In addition, the network-centric technology is in early growth and consequently imperfect.

Leadership commitment in a reengineering project is critical. Reengineering requires behavioral and cultural change that is often "messy." Old ways of doing things can be rationalized and protected. Another element of reengineering is unmanaged expectations. Expectations about the time, effort, or expense required to reengineer a project are often exaggerated to justify the project or convince a work force. Reengineering projects are complex. Michael Hammer suggests: "reengi-

---

[11] Alice LaPlante, "NetWorld keynote examines organizational side of re-engineering," *InfoWorld*. (January 11, 1993), p. 55.

[12] LaPlante "Networld Keynote Examines Organization Side of Reengineering," p. 55.

neering is more like a game of chess than roulette. You lose not because of bad luck, but because you don't know the rules."[13]

TABLE 6-4
Changing Cultural Rules Via Technology

OLD RULE	INTERVENING TECHNOLOGY	NEW RULE
Information is able to be located in one place at one time.	Shared databases	Information can appear in many places, simultaneously.
Only experts can perform complex work.	Expert systems	A generalist can make complex decisions.
A business can either centralize or decentralize.	Telecommunication networks	Business can simultaneously benefit from both approaches.
Managers make all decisions.	Decision-support tools (database access, modeling tools)	Decision making is part of everyone's role.
All field personnel have offices for information retrieval, storage, transmission, and reception.	Portable computers and wireless technology	Field personnel can send, store and receive messages anywhere.
Personal contact with a buyer is best.	Interactive videodisc	The most effective contact with a buyer is the objective.
You have to find out where things are.	Automatic identification and tracking technology	Things tell you where they are.
Plans get revised periodically.	high-performance computing	Plans get updated instantaneously.

Adapted from Michael Hammer and James Champy, "Explosive Thinking" *Computerworld*, (May 3, 1993), p. 125.

---

[13] Rosemary Cafasso, "Rethinking Re-engineering," *Computerworld* March 15, 1993, p. 104.

Reengineering hits middle management hardest.[14] Middle managers constitute 5% to 8% of the workers at corporations but make up 18% to 22% of workers let go. The average downsizing firm lets about 9.3% of its workers go. The changes make some employees redundant, while others find their skills inadequate under reengineering.[15] Most jobs in a reengineered process are upgraded, requiring different skills and more abilities. The implications, then, are not just the initial layoffs, but the increased skill demands of the jobs.

Cultural Issues: Reengineering includes technical, managerial, cultural and organizational issues. It is very complex. Cultural issues are more subtle. Syntex reengineered their R&D process. They found several cultural "rules" that stopped them from being successful. The changes are illustrated in Table 6-5.

This table illustrates the informal "rules" that often permeate an environment. The old "rules" at Syntex describe a culture that was sensitive to hierarchial authority. Violation of these rules result in not being a "team player" or "getting out of hand." They emphasized compliance and enforcing your portion of the hierarchy. These systems are self-reinforcing because people who play this game well are promoted to significant positions.

The new cultural roles focus on direct and open communication related to the horizontal process or program results. None of the subservience to authority relationships is part of the new rules.

Steps in a reengineering process: PHH corporation is a large service company. They perform services like leasing autos and supporting the transfer of executives. Key cross-functional customer-response processes at PHH are Acquisition Services, Member Services, Network Services, and Client Consulting.

PHH undertook a reengineering project[16] within the context of their total quality management (TQM) strategy. PHH's TQM includes such cornerstone pillars as: focus on the customer; individual and team performance; long-term commitment and support; and competitive

---

[14] Al Ehrbar, "Reengineering Gives Firms Efficiency, Employees the Pink Slip," *Wall Street Journal*, (March 16, 1993), p. A13.

[15] Al Ehrbar, "Reengineering Gives Firms Efficiency, Employees the Pink Slip," p. A13.

[16] Sandy Pudifin, Presentation to the Mid-Atlantic Planning Association, March 11, 1993.

positioning.   The logic of working through the organization from the customer's perspective results in the customer value chain.   PHH, like many organizations, found it had systems that sufficed, but didn't give it quality leadership in the current market.   PHH didn't meet the more demanding needs of future marketplaces.

PHH's reengineering process has four-phases:

♦ Phase 1 is process mapping. The steps include defining the team and identifying the processes for analysis.

♦ Phase 2 is the analytical phase. The cost of quality, detailed customer requirements, and beginning process analysis is started in this phase.

♦ Phase 3 begins the design phase of a new process and plan its implementation.

Phase 4 is the implementation phase of the redesigned process.

Delight is a notion from a Japanese marketer named Kano who felt the focus of marketing should be on those product/service features the customer was NOT expecting. This is the delight factor.

PHH is in the implementation phase of reengineering their driver's services processes and its funds/cash management processes.   The first process entails the entire life cycle of a PHH lease from the initial order for the car through its delivery, maintenance, and selling the used vehicle. The intent is to "delight" the driver. The funds/cash business is a key process that connects PHH electronically with vendors, customers, bank lock boxes, and accounts around the world. Managing cash in this business is a critical function that can be very profitable.

Putnam case. The Putnam Companies[17] offer financial products including mutual funds. Formerly, investor correspondence went to mail clerks. Who had to rush to meet federal regulations in opening letters by 4:00 p.m. the day they were received. The reengineered process resulted in scanning the mail into an image system that automatically prioritized and routed the mail to the right departments and employees. Instead of the traditional 3.5 hours to get mail to the right office, it now takes 30

---

[17] Pastore, Richard, "Paths of Least Resistance," *CIO* (April 1, 1993), p. 38.

minutes. Total correspondence has increased 40% without increase in personnel.

SUMMARY

Process thinking is a major message in this book. Process thinking means thinking horizontally across the organization and focusing on customer results. The contrast is with the functionally managed organization which emphasizes results in each functional unit. The idea that every employee is a customer reinforces process thinking. Every employee in the organization is involved in serving either internal or external customer. External customers and their needs for quality, cost, and timeliness become the primary stimuli for action all across the organization. The organization is made up of customer of customers.

This chapter also highlights the importance of the problem-solving process in the high quality organizations. The reason these organizations sustain high performance is they solve problems immediately. Precision and responsiveness continually improve. The design of the organization results in well-trained people in units with the authority to solve the problems they face. Many organizations deal with their problems after it affects the quality of the goods or services. Quality leadership organizations are looking for potential problems and solving them before they affect quality in a significant way.

Problem-solving logic and discipline is straightforward. There are seven steps in the problem-solving process: Diagnosis --> Selection --> Analysis --> Countermeasures --> Results --> Standardization --> Evaluation. A team follows a structured problem-solving process to solve the problems they are facing. It's the rigor of the training and the soundness of the approach that causes reliable decisions to be made in the front-line.

An important component of the problem-solving process is for teams to have the tools that can deal with search, analyze, and report findings on process quality. They also have tools to deal with team problems as they occur. Like any other system, the problem-solving competence has to be maintained and improved. Intensive training efforts and supportive facilitation of difficult situations is an organization responsibility. Units like Human Resources and Quality Assurance provide these efforts.

Quality Assurance (QA) is important in all firms. In the old-design organization, quality assurance is primarily vested in a QA unit that inspects, and tries to achieve a certain level of quality through its presence and intervention in the system. In the new-design organization, QA is vested in teams, an emphasis on designing-in quality, and empowerment.

Leading organizations have intensive improvement strategies. They include maintenance strategies, continuous improvement strategies, and innovation strategies. Maintenance and continuous improvement strategies are centered on the existing technology. Customer satisfaction information stimulates action to improve processes. This generally relates to quality, cost, or timeliness issues. Teams operate across processes and within functions to continuously improve different aspects of the process.

Innovation strategies change the fundamentals of the process. Something enables a major change. Sometimes it is simply the activities within a process that are changed. Other times a technological change allows a major innovation. Automation of tasks or the use of information technology are two enablers of innovation in organization.

Computers provided many opportunities for innovation in processes for the last several decades. The mainframe provided a major boost because of its transaction processing. During the last decade, the personal computer has provided an opportunity to innovate throughout the organization. In many cases, companies use these advances in information technology for competitive advantage. Computing power on the desktop connected through computer servers, is a primary basis for empowerment.

Reengineering is a term that captures the temporal need for many old-design organizations to change the status quo radically. They are faced with transforming their organization. Reengineering provides the methodology for attacking entrenched cultural and structural processes. It uses modern information technology as an enabler of a radical innovation of those processes.

♦♦♦

POINTS TO PONDER

1. What are arguments for and against continuous improvement compared to process innovation or reengineering?

2. How does the PDCA cycle compare to the usual idea of scientific problem solving? What is the significance of the difference?

3. Are the statistical tools of quality a form of common sense, or do they have to be learned like a science form of mathematics?

See the additional questions following the reading.

♦♦♦

READING

Attention to Detail

Core technology is a technical term that refers to the essential technology of an organization. For example, a newspaper's core technology is a sequence from gathering news through printing to distribution; the core technology of the Muppets is creating, writing, and puppeteering; a real estate development core technology is scanning, closing, building, and operating.

Managing the core technology to respond to the demands of the marketplace is the recipe for organization success. It's within this very difficult framework that "organizational sense" serves people well.

Too often managers get away from what their organization does. There are many pitfalls as top managers buy a company and try to manage something they've never laid their hands on. The owner's son or newly hired MBA who has "never met a payroll" are examples. These days it is easy to get wrapped up in the legal and financial aspects of the organization so intensively that managers lose sight of what the organization does.

Microprose has sales of about $40 million. They design, program, and distribute computer games and simulators. "F-15 Strike Eagle" is an example of the record-breaking games they produce.

In order to do well, Microprose has to be excellent in these five technical areas: 1. Software Expertise; 2. 3-D graphics expertise; 3. Game design capacity; 4. Game concept; 5. Hardware. The niches the company targeted within the entertainment industry are adult action computer games, arcade games, and simulators.

Another factor that stands out is Microprose's attention to detail. They are concerned that their games are "fun". It's not important to just get out another game. Many games don't succeed at the "fun" test and are sent back. The importance of early critical input in this process is evident from the fact that a game now takes a year, a team of programmers, and a little less than a $1M to complete. Just a few years ago the games took a couple of months of a person's time to complete.

This relentless attention to the organization's operations occurs in other settings as well. In all the tributes to the late founder of the Muppets, Jim Henson, the consistent theme was his fanatic attention to detail. Hiring bright people and allowing them to succeed seemed to be the essence of his organization theory.

Nissan wanted to emphasize the quality they were expecting their workers to build into the new Infiniti. Their approach was to bus workers to an elite Tokyo country club. While members were out golfing, the workers were running their hands over the seams of their Jags, Mercedes, and BMWs.

Walt Hriniak was the batting coach for the Chicago White Sox in the 1980s. The manager of the White Sox describes Hriniak like this: "Hriniak watches every pitch in batting practice. He goes from one side of the cage to the other. He keeps talking to the hitters, he challenges them, he encourages them, he corrects them...."

There is a critical need for people in an organization to master the operations of the firm. Instilling a fanatical attention to detail deep into the culture is the key. The element that gives the entire effort momentum is a strong strategic vision. Giving humans the context within which they can make micro decisions is motivational and encourages innovation.

4. Reading between the lines, how do these stories illustrate the chapter's theme?

5. Using these stories as a base, give some examples of a person, store or company that seemed to you to do their work very well.

♦♦

CHAPTER 7

DEVELOPING ORGANIZATION QUALITY

◆◆◆

The objectives of this chapter are:

1. To appreciate the challenge facing old-design managers.

2. To follow the change strategies associated with the 5 key quality systems.

Key words introduced in this chapter.

Adaptive change	Dynamics	Network
Archetype	Extrinsic	Phases of
Centralized	Infrastructure	development
Coherent	Interpretive	Planned change
Computerization	scheme	Refreeze
Concurrent	Interpretive	Transformation
Conflict	Intervention	Unfreezing

◆◆◆

INTRODUCTION

Changing an old-design organization to a new-design organization is an arduous task.[1] Almost everything that happened in organizations in the past affects the outcomes in the present and future. The stories of success and failure become embedded in the organization's culture. The ways in which an organization wins or loses become norms and determine the way the organization goes about its present business.

---

[1] E. E. Lawler, "Strategic Choices for Changing Organizations," in Alan M. Morhmann, *Large-Scale Organizational Change,* (San Francisco: Jossey-Bass, 1989), p. 270.

In previous chapters the dynamics of the old-design, hierarchial, authority-driven organization was drawn. This architecture effectively served organizations for decades before and after World War II. The emergence of Japanese organizations and their stunning marketplace successes were initial signals that the times had changed and a new design was required.

> *During the 1970s* the Japanese exploited the quality superiority of their products through effective advertising. This increased the American consumer's sensitivity to quality. The expectation of robust quality has increased, which, in turn, has placed additional pressure on all organizations to be more quality conscious.

International competition wasn't the only trend to converge into a vortex of change for worldwide organization. Customer sensitivity to quality and a more capable and involved employee are other trends. Information technology grew more important during the 1980s. Information technology emerged to affect most activities in the organization and formed the base for the Phase II organization. The satisfaction of customer needs is only limited by the flexibility and timeliness of organizations to respond to them.

MCI is the second largest long distance phone company in the United States. It was formed in 1977 and grew by being more adaptable and faster than AT&T. Dan Akerson, MCI's COO, says "... the company's competitiveness has been guaranteed by our entrepreneurial culture and our flexible organization. They allow us to reinvent the company's structure to meet ever-changing market demands." [2]

Change, then, will be characteristic of organization life in the 1990s and beyond. Organizations fall into two broad categories. One category is the old-design organizations that developed during the post World War II period. These organizations will have to respond to the new marketplace. The alternative is to be defeated in the marketplace.

New York Life is midstream in a transformational change. Lee Gammill, EVP, said "One of our toughest tasks was to dismantle the entrenched departmental fiefdoms. Then, we had to build a framework where teams were encouraged and empowered. We brought people together from across the company, and they worked on ad hoc teams to develop solutions and strategies for our business needs.[3]

---

[2] Corporate Renaissance, *Business Week*, (April 5, 1993), p. 78c.

[3] From "Corporate Renaissance," *Business Week* (April 5, 1993), p. 78b.

Another category includes those firms that started as new companies during the last decade or so. Because these firms were started new during this period, they are likely to use the newer design principles. (At least the organizations aren't fettered by stories embedded in their culture)

A fundamental change in an organization is called a transformational change. When a firm adapts to the evolution of a market, it is called adaptive change. Both types of changes are important, and can be complex.

Transformational change means unraveling the old organization, while building new systems and still competing daily in the marketplace to "meet the payroll." Adaptive change happens within the dynamics of the original organization.

This chapter discusses some fundamental change models and approaches. The first model of change is the Lewin model. Then, an approach that explains the difference between transformational and adaptive change is discussed. Following that, stages are proposed that explains how to transform old-design organizations into new-design organizations.

Some organizations are rocked by crises and find themselves in the mode of constantly fixing something, firing someone, or fretting over some future event. They always are reacting to events. Planned change avoids this insidious chain of events by changing the ineffective components. Once changed, the components can deal effectively with the events. Effective change can result in a proactive component. Being proactive means understanding how the organization is contributing to its own problems.

PLANNED CHANGE

Planned change means reorganizing to respond to changing environmental dependencies. Individuals, groups, units, and organizations go through periods of change. The metaphor freeze or frozen suggest that most organizations develop structure and culture that are interwoven. They become frozen, immovable, and solidified against outside interventions. Indeed, it isn't hard for an organization's management to miss market turns or trends because they are so "frozen" into the existing culture.

Ordinarily change is started by a significant event. A period of change follows, until the firm again feels confident in the marketplace. The new ways of operating become second nature in the next period. This is the pattern described by Kurt Lewin. His framework is unfreeze--> change--> refreeze. It says that a period of unfreezing precedes a period of actual change that is reinforced by a period of refreezing.

IBM is an excellent example of a firm that had decades of success and didn't "see" the changing marketplace. Pressure on earnings created pressure on the CEO to make things happen. Although he took action, the CEO, John F. Akers, couldn't shake his IBM history fast enough. Under pressure, he resigned in 1992, and an outsider, Louis Gerstner, took over.

Table 7-1 arrays the Lewin change cycle against change targets: organization, unit/group, and individual. Unfreezing efforts can be planned in addition to unexpected events that cause an organization to pause and evaluate how they operate. The unfreezing column suggests some natural means of unfreezing and some intervention techniques that sharpen an unfreezing period.

UNFREEZING

Unfreezing suggests that something happens that causes people in the organization to look beyond the existing culture, to scan for a different way of operating. It has long been known that failure, or near-failure, is a good process for unfreezing.

There are many variations on the theme. Sometimes changes are contained within a group or an individual. More often, a breakdown at the individual or group level is symptomatic of wider problems. Sometimes it takes a failure for a firm to investigate and realize that a major problem has been building up for some time. Some incidents can be treated as just another business problem or as a signal for a major investigation. Some examples are: a unit votes for unionization, an individual has a breakdown, a key person resigns, a major account leaves, a group of scientists resign, a key new product is delayed, or a stiff new competition evolves.

The complexity of change is illustrated by an individual's nervous breakdown. An analysis might suggest the problems at the unit or organization level created the pressure causing the personal crisis. For example, the stress from a punitive culture might cause individuals to become sick, quit, or loudly react. The normal organization response is to focus on the individual. Organization responses to individuals seldom take

TABLE 7-1
Lewin's Change Cycle by Level of Organization

Level of Change Efforts	Unfreeze	Change	Refreeze
Organization	*Setting*: Continuing marketplace failures cause scanning for reasons *Interventions**: Strategic planning exercise identifies organizational weakness; Nominal group exercises appropriate	Strategies undertaken to overhaul approach to marketplace and/or fundamental transformation of organization design	Intensive follow-up transition meetings complement the enhanced reward and planning system reinforcers; actual successes help refreeze new behaviors
Unit/ Group	*Setting*: Loss of leadership, continual conflict over resources, or poor results *Interventions**: Nominal group exercises, team building, or training efforts	Planned redevelopment of ways of behaving/change in values/change in core processes	Confirmed by new reward/ administrative structure, successes, diminished conflict, continued positive reports from unit(s)
Individual	*Setting*: Feeling of anomie, severe role conflict, and health or mental stress *Interventions**: Counseling efforts, suggestion box/open-door policy	Work through the details of personal strategy to cope with, and then master, the new situation	Confirmed through work on a support network and reported successes in new behaviors

KEY: *: See Glossary for definitions.

into account the wider issue facing the organization. If the crisis increases to a sufficient degree, then the organization widens its scan for solutions. It might be "ready" for an unfreezing effort.

If the organization chose to look at this as a problem to be solved, it could be an unfreezing opportunity. The individual breakdown causes people to be momentarily concerned, worried, and open to problem solving. A carefully planned survey, focus group or team meeting to gather data could involve people in developing a solution.

CHANGE

During the change period, planned strategies address factors that limit organization, unit, or individual performances. The focus of the intervention effort can be any one or combination of these variables: structure, policies, systems, operations, groups or individuals. Because of the interconnected nature of organizations, there are intended and unintended results from any intervention.

When change in the culture, in group/team norms, or in individual attitudes is required, the demands for competency in organization change increases.[4] Operating managers seldom have the insights to manage the complexity of a change effort. Ordinarily, professional change agents are used. Change agents use sophisticated tools to create a period of planned change. Under these conditions the outcome is likely to be achieved.

Intended positive outcome	Unintended positive outcome
Intended negative outcome	Unintended negative outcome

TABLE 7-2
Intended and Unintended Outcomes

There is considerable risk in intervening in an organization. Table 7-2 illustrates the situations a change agent has to anticipate and deal with effectively. The table suggests that in addition to the intended positive outcomes activities, there are unintended positive and negative

---

[4] For a review of this literature see Allan M. Mohrmann, et al., *Large-Scale Organizational Change,* (San Francisco: Jossey-Bass, 1989), also see Peter Senge, *The Fifth Discipline,* (New York: Doubleday, 1990).

outcomes. In most cases, there will be no intended negative outcomes. Two examples of an intervention are:

Intervention: Reengineer a process: Positive intended outcome: Increase responsiveness to customer needs.
Positive Unintended Outcome: Increases suggestions from other units and process owners; Negative unintended outcome: Key personnel in other units resign in anticipation of a reengineering project.

Intervention: Tighten selection process: Positive intended outcome: increase skill level of personnel in organization, followed by performance declines; Positive unintended outcome: existing personnel attempt to do a better job; Negative unintended outcome: newly hired people are harassed.

Planning for change is very complex. The unintended consequences require sophisticated management. Implementation of the change is as much art as science, because of its complexity. Inadequate efforts in any of these steps will result in an unsuccessful or delayed change effort. Resistance to change is natural for organizations, units, or individuals. People are limited by the constraints of the old ways of behaving. Culture reinforces these behaviors.

Later in this chapter a framework for introducing the quality systems will be introduced, within the context of organization development. These are fundamental transformational changes to be introduced after appropriate unfreezing.

REFREEZE

Following a successful change period, time is required so the change effort becomes second nature. This period results in the new behaviors and norms becoming established in the culture. Inadequate practice during the refreezing period lets the old norms control behaviors. Without a successful refreezing period regression to the old set of norms is likely. Another set of influences is more insidious. There are still stakeholders like customers, vendors, employees, unions, and business partners that unconsciously prefer the old way of behaving. Changing these stakeholders requires a consistent strategy over many years. Stakeholders harbor stories about the old organization. They need to be convinced that the changes are real. Supervising, monitoring, problem solving and rewarding are some general refreezing tactics.

> *"When people* *in organizations focus only on their position, they have*
> *little sense of responsibility for the results produced when all posi-*
> *tions interact. Moreover, when results are disappointing, it can be*
> *very difficult to know why. All you can do is assume that "someone*
> *screwed up".*
> Peter Senge, *The Fifth Discipline,* (New York: Doubleday, 1990), p. 19.

Change timeline: The time required for unfreezing, change, or refreezing is not very clear. Most people want uncomfortable situations to be over quickly. Most change efforts take a long time, however. Each phase takes more, or less, time depending on these factors:

the severity of the problem. The more severe the pressure, the more likely the firm will undertake a change effort. Severe problems are likely to take a long time to finish.

whether it was anticipated. It takes more time to recover from an unexpected failure than one in which there was a dawning realization that events would turn out badly.

the expertise involved in planning and implementing the change. Finally, most organizations try to treat problems with a business-as-usual, problem-solving approach. Often this approach simply makes the situation more complex and difficult to untangle. The danger is a simple problem becomes more complex and damaging.

Changes sometimes take years, and each stage is equally important. Unfreezing activities sets up the change strategy, which sets up the refreezing activities. Firms often make it through the change period with some changes intact. Unfortunately, they don't often have effective follow-up to ensure that the new way of behaving becomes second nature. The period of refreezing is important to the success of the change effort.

TRANSFORMING THE ORGANIZATION

The Lewin model is helpful in framing the general process of change. All planned change, large and small, falls within this framework. Keep in mind that many change opportunities are ordinarily missed. Organizations discount, and otherwise rationalize, if they notice, many events in their internal and external environments. Some events can be ignored, but many are symptomatic of underlying problems in the organization.

Further Complications:
An Unsuccessful Track-Record

An organization's history of marketplace success is important in any change effort. For example, if the firm historically has not been a strong competitor, the culture will present a major barrier to any change effort. Poor problem-solving, decision-making, a lack of planning, insistent bankers, cautious suppliers, and suspicious clients all remain distrustful, even after an open commitment to change has been made. This history is embedded in the culture. The problem isn't only the overt behaviors that affect how customers are treated or work done. The problem includes the underlying assumptions made by employees about customers and about work that continue to guide behaviors. So, compliance to a new way of doing things can be deceptive. People might behave right temporarily, but lurking right underneath are beliefs that reinforce the old way of behaving. Thus, some changes can be superficially attained, but are unlikely to be sustained.

People are part of the problem. An organization with a lack of success is unlikely to attract employees who are used to winning consistently. Selection standards diminish to meet the likely candidate, the quality of customer lists degrades, financing becomes more difficult as financiers become suspicious, and energy becomes less focussed as inspection and rework takes more time. The problems go deeper because less successful firms are less in control of how they go about producing and selling their product or service. People are more distracted and managing is less methodical.

Planned change becomes more complex and subject to surprises under these conditions.

This section highlights what happens to organizations as they try to win in the marketplace.

Earlier in the chapter, a distinction was suggested between adaptive change and transformational change. The more radical and rapid the change in the environment, the more likely the firm will undergo a transformation. Most organizations react to changing environments with adaptive change techniques. This is a result of the firm's using the same adaptive strategies they used successfully in the past.

> *"A new paradigm might emerge if the organization's ways of looking at the world and ways of doing things no longer address the problems and realities that are being confronted and the social matrix that supports the status quo begins to disintegrate."*
> From Gerald Ledford, et al., "The Phenomenon of Large-Scale Organizational Change in "Allan Mohrmann, et al., *Large-Scale Organizational Change*, (San Francisco: Jossey-Bass, 1989), p. 14.

Greenwood and Hinings suggest an approach for describing organization behaviors when facing the need for transformation.[5] They explain why organizations act as they do when faced with change. The terms of the model are explained in the terminology box accompanying this discussion. Figure 7-1 pictures the model in action.

DESIGN ARCHETYPE

In their terms, a design archetype evolves because it solves problems effectively in a certain environment. As time passes, the archetype is refined and develops a high degree of coherence. The old-design organization that has been carefully elaborated throughout the text is a design archetype. Policies, strategies, and systems intertwine consistently/coherently to make this a powerful design for its period of history. Most large-scale organizations, from the government through General Motors, have some common characteristics tying their dynamics to the old-design organization.

Over the 70 or so years that the latest rendition of the bureaucratic model was dominant, scholars, and practitioners refined the understanding of its internal dynamics. According to Greenwood and Hinings, the old-design archetype generated a coherent set of internal dynamics that interpreted marketplace changes predictably. The development of the stable bureaucracies responded to the reliable 1950s and 1960s marketplace. These terms describe a strong culture and tightly interwoven formal organization. Many institutions were successful and reinforced the archetype. Labor unions, for example, emerged in response to the impersonality of this archetype. Schools of business and the study of political science on most campuses teach the principles of this archetype.

---

[5] C. R. Hinings and Royston Greenwood, *The Dynamics of Strategic Change*, (New York: Basil Blackwell Ltd., 1988). James G. Hunt and his colleagues are doing research on this model in the United States. See Arja Ropo and James G. Hunt, "Leadership and Organizational Change: Development of a processual Grounded Theory," an unpublished manuscript, Texas Tech University.

TERMINOLOGY BOX
Greenwood and Hinings Model

Design Archetype: This is defined as a general architecture that most organizations follow because it is successful. As environmental forces change the organization either adapts to the change or transforms itself to a new design archetype that is more effective in the new environment. Design archetypes develop internal dynamics which become strong the more coherent the structure, systems and culture.

Tracks: Their approach suggests that organizations follow predictable paths through their histories. Track 1, inertia, is an organization that stays within its design archetype and evolves with its marketplace. Adaptive change applies to track 1. The rest of the tracks represent firms attempting transformational change. Track 2 is a successful transformation; track 3 is a failed transformation and regression to the old archetype; track 4 is a continuing, but unsuccessful, attempt- a never-ending-journey.

Interpretive Schemes: How an organization interprets an environmental event is the organization's interpretive scheme. Internal dynamics resulting from culture, systems and structure result in a strong interpretive scheme.

INTERPRETIVE SCHEME

The interpretive scheme is a web of structures, policies, and strategies. The new-design organization reflects the major changes in information technology, internationalization, and increasing customer sensitivity brought to the external environment. Japanese organizations reflected these changes well, as attested to by their market successes. Japanese organizations represented the essence of the new-design archetype during the 1980s.

These points summarize change, thus far.

♦ Bureaucracy is an archetype, and the new-design organization is a new archetype.

♦ Adaptive change occurs within an archetype, but not between archetypes.

♦ Transformational change is distinguishable because they aim for fundamental changes.

American business has a tendency to use the "quick fix" and "program du jour"[6] to change within an archetype. Some managements use words or gimmicks instead of going through the painful period of change to respond to problem areas. The quick fix was used while the marketplace was relatively stable as a common reaction to problems. Now the fundamental changes in the marketplace require equally fundamental changes in the organization. Yet many managements still use the quick fix response. Some of the recent failures by firms trying to use total quality management failed because they use the concepts as a quick fix instead of as a technique for fundamental change.

Student Crisis

A student fearing all "E's" in his first semester in college goes to an academic advisor to get some magic advise to pull the semester out. The advisor, though, tells the student he has to change his attitudes toward education, study habits, and drop most of his friends, if he intends to succeed at this school.

The professor might have said the design archetype from home didn't allow the student to compete successfully. His interpretive scheme gave the wrong value to assignments versus social activities. A new design archetype is required and here are the change strategies (new friends, etc) that need to be adopted in order to get on the right track to a successful change. The new design archetype will likely result in better grades.

The dynamics of his present way of behaving are a powerful pull to continue on the same path. Maybe some ideas can be adopted to see how it goes. The inertia of the design archetype results in what is minor adaptive change instead of the required transformational change suggested by the advisor. The student's parents weren't very pleased with the coherence of the student's present design archetype when he brought home the semester's grades.

This problem is illustrated by the reaction of some companies to Japanese successes. One classic old-design firm developed a joint venture with a major Japanese firm. The Japanese firm took over management of the U.S. company's domestic plants. The Americans hoped to see Japanese manufacturing "secrets" because they had access to the plants. Company

---

[6] Michael McGill, *American Business and the Quick Fix*, (New York: Henry Holt, 1988), and Ralph H. Kilmann, *Beyond the Quick Fix*, (San Francisco: Jossey-Bass, 1984).

engineers toured the facility many times. They discussed, measured, and took pictures of different aspects of the line.

After the engineers left, an employee who had worked for both the previous American management and the newer Japanese management shook his head. He said: "They missed the point. They only saw the places where there was some unique automation. That stuff doesn't amount to a hill-of-beans around here. It's the teams and human resource effort that makes the difference."

FIGURE 7-1
Pictorial of Greenwood and Hinings Model

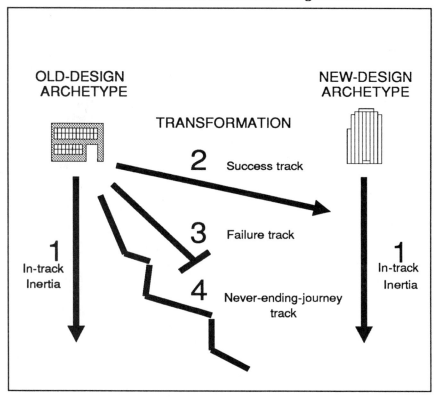

The interpretive scheme of the old-design American manufacturer colored its observations. They never saw the empowered status of the employees and the power of teams. They only saw the "control" dimensions of the situation. They were under the old bureaucratic principle that automation is used to minimize the number of, and errors from, employees.

TRACKS

The challenge is how to transform old-design organizations into new-design organizations. Greenwood and Hinings suggest organizations follow different tracks in their quest for change. Old-design organizations have established a track within which they have used adaptive change to stay successful. There is inertia that keeps the organization in-track. Inertia results from the strength/coherence of the internal dynamics of the archetype.

To illustrate this point, both old- and new-design organizations responded to the information technology trend by buying computers. Both types of organizations have large investments in hardware and software. The old-design organization computer architecture (hardware and software) supported the centralized authority patterns of the bureaucratic archetype. This meant a highly centralized large-scale computer and highly control-oriented software that guarded the company's information.

The new-design organization has hardware and software that complements the communications and problem solving requirements of the decentralized organization. The new-design organization has decentralized computing that puts information close to the front-line. Personal computers give the desktop immense power. They are connected through local area networks to servers which are computers that hold information. A large firm then has to connect hundreds of servers to have enterprise-wide coherence. Software has developed to take advantage of this decentralized structure.

This dual use of computers and information technology to monitor or to empower has been noted by other authors. Walton[7] calls it "compliance effects" and "commitment effects", while Zuboff[8] names the uses "automate" and "informate."

The magnitude of the transformational change between the old-design and new-design archetypes can be seen as a company tries to change its information system to reflect the new environment. Not only is the change from one computer architecture to another costly, but it requires a complete change in business processes. Computer systems mirror the business processes of a company. Without a computer change, there will

---

[7] Richard Walton, *Up and Running: Integrating Information Technology in the Organization,* (Boston: Harvard Business School Press, 1989).

[8] Shoshanna Zuboff, *In the Age of the Smart Machine: The Future of Work and Power* (New York:Basic Books, 1988).

be no change in processes. This is the focus of the strategy of reengineering.

This says nothing about the establishment of teams, improvement in employee competence and change in culture that has to accompany this change. Imagine the inertia when the centralized computer unit sees their fiefdom threatened by a decentralized framework. With so many competing needs for capital, how easily is the financial decision going to be made to junk the mainframe and buy personal computers and LANs. Keep in mind, the executive mind-set is still deep into the old interpretive scheme. They will have a tendency to regress to their old way of thinking and reject a rapid change to the new-design archetype. Inertia of the old-design archetype will likely dominate the thinking.

The newspapers are full of stories about companies that are disappointed with their attempts to implement total quality management. The tendency is to blame TQM and say it's not a worthwhile goal. By now you can guess the problem isn't the quality goal... it's the challenge in transformational change. Even the most astute firms have problems.

The dynamics of the archetype are positive when the external environment is supportive. When the external environment changes, the usual adaptive strategies cease to be effective. The inertia of the old-design archetype results in little or no change for many firms. Others undertake a legitimate, planned, transformational change. Those firms trying a transformational change fall into one of four tracks.

Most firms never escape the web of the old-design archetype. The inertia conceals the extent of the change.

One track includes those firms that succeed in transforming from being an old-design to a new-design archetype.

Another track includes those firms that try, fail, and then regress to the old-design archetype.

The last track includes those that expend lots of resources and always come tantalizingly close to success, but never achieve it. These organizations are on never-ending journeys.

These four tracks describe the situation facing many organizations trying to respond to the environment of the 1990s. The tracks are (1) inertia, (2) success, (3) failure, and (4) never-ending journey. General Motors has tried to transform their automobile division over the last fifteen years with mixed success. This next section ties their efforts to the Greenwood and Hinings model.

CHANGE IN WORLD'S LARGEST CORPORATION

General Motors is the world's largest corporation with about $140 billion in sales. GM is the world's largest automobile company, as well, and has giant computing, finance, and electronics subsidiaries. In spite of its size, this company has been under constant pressure since the 1970s, particularly in the giant auto segment. In spite of some positive accomplishments, the overall corporation is still under siege in the 1990s. Japanese automobile companies, as a group, increased their market share in the U.S. from 10% to over 30% by the early 1990s. A large part of this gain came from General Motors' failures in the market place. During the same period, GM's market share slid from nearly 50% to less than 30% during the summer of 1993. It has since recovered somewhat.

Other American car companies faced the same problems as GM, but weathered the competition more effectively. Ford lost billions of dollars in 1981 and used this to unfreeze a hide-bound bureaucracy and adversarial union to go through a decade of transformational change. At the end of the 1980s it produced half the top 10 selling cars world-wide. Ford's quality ratings were also very high. Chrysler waited until the late 1980s before they "Hondaized" their company. They studied, then emulated, Honda's successful company. They are on track to be one of the success stories of the 1990s.

Many of General Motors's problems in the 1980s are due to the success it had over the years. From the time of Alfred Sloan in the 1920s through the 1970s, most large organizations tried to emulate the way GM was organized and managed. An ex-president of GM said, "What is good for General Motors, is good for America." This arrogant statement of the 1950s has been followed by, "When General Motors gets licked in the marketplace, so does America" in the 1980s and 1990s. The dynamics of the old-design archetype and the resulting interpretive scheme made it difficult for GM to "see" the severity of the change and made it almost impossible to change.

The inertia of the old-design is what had made it difficult for GM to change. Roger Smith, the president of GM during the 1980s, suggested that changing GM was like changing the course of the giant Queen Elizabeth ocean liner (QEII). The forward motion (inertia) of the QEII resulted in taking miles to turn the ship. In GM's case, the analogy implied that Smith thought a long term adaptive change would accomplish the goal of turning GM. Most observers agree that time isn't on GM's side. Inadequate change might result in more agonizing defeats in the marketplace and eventual withdrawal from the auto industry.

The corporation is going through a difficult transformation. The success or failure of the effort won't be known until well into the 1990s. Since the transformation has been underway since the 1970s, it's possible that corporate GM is on a never-ending-journey.

GM experimented during the 1980s to try to find the appropriate strategy to make them more competitive. Some of GM's strategies included

the development of Saturn automobile;

a joint manufacturing venture with Toyota;

the independence of Cadillac; and

numerous initiatives with the core automobiles companies.

The first three strategies indicate GM's recognition of the need for a transformational change. The last strategy indicates their quandary regarding the appropriate strategy to use. The core auto companies constitute the largest part of GM. These strategies are adaptive change attempts. Using such a wide variety of approaches appears to support GMs argument that it both takes a long time to change a giant company and that GM has enough time to change.

Table 7-3 uses the Greenwood and Hinings model to analyze GM's strategies. The following discussion gives some background on each of the strategies.

Saturn: In 1983, a group of GM executives were given the charge to develop a new car. They were told explicitly to use resources outside GM. They had an open checkbook for this project. Utilizing the latest technology they built a "greenfield," new-design operation in Tennessee. In 1991, the first Saturn rolled off the assembly line. The UAW negotiated a special contract that gave unprecedented flexibility to management.

NUMMI (New United Motors Inc) joint venture: In the early 1980s, GM sales dried up on the West Coast as the Japanese dominated. The lack of sales caused GM to close its Fremont, California, plant. GM, in effect, conceded the territory to the Japanese. The Japanese were superior manufacturers and the quality of their cars humbled their American counterparts.

Searching for answers to the Japanese manufacturing superiority, GM proposed a joint venture to Toyota. Toyota was searching for a manufacturing facility to keep up with demand. The joint venture agreement provided for Toyota to manage GM's old Fremont plant with American UAW workers. The union was anxious to put workers back to work and agreed to relaxed work rules.

They produced the Toyota Camry in the facility. Toyota would take half the output for its dealers. The other half would have the name Nova (it is now the Prizm) and go to Chevrolet's dealers. The results were instructive. Within a short period of time this facility produced autos with quality equivalent to Toyota's Japanese facility. Both companies benefitted from the effort. The agreement between Toyota and GM was renewed in 1993. This was a greenfield, new-design strategy.

Cadillac: In 1984, GM split GM into large- and small-car divisions. Robert Stempel headed the large-car division, which contain Cadillac, Buick and Oldsmobile. With the increased authority within the division, the plans called for more autonomy for Cadillac. Instead of relying on centralized design, purchasing, and manufacturing, Cadillac assumed responsibility for all these functions. In addition, it began a major quality intervention.

Over the next few years, Cadillac lost market share and reputation like the rest of the corporation. However, the quality initiative grew dramatically. Building in quality systems resulting in higher-quality automobiles. New initiatives with customers resulted in higher satisfaction. By 1992, Cadillac contended for America's Baldrige National Quality Award and won it. The first car design independent of GMs central facility was introduced in 1992. It won car-of-the-year awards, and is one of the highest-rated cars on the Powers' Quality Survey.

The Rest of the Units- The rest of the corporation has been relatively untouched. It was subject to many interventions during the 1980s, however. The UAW didn't change any work-rule or seniority provisions in these contracts, as they did at the smaller units, NUMMI and Saturn. GM's recourse was to automate to minimize unionized employees. The results of their automation initiative at their Detroit-Hamtramck plant was nearly disastrous. Robots turned on each other, painted each other, and smashed windows. It became a nightmare of bugs and glitches.[9] Joint UAW-GM initiatives to increase worker productivity continue. All this within the old archetype.

GM bought a computer organization (EDS) to increase the effectiveness of information technology in designing manufacturing facilities. They also bought Hughes Electronics in 1985. EDS and Hughes were both good independent companies that have prospered and they made an impact on the automotive division. EDS assumed management of all computing in General Motors. Computing is conceded to be excellent at GM. Hughes influence is felt in the quality of electronic equipment and some advanced design inputs. These are welcome additions to a situations that still harbors old-design assumptions. The relationship with the UAW in the core auto component is a major constraint to General Motors's progress. It is reported that GM's costs are about $2000 above its American competitors.

ESTABLISHING QUALITY-LEADERSHIP

The new-design organization is a relatively open system organization comprised of the quality systems and supporting infrastructure. Any organization intending to become a new-design organization has to develop each of these systems.

From Lewin, the unfreezing probably results from marketplace failures. The change process includes strategies to implement each of the strategies.

Greenwood and Hinings' research suggests that a transformation might succeed when the interpretive scheme changes. The interpretive scheme is a product of the dynamic web of structure, customs, and systems. Over time employees adapt to this dynamic web. They are reinforced by the structure, help establish customs, and work with these systems daily. After a while, many stakeholders resist any change from this dynamic web. In a transformation, a new structure, customs and systems replace the old. They alter the old dynamics and the interpretive scheme significantly. A new set of dynamics consistent with the new environment takes their place when the organization is successful.

---

[9] Maryann Keller, *Rude Awakening: The Rise, Fall, and Struggle for Recovery of General Motors*, (New York: Wm. Morrow and Co., 1989), pp. 207-8.

TABLE 7-3

Selected General Motors Strategies

STRATEGY	PROBLEM	TRACK	RESULTS
Saturn	Suspicion that the source of GM's quality difficulties was the GM culture	Start a new-design archetype	Successful development of a high-quality, mid-sized automobile, large capital costs make profitability a question mark
NUMMI	Searching for insight into the Japanese superiority in manufacturing	Successful transformation	The joint venture was a success; the question is whether GM learned the secret to Japanese manufacturing
Cadillac	Suspicion that divisional structure and common design and manufacturing systems limited products from being competitive	Successful transformation	After 5 years, the organization won the Baldrige Quality Award; the 1992 automobiles won quality and design awards
Rest of units	High costs, adversarial union relations, poor quality, and unimaginative designs cause marketplace problems	Never-ending journey at corporate level with some major subsidiary successes and failures	GM has had mixed results. Costs are still about $2,000 per car more than competitors; design and quality have improved; lack of capital resulted in lagging new designs; executive resignations in the early 1990s increased the urgency to change

A new design organization is the target of most old-design organization. Transformations are challenging. The key quality systems and infrastructure have to be built. The next section suggests a pattern for change of each of the key quality systems. A four-phase model is used.

PHASES OF THE TRANSFORMATION

This section builds each of the systems using a four-phase model.[10] In general, the four phases suggest the changes necessary to go from the closed-system, old-design organization to the new-design organization. The general spirit is one of a transition from an old-design organization characterized by control to one characterized by new-design flexibility, empowerment, and teams.

The situation is that the old-design organization has to build the five quality systems and infrastructure. The key quality systems are benchmarking, supplier partnerships, design system, people systems, and the integrated technical core. They were featured in Chapter 3. Most organizations have to build each system. The development of each system depends on the concomitant development of other systems.

Figure 7-2 is a general depiction of how this transformational change might work. Center Bank is pictured on the left side of the graphic. It's goal is to look like Center's Quality Bank on the right side of the graphic. These are the old-design archetype and the new-design archetype. The lines between the old-design and new-design Center Bank depict the strategies they have to complete. The top lines shows the competitive strategies required to sell products and services in the marketplace. The bottom lines describes building the key quality systems. It is easily seen that this period is very complex for most organizations.

As the organization develops quality systems, competitive strategies adjust to take advantage of the new-found potential. There is a constant interplay between these systems. For example, with the development of the design and integrated core system, the product has higher quality. This allows a more aggressive strategy against lower quality competitors.

Table 7-5 arrays the key systems shown in Figure 7-2 along a four phase change. The first phase is close to old-design and represents a start. The fourth phase represents the peak development of the systems. Together they represent the new-design archetype.

Table 7-5 is a narrative describing the steps in building the systems. Following the table, each system's development is elaborated. Because each system is listed separately, it appears that the subsystems can be developed independently. It'll be clear going through the discussions that

---

[10] AT&T, *Quality Manager's Handbook*, (Indianapolis: AT&T, 1990), p. 12.

each subsystem depends on the development of others in concert. There is a balance in their development. Superimposing the four phases development in Table 7-5 over the transformation of Center Bank in Figure 7-2 hints that the changes will take many years. Another factor is that there are many limitations to the smooth development of any of the

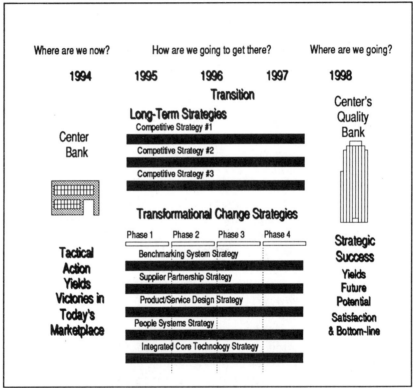

FIGURE 7-2
Transformational Strategies and Design Archetypes

The Lewin model's unfreezing efforts to prepare for rapid change occurs in phase 1. The second phase is characterized by building systems and changing norms. The third phase develops each of the systems and begins refreezing. The final phase fine tunes the systems and finishes the refreezing process.

subsystems. Barriers include the old customs, limited resources, intensive competition, limited employee competencies and more.

BENCHMARKING

Summary: Benchmarking is a system that provides for a continual scan for organizations that do something particularly well. It can provide the basis for continual improvement through the team network. In addition, it can provide the input for major "breakthrough" changes.

Phase 1: Benchmarking competence lags the development of a basic information system and a team network. Firms aren't doing well enough to benchmark or have too many other projects under way to do it well.

Phase 2: Benchmarks of primary processes taken from "local" or literature benchmarks are initial efforts. Linkages from the benchmark are being developed into the team network, planning system and design system.

Phase 3: Refined internal measurement systems generates more sophisticated benchmarking requests. Competent quality network and a vigorous planning system increase deployment of information.

Phase 4: Benchmarking teams take the initiative to look for "best of best" benchmarks of increasingly more sophisticated processes. Benchmarking is an integrated component into quality network and planning systems.

According to the International Quality Study, benchmarking benefits higher performing companies only. "In the lower-and medium-performing groups, there is no compelling positive impact from any of the benchmarking practices." "Best of best" benchmarks are unachievable by this group. In addition, these organizations "need to focus their resources on their core infrastructure... "
Ernst & Young, *Best Practices Report.* (Cleveland: Ernst & Young, 1992), p. 38.

SUPPLIER PARTNERSHIPS

Summary: Successful deployment of a partnership program depends internally on strategies improving product or service design system, a developing team network, and the implementation of a problem solving norm in the core technology. Externally, the awareness of quality in the supply chain is important. Partnerships start as the companies in the supply chain consider being certified or audited. Reengineering often brings suppliers into a just-in-time relationship with the organization. Care has to be taken not to demand more from the supplier than the

TABLE 7-5
Development of the Five Key Quality Systems

	PHASE 1	PHASE 2	PHASE 3	PHASE 4
Benchmarking	Benchmarking efforts aren't effective without other systems being developed	"Local" benchmarking broadens as internal systems develop	Refined internal systems result in world-class benchmarking	Benchmarking teams take initiative to look for "best of best"
Supplier Partnerships	Communicate quality requirements; establish audits or certification options.	Quality feedback increases to a few qualified suppliers.	Initial supplier partnerships and preferred supplier programs.	Partnerships result in a tightly integrated supply chain
Design system	Project teams and increased customer information are highlighted	Formal concurrent team experiments with supplier and customer membership	More customer information in a team-based design process	Supplier/customer partnerships and concurrent design processes
People systems	Basic training in problem solving and quality awareness representative	Focused reward, training, selection, development, and teams	Real team successes begin to characterize rallies and awards	Discretion at the shop floor and self-managed team
Integrated core Technology	Map key processes and begin to measure basic results	Exploring supplier and design system relationships	Reengineered processes	Core competence results in strategic advantage for firm.
Infrastructure	Leadership commitment and quality council are set up	Deployment/management by plan becomes key initiative.	Power shifts from the functional hierarchy to the quality hierarchy	Characterized by diminished hierarchy, and problem solving teams.

company can provide itself. The key is to build quality leadership together, and methodically.

Phase 1: Initiated by measuring obvious internal quality processes and communicating requirements to supplier. Expectations for possible exchange of quality information are formed.

Phase 2: Characterized by increasing flow of information to and from suppliers. Beginning to select the most responsive suppliers to develop closer relationships. Audits and certifications become criteria for supply contracts. Members of special design project teams.

Phase 3: Supplier audits and certification are typical. Suppliers included in more complex design system and part of planning for reengineering core processes. Just-in-time systems require partnership status. An open two-way communication capability characterizes the relationship.

Phase 4: Close and intimate relationship with supplier's organization exists through shared design and production information and facilities.

DESIGN SYSTEM

Summary: The design system becomes even more important in the new-design firm. Cycle time and increasing interaction with the customer are components of the design system. Shifting the emphasis from inspecting and fixing it in, to designing it in is a major effort. An effective design system depends on concurrent development within a team network, an integrated core technology, a customer information system, and a mature culture.

Phase 1: Measure cycle time and cost of quality for organization to focus effort. Begin increasing participation by customers and customer data in design process.

Phase 2: Assign a project team to manage special project. Continue refinement of database of customer-need information and invite supplier participation. Initiate concurrent teams' experiments.

Phase 3: Integrate customers and suppliers into a sophisticated concurrent engineering design process.

Phase 4: Integration into supplier/customer partnerships and integrated core result in accurate and rapid reflecting of customer needs in product/service.

INTEGRATED CORE TECHNOLOGY

Summary: How a product is manufactured, or a service delivered, is the heart of the organization. The effort is to transform the core technology from one designed to simplify and control to the integrated core where the intelligence of individuals and teams are integrated into the core technology.

Phase 1: Develop metrics for key processes and awareness of process management.

Chrysler radically changed their system in 1988. Faced with survival, it emulated Honda's design system. The first step was to organize a makeshift design center at an empty hangar that would allow teams to work together. The engineers were told to build the best car. No interference from headquarters (phase 2). The award winning LH cars were the result. Chrysler followed through with a $500 million design center that supported concurrent engineering (phase 3). The results are a 3.5 year design cycle (down from 5 years) and a new car every 6 months from 1992 through 1995 from this design cycle. They are now improving their manufacturing quality to match the "car of the year" awards they got for the LH series. Chrysler has improved its market share to over 14% in 1993 from less than 10% in 1990.

Phase 2: The goal is to increase knowledge of processes through the sophisticated development of metrics. Increased understanding of customer requirements, determining cost of quality and increasing supplier possibilities create need for additional change.

Phase 3: Understanding the limitations of the organization core to respond to customers, benchmark information and other ideas from industry, and increasingly strong quality team network results in pressure to re-engineer processes.

Phase 4: The integrated core is further refined as existing benchmarking teams, quality teams, and customer/supplier partners focus on a world-class quality product or service.

Mikio Kitano is Toyota's production guru. Kitano rejects machines that over complicate production. "The key to productivity is simplicity. Men control machines, not the other way around."
Karen Lowry Miller, *Business Week*, (May 17, 1993), p. 95.

INFORMATION TECHNOLOGY

Summary: Information technology is a major design variable. It makes the new-design organization possible. Information technology is involved in the development of each of the quality systems.

Large old-design organizations centralize computing power (mainframe computers). Control is the focus of computing in old-design organizations. The advent of smaller computers during the 1980s connected by local and wide area networks (LANs and WANs) has complemented the need for organizations to be more responsive to a faster-paced external environment by empowering front-line employees.

Phase 1: Information is centralized with the intent to control access to information. The information architecture complements the old-design structure. Pressure to get information to the front line begins to increase. Groups of PC users emerge. Decentralization, downsizing, and rightsizing begin to invade thinking.

Phase 2: LANS emerge in units around the company. They connect the desktop personal computers. Questions of data availability, data security, and developing internal standards for hardware and software become important. Electronic mail is one of the first applications to drive the connection of the dispersed local area networks. Communication is important to many of the developments in the organization. The mainframe data is distributed to computer servers for local use on computers.

Questions about how to migrate from the mainframe to decentralized computing begin to dominate strategy.

Phase 3: Decentralized computing increases the communication and coordination available at the shop floor, further weakening the hierarchy. Strengthening teams, and more frequent customer information, increase pressure to expand the responsiveness of the core technology. Reengineering important processes with heavy information technology input highlights this phase. Supplier partnerships are enhanced with electronic data interchange (EDI).

Phase 4: Reengineered integrated core supports team and individual responsibilities for quality efforts. Application of information technology to coordination applications and mission critical processes further flattens hierarchy and makes the switch to distributed processing complete.

> *"By virtue of its power and popularity, no single business resource is better positioned than information technology to bring about radical improvement in business processes."*
> Thomas Davenport, *Process Innovation*, (Boston: HBS Press, 1993), p. 17.

INFRASTRUCTURE

Summary: Infrastructure refers to the systems that support the effectiveness of the quality/value chain. Marketing, finance, information technology, and human resource systems are important infrastructure elements.

Marketing's focus shifts from "pushing product" to supporting the customer satisfaction effort and helping to highlight the "delight" components of the product or service. Finance has an important role in financing the drive to quality leadership in the marketplace. This sometimes requires a shifting of power away from financial planning to quality planning (managing by plan). Information technology and people systems are described in detail in this chapter.

Phase 1: The old-design infrastructure is a centralized, financially driven organization with a self-contained marketing unit focused on exploiting market opportunities. Initial demands of the quality-aware organization begin to refocus these infrastructure components.

Phase 2: As the team network evolves and the supporting quality planning/management by plan become more important, the financial function becomes more supportive of the quality effort. The increasing need for customer-need information (design system) and satisfaction data (design and production systems and team network) integrates marketing into the quality network.

Phase 3: The emphasis is on managing the power shift from the functional hierarchy to the flattened quality hierarchy. Refining managing by plan through increased interaction with quality information and more competent teams is important. Marketing and finance become fully integrated into the team network and manage by plan efforts that support satisfaction of customers' needs.

Phase 4: Attaining world-class status requires constant refinement of the existing systems in a coordinated focus on customer satisfaction.

> *"For now the actual process of managing is exempt from process innovation, for--as researchers have shown--it is unstructured, discontinuous, ad hoc, intuitive, and cognitive."* Nannette Fondas, "Process Innovation," *The Academy of Management Executive*, VII, No. 2, (May 1992),p. 102.

PEOPLE SYSTEMS - PS

Summary: People systems are very complex.   They include the entire team network and the supporting selection, training, assessment, and development subsystems. These systems determine the potential success of the entire transformation. However, people systems depend on the logical development of the other systems. Increasingly sophisticated teams and individuals need increasingly sophisticated information and quality systems to continue their development.

Phase 1: Initially, there is an emphasis on training for basic problem solving. Employee teams are formed to get the increasing workload done.

Phase 2: People systems proliferate in stage 2 with initiatives in reward systems, selection systems, and management development. The quality team network increases in complexity and demands increasingly sophisticated training and selection support.

Phase 3: With a quality network and emerging support infrastructure, the integration of quality processes into the business processes begins. Real team successes begin to characterize rallies and award ceremonies.

Phase 4: Individual decision-making discretion and self-managed teams distinguish operations and other front-line positions. The integration of information technology, people systems, and elements of the core technology are refined into world-class status.

> *Lee Boatwright, CEO of Baltimore's CentraBank, recalled the transformation he led a medium-sized savings bank in the early1980s. "The reason we were a success was our immediate focus on building a team structure, along with tightening selection and expanding training. This allowed us to tackle the increasing workload with more qualified and higher skilled people."*

TABLE 7-6
Changes in Key People Systems

	PHASE 1	PHASE 2	PHASE 3	PHASE 4
Quality Network	Quality Council started	Expanding teams and growing information systems enhance growth	Refinement of management by plan and quality network	Differences between quality responsibilities and functional role transparent.
Teams	Ad hoc team projects started	Pseudo-teams evolve but full development is still limited	Full team development depends on process re-engineering	Self managed teams are fully supported through quality network
Selection	Selection system is expanded to include teamwork criteria	Selection system is tightened with criteria complementing needs of teams	Team-based selection includes team competence	
Rewards	Some extrinsic rewards for quality participation	Quality networks and teams increase reward opportunities	Teams and re-engineered processes increase reward occasions	Culture is characterized by an embedded web of extrinsic and intrinsic rewards
Assessment	Traditional hierarchial appraisal system focussed on individual	Slow evolution to team-based evaluation and customer indices	Managing by plan and team-based reward system guide appraisal	Assessment is team-based and related to customer needs
Training	Initial training is on quality awareness and basic problem solving	Training proliferates to lead growth of quality effort.	Training adapts to changing culture	Training and coaching become ubiquitous

Several important subsystems develop in concert with the key quality systems. They play a key role in the development of the infrastructure that supports the viability of the new-design organization. This next section starts with capsule comments in Table 7-6, which summarizes the development of the key people systems.

QUALITY NETWORK

Summary: The quality network is organizational quality's beachhead in the organization. It provides a power base from which to launch the team effort, establish priorities in organization activities, and acquire resources. It enhances leadership opportunities to establish the quality value.

Phase 1: The quality network is initiated by an executive-level quality council. Training in problem solving precedes the initial projects. Intradepartmental, voluntary quality circles are established.

Phase 2: The quality network proliferates through the organization as training achieves a certain intensity and the number of teams achieves a critical level. Processes are identified, information is available, and the benchmark teams are active.

Phase 3: The network is integrated with the management by plan system. Real teams develop with some initial forays into self-managed teams.

Phase 4: People transfer easily between team and individual roles almost unsupervised. The team is an integral part of all core and infrastructure processes and systems.

TEAMS

Summary: Teams are the heart of the improvement effort. They become the primary means of getting work done, outside the day-by-day operations. Process improvement activities and most innovative work are done by teams working on projects. Teams in the core technology teams evolve from ad hoc quality teams to self-managed teams if the process is supportive. Reengineering is undertaken to provide the appropriate environment. Middle-management teams evolve from directing activities to tackling complex process and strategic problems.

Phase 1: Because of the limitations of hierarchy and design of the core technology, teams don't exist. Minimal team activity at this stage.

Phase 2: Team activity increases, but full development is still limited by the entrenched old-design authority relationships. Problem solving teams are started and begin to blossom in middle management; voluntary quality teams (e.g., quality circles) in core technology are moderately successful. The design of operations is a limiting factor.

Phase 3: Inadequate systems to respond to customers, and pressure to redesign core technology heighten early in this phase. Strategies are made to reengineer processes. The quality network undertakes reengineering projects. Use of information technology with the intent to empower flattens the hierarchy and refocuses middle managers. Problem solving, training, and coaching become middle management responsibility.

Phase 4: Aligned with core technology and supported by team infrastructure, teams are self-managed.

SELECTION
Summary: Continually tightening the selection process to improve human resources is the goal of the high quality organization. As the new-design systems take hold, the demands on and for people increase dramatically. Quality of personnel is a key factor in the success of the transformation. Criteria increase for competency and broaden to include team compatibility.

Phase 1: In line with quality commitment, selection system is expanded to include criteria for teamwork.

Phase 2: Selection system is tightened to include tests and experientials for interpersonal competence.

Phase 3: Selection for problem solving and team competence become the heart of the selection process.

REWARDS
Summary: The reward system is an important enabler of the entire transformation process. Then it becomes a major feature of the new-design culture.

Extrinsic rewards (those generated by the organization) and intrinsic rewards (those that come from success in challenging jobs) combine in a complex reward system. In the hierarchial organization, extrinsic rewards are available. Design factors make the jobs too simple. Intrinsic rewards accumulate as the team network develops and processes are reengineered. As the quality network develops, additional extrinsic reward opportunities are initiated.

Phase 1: Extrinsic rewards are given for participation in the quality efforts. This includes money for suggestions and recognition mementos.

Phase 2: In general, the reward system becomes more widespread as teams begin to proliferate. This includes additional recognition ceremonies generated from accomplishments within the quality network.

Phase 3: Intrinsic reward opportunities increase as processes are reengineered. Extrinsic performance rewards, rallies, and parties proliferate as the team network is fortified.

Phase 4: Positive reinforcement is evident in the entire culture from the monetary rewards, team rewards, self-managed environments, and coaching, all supported by a myriad of intrinsic rewards from the way the business is organized.

ASSESSMENT

Summary: Feedback is ample in the new-design environment. Assessing teams and individual performance is difficult, though, because most efforts are intertwined with other people in teams and elements of the core technology. Assessment occurs frequently in these organizations because assessment information feeds into the team problem solving. If performance is low, the system is evaluated to establish the reasons for low performance. Rewards go to teams based on overall performance of the unit or organization.

Assessment in the old-design organization is focused on the individual. If the assessment determined the individual didn't achieve pre-set objectives, then minimal reward or no promotion resulted. The system's unintended result was that people protected their own performance, often at the expense of others and the organization.   The evolution from this system to the new-design system is difficult. Elements of the individually based system exist until phase II, when the spirit of continual improvement and teams take root.

Phase 1: The traditional appraisal system evaluates behavior against hard criteria like cost and sales criteria and soft criteria like manifesting certain traits. The system is administered through the hierarchy. Early in this stage, the system is moderated by the quality notion that most performance problems belong to management not the individual.

Phase 2: As the team-based quality network develops, the traditional system fades. Constant feedback to teams on all elements of the work process supports continual improvement. This diminishes the importance of the old yearly assessment process.   Selection   and   training systems are featured in the new-design organization. These systems increase the competency of the employees, which, in turn, feeds into the team problem solving. The use of assessment systems to weed out incompetent employees diminishes.

Phase 3: Managing by plan focuses people and teams on follow through. Team-based reward system increases nonhierarchial assessment of significant performances. As the business process redesign makes the processes more responsive to the customer, customer satisfaction data become assessment criteria. This data becomes more important to the assessment of the organization.

Phase 4: Assessment is team-based and results from performance on customer indices.

TRAINING
Summary: Training is an essential component of the success of nearly all efforts during the transformation. New skills and attitudes need to be introduced, reinforced, and increased during the transition. The new-design organization is communication-intense and training is a component of that.

Phase 1: Training needs in the hierarchial organization are moderate owing to the simplified jobs and elaborate hierarchy. Increases in training are focused on future problem solving needs of the organization.

Phase 2: Training needs increase dramatically as the team network grows. The increasing complexity of the work and demands for communication skills result in new demands for training. The decline of the hierarchy increases the importance of training as a communication and control system.

Phase 3: Training needs expand to include technical-, group-, and individual-level needs. As the hierarchy diminishes, training and coaching increase in scope.

Phase 4: Training and coaching become ubiquitous. Training through formal and informal means covers all elements of technical, administrative, group, and individual needs. The organization is characterized as the learning organization.

PROBLEM SOLVING

Summary: Problem solving is a core process in the new-design organization. Once people have the tools and the team network, the basis for continual improvement, kaizen, is established. Problem solving potential is limited in the old-design organization because jobs are simple and teamwork is difficult to organize. Increasing information technology begins to provide problem-solving opportunities in middle management. Reengineering exercises create more opportunity in the front-line.

Phase 1: The problem-solving process is highlighted as core to the quality effort in the quality awareness efforts. Initial training efforts highlight the basic problem-solving tools.

Phase 2: Problem solving training includes additional ways to structure problems, collect and analyze data, as well as implement results. Limited by developing team network and old-design core technology.

Phase 3: Language of, and priority of, problem solving is recognized and rewarded. Training becomes more complex as the organization approaches full statistical process control. Partners (suppliers and customers) are introduced to the company's problem-solving process.

Phase 4: Problem solving becomes the guiding discipline of self-managed teams.

CUSTOMER

Summary: The customer is the entire focus of the quality organization. Customer needs drive the design process. Customer satisfaction drives the production system. Marketing finds ways to support the information needs of the units and help drive the quality leadership goal. Internally, tasks in cross-functional processes are connected by a chain of "customers of customers." Employees think of themselves as customers of the employee of the task upstream from their task. They, in turn, have customer's downstream.

Phase 1: The initial strategy entails finding any available customer information and putting it into a format to help improve design on future products and adjustments for current products.

Phase 2: Other systems just emerging demand more customer information. Increasing awareness of customer needs for design systems increases sophistication of customer research and related information systems.

Systems that respond and categorize customers' warranty claims and complaints become more sophisticated.

Phase 3: A sophisticated customer information system (CIS) supplies information increasingly demanded by teams to refine existing products or services. Marketing becomes more pervasive using surveys, interviews, and focus groups. Metrics are increasingly tied to demanding benchmarks. Customers are partners in several internal processes.

Phase 4: Sophisticated information systems fine-tune the development and building of quality products or services. Customers are members of teams.

SUMMARY

The change process includes three phases: unfreeze, change program; refreeze. Unfreezing makes the organization/unit/ individual prepared for the change program. Unfreezing can result from a planned change effort by an organization development expert. The unfreezing can happen because the organization fails. A failure causes concern and a scan of the environment for a solution. These situations prepare the way for the change program. This phase implements the changes. The final refreezing phase ensures the change program becomes part of the culture. It ensures that the infrastructure supporting the change is complete.

Organizations are challenged to make the appropriate change to maintain their success. As the market evolves, organizations have to make adaptive changes in order to maintain their success. The dynamics of the marketplace stay the same and the fundamental design is the same. This is called a design archetype and it is complementary to the environment it faces. If the environment changes fundamentally, then the underlying design assumptions change as well. This is a new design archetype. The key for the existing organization is to undergo a transformational change. This results in a change that alters the internal dynamics and interpretive scheme so the organization can be successful under the changed market conditions.

Organizations follow one of four tracks in the transformational change effort: track 1-- organization inertia results in the organization staying in the same track and not undergoing the fundamental change; track 2-- the organization successfully makes the fundamental changes; track 3-- the organization tries, but fails and gives up; track 4-- the organization expends enormous efforts, never gives up, but doesn't succeed as in a never-ending journey.

Within the planned change phase, a model of four phases of change is presented. The four phases take an organization from the old-design archetype to the new-design archetype. The four phases are characterized as a transition: phase 1--Control to Awareness; phase 2--tentative to Feedback; phase 3--relationship to partner; phase 4--partner to team.

Each of the key quality systems are arrayed against the four phases. Benchmarking, product or service design, partnerships, people systems, and integrated core technology are tracked through the four phases with some reference to how they depend on concurrent development for a successful transformation.

◆◆◆

POINTS TO PONDER

1. It's been said that nothing is so constant as change. Do you agree with this?

2. In the sense of Lewin's change model, can a quality process be "re-frozen" for the long term (like ice-cubes)? Or do we need to keep working to keep the frozen process effective?

3. How can one deal with typical forms of resistance to change with quality processes that must be seen as changes?

4. If change is a continuing and never-ending journey, when will we ever have any stability in the work place that people can count on and relax a little?

Please find additional questions at the end of the reading.

◆◆

READING

The New Paradigm

What do Ptolemy, Copernicus, and Jack Thompson have in common? No they aren't on a TV sit-com.. nor are they three ancient deities. The former two are ancient astronomers, and the latter is a modern day vice-president at McCormick and Co. It took 1400 years for the wrong ideas of Ptolemy to be replaced by the right ideas of Copernicus. Jack and his colleagues brought McCormick through an analogous breakthrough in business in just a few years.

Ptolemy was an astronomer. His paradigm had the Earth at the center of the Universe. It took 14 centuries until Copernicus showed that the errors astronomers were vainly trying to explain resulted from a faulty paradigm. No amount of fancy word-smithing could explain away the errors. The fundamental paradigm had to change. Surprising to many of Copernicus's followers, the earth wasn't the center of the universe. The sun was. Once the new perspective was adopted, the errors and mistakes in many other areas were put into context and explained.

The Ptolemy-Copernicus example illustrates the way people have learned through the ages. Jumping to the present, modern corporations are changing in much the same way. The old bureaucratic, finance-driven organization represented by GE, Westinghouse, and IBM of a few years ago, is analogous to a Ptolemic paradigm. For decades the marketplace seemed to revolve around their companies. Over the last couple of decades these companies were surprised as increasing customer sensitivity to quality, voracious international competition, rapid advances in information technology, and new approaches to human resource management set up the organizational equivalent of the Copernican revolution. This changeover didn't take a few centuries. It only took a decade.

Leading companies adopted total quality management as a corner-stone to change. In addition, these companies adopted intensive human resource programs and used new advances in information technology. TQM can have a positive impact on any organization, even some of the traditional organizations. What distinguishes the leading companies is their emphasis on human resources, and even more importantly, the use of information technology to leverage the talent of the company's human resources.

Information technology is the component that turns adaptive change into a transformation. Computers have been used to automate old ways of doing things.   This is called "paving the cowpath."   Leading organizations use computer to enable transformational change. This is a new road, more direct, and much faster. The term is reengineering. Reengineering processes help companies become more competitive by responding to customer needs more quickly.

This is why Jack Thompson is featured in this article. The information technology strength in an organization is a key element in the foundation for most organization successes in the 1990s. Not only does it enhance organization change, but it provides the basis for competitive advantage. This is exactly what it did at McCormick during the 1980s.

The problems in the 1980s were partially due, ironically, to successes during the company's prior 100 years. McCormick is a proud company that has always excelled in the marketplace. The quality of their spices was its calling card. The earliest motto, "Make the best, somebody will buy it," was superseded by "Quality is our signature" a couple of years ago. What organization wouldn't like to build its modern quality effort on the depth of this history?

McCormick people are a decided competitive advantage.   Few workforces are nurtured like McCormick's. For example, they have a complex management development infrastructure called Multiple Management, "the management of the business by many." Governed by its own by-laws, it presents an opportunity for middle managers to manage and participate in large-scale projects. It represents a tremendous problem-solving resource for the company. In addition, the system provides the corporation with a proving ground for future leaders.

The roots of the multiple management system go back 60 years to the problems of the depression.   C.P. McCormick took over the nearly-bankrupt corporation amid many threats including the rise of powerful messages from socialists and unions. CP developed a missionary zeal on what "free management" could do. He captured his successful management theory in a book titled *The Power of People*. His efforts are the roots of the modern multiple management. Sixty years of refinement. This is a textbook example of building a winning culture.

Interestingly, this cultural strength turned into a liability as employment at McCormick began to be taken for granted. It had a people-oriented culture. The tone of the culture was more in the paternalistic tradition of the bureaucracy. The 1980s revolution required changing this paternalism into a culture where individuals are empowered in their roles and the structure allows wider participation.

McCormick's wake-up call came when a raider attempted to buy control of the company in 1979. They fought off the bid, but nearly lost the company. McCormick had a real estate subsidiary that was very successful, but detracted from the stock market value of the company. If

McCormick could be bought, the real estate subsidiary could have been sold for more than the present market value of the entire company. Then the spice company would have been free. The rapid growth of the real estate subsidiary had the effect of taking executive management's eye off the manufacturing side of the company. The spice part of the company was high-cost, rather arrogant, and slipping.

With this as a backdrop, Jack developed a strong team in information systems that supported changes in McCormick's manufacturing capability. Internal changes included a major program in total quality management, development of work teams, and improved information systems at all levels. The core manufacturing capability gave the company cost and flexibility advantages. Buzz McCormick and Bailey Thomas unleashed a vastly improved marketing strategy partially based on this manufacturing capability. Competence in international communications and electronic data interchange set the stage for McCormick's adoption of supply-chain management. Not only did the company follow their customers like McDonald's internationally, but it began to work with growers and processers of spices worldwide to improve quality and quantity.

McCormick is a survivor. Over the last five years, its profits have grown rapidly. After his retirement, Jack Thompson said "McCormick knows how to use quality, information, people, and internationalism to its strategic advantage. Competitors have a real challenge in front of them if they want to beat McCormick in the marketplace."

5. What elements of adaptive change and transformational change are evident in this reading?

6. What key quality systems are explicit and which ones are implicit in the reading? Do you see any evidence of the four phases of growth in the reading? How must the change have progressed based on your knowledge of change in the key quality systems?

◆ ◆

CHAPTER 8
THE WORLD QUALITY REVOLUTION

The objectives for this chapter are:
1. To understand the importance of the quality award and prize competitions.

2. To understand the comprehensive nature of the models driving the competitions.

Key Words introduced in this chapter.

Audit	Enabler	ISO 9000
Baldrige Award	European Quality	Network
Benchmark	Company Award	Senseii
Deming Prize	Innovation	Transformation
Deployment	Intangible	

INTRODUCTION

Quality is being adopted by companies around the world. It is a key element to the competitiveness of a company that intends to win in the marketplace. As a testament to its importance, national and local governments sponsor many awards and prizes. Ordinarily, there are criteria to be met, evaluations, and visits before selection of winners.

Prizes/awards are given to the organization that achieves control over a comprehensive quality infrastructure, and show results from that effort. They all offer a framework against which a company is evaluated. The framework represents the basic systems/processes that support an organization's quality initiative. It is sufficiently general so organizations can reflect their own unique situations.

An analysis of the prizes is important to all interested in managing the quality organization. Using one of these frameworks is likely to be the way a firm becomes introduced to the rigors of achieving high levels of quality. The international comparisons only reinforce the importance of quality. They increase the awareness of the world-wide applicability of the quality model of organizations. In addition, they make organizations aware of all the potential competitors emerging with quality products around the world.

This chapter discusses three major awards: the Deming prizes, the Baldrige National Quality Award, and the European Quality Award. They come from, respectively, Japan, the United States, and Europe. The Japanese award was first offered during the 1950s by the Japanese Union of Scientists and Engineers (JUSE). The American award was legislated by Congress in 1987. The European award is privately sponsored and was first given in 1992.

These programs evolved from national concerns about their competitiveness. During the 1950s, the Japanese had little capital and a terrible worldwide reputation for quality. The Deming prize was created to focus attention and resources on the need to conserve capital and increase exports. The Baldrige came about because of the Japanese success in building quality into their products. Congress saw the connection between the devastating marketplace defeats of U.S. companies and the low quality of their goods. Passage of the law was its attempt to enhance the focus of American firms on quality.

Europe put up barriers to Japanese competitors. Consequently, Japanese influence was delayed in that marketplace. One professed goal in the early drive for unification of Europe was to protect the European way of life. Most of the countries have institutions protecting a balance of work life within a complex social-welfare society. Most organizations historically developed internal human resource programs that reflect this value system. Massive unemployment in most countries have increased criticism of some of these practices. There is a concern in Europe that they aren't keeping up with the quality revolution racing across rest of the world.[1]

THE DEMING PRIZE

W. Edwards Deming is a giant in the world quality revolution. In Japan the quality revolution built its momentum on Deming's ideas. It was his understanding of the Japanese predicament, sensitivity to the

---

[1] Lucy Walker, "Delors Counts the Cost of War on Jobs," *The European*, (May 27-30, 1993), p. 33.

people, and his predilection to teach that increased his influence. Deming, apparently, had a way of explaining statistics that was understandable. He had respect for the Japanese development effort. In order to help that effort he donated the royalties from the translation of his book and his lecture fees to JUSE to continue its work on quality. In 1958, JUSE devised the award to focus Japanese attention on statistical quality control. As a measure of their respect for Deming, they named the award for him.

> *Toyota saw* to it that 11 of its major suppliers had won the award by the late 1980s. Besides Toyota, other winners include familiar names like Komatsu, Ricoh, Toshiba, Bridgestone, and Matsushita Electric.

THE PRIZE

The Deming Prize rewards the firm for absolute control over all elements that have any impact on product quality. The philosophy is total quality control (TQC) and is deployed organization wide. There are three categories of winners of the Deming Prize: the Deming Prize for individuals, the Deming Application Prize awarded to companies, and the Deming Factory prize. In 1970, another award was created that can be called the Japan Quality Control Award. This is the highest award for quality given to a company. The requirements are that the company must have won the Deming prize, and waited 5 additional years to apply.

> *TQC-- Total quality control-- A company-wide focus on Kaizen activities through an integrated, cross-functional effort. Improvement of cross-functional goals like quality, cost, scheduling, manpower development and product development become the core of the effort. TQC includes sales, marketing, and service, as well as production. Policy and quality deployment, plus organization development, all fall under the TQC.*

Firms applying for the Deming, are prepared to spend years increasing their control over quality. Counselors (senseii) approved by JUSE work closely with the company to raise it to a competitive level. These counselors drill the company officers and managers until they have a superior understanding of how their organizations control quality. When the counselor says it is time, the company applies to compete for the award. If the application is accepted, the company prepares for an intense two-week audit of its facilities by prize officials. The audit determines the caliber of the firm's methods and mastery of TQC. The prize emphasizes education, self-improvement, and cooperation.

DEMING PRIZE AUDIT CHECKLIST

The Deming prize's approach to quality is heavily analytical.[2] The intent is to organize to collect, analyze, and use appropriate quality data. The following discussion highlights the key questions asked in the competition:

♦Corporate policy: Are the quality plans, goals, policies, and deployment systems consistent, constantly rationalized, and focused on the supply, processing, sale, and delivery of the product or service?

♦Organization and its management: How extensive is the structural change to reflect authority redistribution, the full development of the quality network, and communication and coordination requirements among the quality entities?

♦Education and Dissemination: How pervasive is education across the organization units, including subcontractors and vendors? Is the training intensity of analytical tools, like statistical quality control, adequate to make everyone understand the concepts?

♦Collection, dissemination and use of information on quality (implementation): Is the firm organized to ensure that quality information from inside and outside the organization, is processed, analyzed, and transmitted quickly throughout the organization?

♦Analysis: The following questions focus on the critical aspects of the infrastructure that ensures the appropriate intensity includes: How is quality information collected and analyzed across all units? Are quality problems defined and analyzed using appropriate tools (especially statistical methods)? Are the results utilized assertively?

♦Standardization: Are standards established, used, revised, and rationalized?

---

[2] Masaaki Imai, *Kaizen,* (New York: Random-House, 1986), p. 243-5. See also Joseph Duffy, "The Deming Prize vs. The Baldrige Award," *Quality Digest,* 1991, pp. 48-49.

♦Control: Are control points and countermeasures established for the organization for normal and emergency conditions? How effective is the administration of this process?

♦Quality Assurance: Is there appropriate intensity in the administration and problem solving for the quality assurance system? Are their systems ensuring the competence of new-product development, quality function deployment, safety and liability analysis, process control and improvement, and process capability?

♦Results: What results can be shown from the introduction of TQC on product quality, service, delivery, cost, profits, safety, and the environment? Are there any intangible benefits?

♦For the Future: Does the company base its future strategies on an analysis of current strengths and weaknesses and information from the TQC program?

RESULTS OF THE COMPETITION

The Deming prize is a rigorous competition. The results for the winners have been positive. Table 8-1 outlines the tangible and intangible effects as recounted by the winners.

Professor Tetsuichi Asaka is the leading Deming Prize consultant. He strikes fear in companies because he is so good. Every few weeks he, or an associate, grills one of the company's top managers for hours on what they know and understand.

Texas Instruments's Japanese subsidiary (TI Japan) had difficulties before 1980 in manufacturing semiconductors. The company was full of dissension and problems. It was the acknowledged technology leader, but not the quality leader. There were visible problems like bent leads, cracks in some packages, and improper labeling. Job standards problems made machinery adjustments difficult. During the preparation for the Deming, TI Japan virtually eliminated visual inspection. Production problems were down by 50% and worker productivity up by 30% between 1980 and 1984. TI Japan won the Deming in 1985.

Achieving the prize is an all out effort. Not all firms are successful in their attempt to achieve it. Other firms believe that the TQC model is too

TANGIBLE EFFECTS	INTANGIBLE EFFECTS
o Increased market share o Increased sales volume o Increased production volume o Successful development of new products o Shortening of product development time o Development of new markets o Improved quality o Fewer complaints o Reduced defect costs o Fewer processes o More employee suggestions o Fewer industrial accidents	o Increased involvement in management o Increased quality consciousness and problem consciousness o Better communications, both horizontally and vertically o Improved quality of work o Improved human relations o Improved information feedback o Improved management skills o Permeation of market in concept o Clear delineation between responsibility and authority o More confidence in new product development o Conversion to goal-oriented thinking o Improved standardization o More active use of statistical quality control

Adapted from Imai Masaaki, *Kaizen* (New York: Random House, 1986), p. 246.

TABLE 8-1
Reports of Competitive Effects from Deming Winners

constrictive. It might, indeed, limit their ability to respond to the marketplace. Companies spend three to five years honing their operations for the prize. It involves everyone in the corporation. Once a company declares itself a candidate it can't afford to lose. Seiko lost during the 1960s and never reapplied. It's said that after losing, pride doesn't let a company reapply. Kenichi Ohmae of McKinsey & Co. sees the Deming Prize winners as comprising a cult. He says that some of the many companies that won the prize "are suffering an overdose of dogma."[3]

It's said that conventional TQC is too inflexible and erodes the creative components of the organization. Developing advertising campaigns and wooing clients are marketing processes that don't lend themselves to TQC. Fuji Xerox observes that justifying everything with data inhibited laboratory creativity. Shimuzu Construction won the Deming in 1983. The award came the same year the company had serious financial setbacks. In retrospect, they observed, "The fervor shown by proponents of total quality control is exactly like what is seen in adherents of some religious cult." Two household names, Canon and Honda, avoided the competition altogether, because it would rob them of their spontaneity.

JUSE organized a second quality medal to encourage organizations to continue the intensely managed quality. The Japan Quality Control Medal was created in 1969. Companies can compete for it five years after they win the Deming prize. Twelve companies have won this new medal. Toyota, Komatsu, and Nippon Steel Corp are among the better known winners. In spite of what the detractors of the prize profess, those companies are still world-wide leaders.

THE BALDRIGE AWARD

The Deming prize is offered through JUSE, largely an academic group. They became both the tutors for and judges of the award. The Baldrige award was originally designed to be a peer review award offered by an industrial foundation that judges industrial companies.

The hero in this story is Admiral Frank C. Collins, Jr. In the early 1980s,[4] Collins was executive director of Quality Assurance for the Defense Logistics Agency. The stimulus for his effort was a half page ad in an American newspaper by a Japanese company. It said, "The most important name in quality control in Japan is American." Of course, the reference was to W. Edwards Deming, for whom the Deming prize was named. The company had won the prize 23 years earlier and was still proud of that fact. To Collins, this spoke of the power of the prize to concentrate a company's management on quality.

Working hard, Admiral Collins presented the quality award idea to the National Academy of Sciences. He felt it was prestigious and nonpolitical. It turned out that they weren't interested. Collins didn't let

---

[3] Masaaki Imai, *Kaizen*, (New York: Random House, 1986).

[4] F. C. Collins, "The Malcolm Baldrige National Quality Award-- A Dream Realized," *Quality Digest*, (April 1989), pp. 38-49.

the idea die, however. He took it to the Department of Commerce in early 1983, where it got a hearing. The U.S. President's Council of Economic Advisors was also cool to the idea, and it faded away.

Later in 1983, there was a White House Conference on Productivity. This conference was focused on the issue of the diminishing American productivity. The National Productivity Advisory Council sponsored the conference thinking the outcome would be a National Medal for Productivity. Although people were interested, the idea was tabled because no thought had been given to the criteria for achieving the medal.

A book summarizing the conference, Productivity Growth: A Better Life for America, was published in 1984. The book consisted of 82 recommendations for government action, 66 private sector recommendations, and 7 specific quality recommendations. During this period an advocate for national productivity, C. Jackson Grayson, became acquainted with Admiral Collins. Grayson was a member of both the White House Conference and the National Productivity Advancement Council.

After Collins retired from the Navy in the fall of 1984, he became vice president of a company named AVCO. He and Grayson decided to create a National Quality Productivity Award. Late in 1985, a group of business people got together in Washington, D.C.. They decided to: (1) press for a quality award rather than the combination productivity-quality award, (2) develop criteria that would fit both service and manufacturing, and (3) meet two times per month until they developed the criteria to achieve the award.

Initially, they had no official name -- they were known as "Marty's Group." They met over 50 times to establish the criteria for the award. Marty was the hard-working executive secretary that coordinated all the activities. Near the end they officially named the group the President's Quality Award. They became aware of work being done by the Senate subcommittee on Science and Technology on a quality award bill. Florida Power & Light's representative served as liaison between the private group and the Senate committee. Both groups worked well together.

The American Society for Quality Control (ASQC) is a major association of quality professionals. They were part of Marty's Group. In a total surprise testimony to the Senate subcommittee, the chair of ASQC testified, "The last thing American industry needs is an internal competition of a national quality award, especially since the award implies winners and losers. We need to carefully and fully understand the proper context for a national award."[5] In a further blow, he said ASQC would participate only if there was "a substantial technical assistance support

---

[5] Collins, "The Malcolm Baldrige National Quality Award-- A Dream Realized," p. 42.

program to provide guidelines, training and sharing of effective strategies with all industry and government." ASQC dropped out of Marty's group. To be snubbed by the leading quality association was a shock.

The congressional subcommittee, though, pressed the Collins group to finish. The group, intent on making this a peer judged affair, developed a foundation with about $3 million. In another surprise, the popular secretary of commerce at the time, Malcolm Baldrige, died when he was thrown from a horse. In the midst of the reaction to this popular Secretary's death, Congress acted on the quality award and passed Public Law 100-107, The Malcolm Baldrige National Quality Improvement Act of 1987.

> Public Law 100-107: "To provide for the establishment and conduct of a national quality improvement program under which (1) awards are given to selected companies and other organizations in the United States that practice effective quality management and as a result make significant improvements in the quality of their goods and services, and (2) information is disseminated about the successful strategies and programs."

Congress reflected the public's concern about the quality of products and services in the United States with the passage of the act. There were three objectives of the legislation. The first was to promote quality awareness. The second was to recognize quality achievements of U.S. businesses. The third was to publicize successful quality strategies.[6] The work of the Collins group became the nucleus of the Baldrige Prize.

President Reagan wanted the first awards to be given before he left office in 1988. The award office was placed in the National Institute of Standards and Technology (NIST) because of its reputation and objectivity. The first awards were given in the fall of 1988, largely because the administrators of the office were able to build on the comprehensive work accomplished by Admiral Collins and his group.

CORE VALUES

The Baldrige's vision is to focus organization efforts on being the best. Quality leadership in the marketplace is the goal. Underlying the quality model they developed are several core values:

♦ <u>Customer</u> <u>driven</u> <u>quality</u>: Customers get value, satisfaction and preference in their experiences with the organization. These

---

[6] *National Institute of Standards and Technology. 1993 Award Criteria*, (Washington D.C.: Government Printing Office, 1993).

include the gamut of interactions from the purchase through servicing. The entire strategic focus of the firm is to retain customers and increase loyalty and satisfaction. Flexible responses to changing market and customer needs are part of the value.

♦ Leadership: The emphasis for leadership is to "create a customer orientation, clear and visible quality values, and high expectations" through active participation in all aspects of quality and strategic planning. Leadership should be participative and highly visible.

♦ Continuous improvement: All work unit activities try to continually improve in addition to searching for "breakthroughs." The areas of interest are: improve products; reduce errors, defects and waste; improve cycle time; improve productivity; and improve companies' community leadership responsibility.

♦ Employee participation and development: Workforce quality and involvement are essential ingredients to the quality leadership company. Employee satisfaction is an element of a company's success in instilling this value.

♦ Fast response: Response, quality, and productivity all improve as an organization develops ever-shorter cycles for new or improved products.

♦ Design quality and prevention: Designing-in quality minimizes downstream problems and increased costs. This value is focused on working out problems upstream and preventing downstream problems.

♦ Long range outlook: Quality leadership in the marketplace requires a long term commitment. Commitments to customers, suppliers, and others require this orientation. Strategic planning anticipates many changes, and supports a firm's long term commitment.

♦ Management by fact: Information extracted from multiple sources support organization decision making and problem solving. Some examples include benchmarking, team problem solving, planning, customers, performance, and marketplace comparisons.

♦ Partnership Development: External customer and supplier partnerships and internal partnerships with unions are examples of this value. At the strategic level alliances and joint ventures are becoming increasingly important manifestations of partnerships.

♦ Corporate responsibility and citizenship: The company's concern includes the society in which it does business. The organization's concerns include supporting social and economic stability and minimizing the negative impact of the business on the society.

THE BALDRIGE MODEL

With these values underlying the effort, the Baldrige has a model of organization that targets the key variables that describe an organization's quality infrastructure. The flow of the Baldrige model is illustrated in Figure 8-1. It is described like this:

The leadership driver focuses the four system components so that measurable quality results succeed in meeting the **customer satisfaction** organizational goal.

Figure 8-1 puts these words into the sequence described above.

FIGURE 8-1.
The Baldrige Organization Model

▾ Leadership (95 points)	▾ Information analysis (75 points) ▾ Strategic quality planning (60 points) ▾ Human resource utilization (150 points) ▾ Quality assurance of products or services (140 points)	▾ Quality results (180 points)	▾ Customer satisfaction (300 points)

From Curt W. Reimann, "The Baldrige Award: Leading the Way in Quality Initiatives," *Quality Progress* July 1989, p. 38. See also 1993 Award Criteria: pp. 5,15.

Leadership is the driver on the left with systems, results, and satisfaction resulting from the leadership efforts. The numbers following each variable are estimates of the relative importance of each variable in the achievement of high quality. This model simply lists the variables. They act together in complex ways to achieve the quality results and customer satisfaction.

Each of the seven criteria in Figure 8-1 is weighted according to the importance of the criteria in achieving high quality.[7] They are listed in the figures by each criteria. The individual weights add up to 1000 points. An initial observation of the exercise might remind you of the puts of components of college entrance tests like the Scholastic Aptitude Test.

The seven major criteria are broken into 92 areas to address. These "Areas to address" focus attention on key attributes of the criteria. The comments help a company tie the criteria to the core values described earlier, and they help link the criteria to each other. Even with this level of coaching, there are numerous approaches a company might take to improve their quality.

Customer Satisfaction: Customer satisfaction is the primary organization performance goal. Quality is attained if the customer is satisfied. The model emphasizes quality results. They indicate the level of customer satisfaction. The elements of customer satisfaction are:

- Customer satisfaction measures

- Customer satisfaction relative to competitors

- Customer retention

- Market share gain

All the efforts expended in the organization are focused on meeting customer needs.

Quality results are objective measures that mark the organization's progress in meeting customer satisfaction. Some examples include:

- Product and service quality

- Productivity improvement

- Waste reduction and elimination

---

[7] U.S. Department of Commerce. *1993 Application Guidelines*, (Washington D.C: Government Printing Office, 1993). p. 5.

♦ Supplier quality

These measures add to the management by fact core value. These facts give the organization a basis for channeling action for improvement.

Systems: There are four broad systems that support the quality effort. These broad systems integrate the organization together. These systems include:

♦ Information and analysis-- scope, management, reliability, timeliness, and access of the data and information used to align and integrate the quality system. It concerns planning, day-to-day management, benchmarking, and evaluation of quality.

♦ Strategic quality planning-- the system documents the organization's formulation process and implementation plans for quality leadership in the marketplace.

♦ Human resource development and management-- the system that enables the full potential of the organization's workforce in pursuit of personal and organizational growth and quality leadership. This key system contains numerous subsystems that include training, development, recruiting, selection, and team infrastructure.

♦ Management of process quality-- focuses on systematic work in improving process design and control (materials, parts, and service). It examines management of the core technology, supply chain management, and research and development to achieve ever-higher quality and operational performance.

Leadership is an enabler of quality in the Baldrige model. The Baldrige recognizes the importance of leadership in both establishing direction and sustaining a higher set of standards. Leadership energy ensures the values that support the quality initiative are woven into the culture. Leadership enhances establishment of the high levels of performance of internal management systems along with relations with the external community.

COMPETITION FOR THE AWARD

Companies use the Baldrige criteria as guidelines for development. Each of the systems are developed so that quality results and customer satisfaction are achieved. As their systems mature, the company applies to compete for the Baldrige award. The application is limited to 75 pages, and addresses each of the criteria. It pays special attention to how the firm handles the areas within each criterion. After the application is accepted, a four-stage review process starts. The stages are:

Stage 1. Evaluation of the applicant's written examinations by five Baldrige board members.

Stage 2. Consensus review of evaluations of best firms from stage 1.

Stage 3. Site visits for best of stage 2 firms.

Stage 4. Judges review site visits and make recommendations to the Baldrige office. The companies are further evaluated for other factors that might threaten the lustre of the award.

The firm gets feedback on the state of its preparation at several points. The criteria and point system result in a constant benchmark for the firm as it prepares. At each stage after deciding to compete, the firm gets feedback from outside judges. First, the application is judged, then the firm is judged during the site visit. The evaluation and feedback cycle is one of the major benefits of the competition. In perspective, the award itself is not as important as the competitiveness of the firm. This makes the feedback invaluable, because there is "life after the award."

There was a limit to the number of awards given in any one year. The original limit was six firms: two manufacturing firms, two service firms, and two small businesses. There is no minimum number of awards that have to be given in the present rules. There is a growing consensus that the limitation might be unfair to firms that meet the criteria, but happen to do so in a year with "too many" winners in the category. Five firms won in 1992, and three won in 1991. Only five service firms have won the Baldrige from its inception. The winners of the Baldrige are listed in Table 8-2.

EVALUATION SCALE

The Baldrige examiners scrutinize each criterion to see how the organization implemented the requirements. The general evaluation framework is described in Table 8-3. The key variables are:

♦ Scores: The scores are an accumulation of points on each of the seven major criteria. The cumulative number is then arrayed as a percentage of the total possible points.

TABLE 8-2
Winners of the Baldrige National Quality Award

YEAR	SMALL BUSINESS	SERVICE	MANUFACTUR- ING
1988	• Globe Metal- lurgical Inc.	None	• Motorola, Inc. • Westinghouse Commercial Nuclear Fuel Division
1989	None	None	• Milliken & Co. • Xerox Busi- ness Products and Systems
1990	• Wallace Co.	• Federal Ex- press	• Cadillac Motor Car Co. • IBM Rochester
1991	• Marlow Industries • Zytec Corp.	None	• Solectron Corp.
1992	• Granite Rock Co.	• AT&T Uni- versal Card Services • The Ritz- Carlton Hotel Co.	• AT&T Net- work Systems Group Transmissions Systems • Texas Instru- ments Defense Systems and Electronics
1993	• Ames Rubber		• Eastman Chemical Co.

categorizes a company's development by the percentage of total points it achieves.

♦ Approach/deployment: The examiner looks at the appropriateness, effectiveness, and consistency of the approach used by the company. Key elements include an evaluation cycle that is quantitative and prevention-based. Deployment refers to how effectively the firm implements its approach to each of the criteria.

♦ Results: Results are evaluated using factors such as the firm's performance levels, how the firm compares to industry benchmarks, the rate of improvement, and the record of sustained performance.

The Baldrige framework is useful to an organization whether it applies or not. The criteria with the 92 Areas to Address are complete enough that a firm can benchmark its progress against the scoring guidelines. Examiners use the same scale in evaluating companies competing for the prize.

DISCUSSION
There are several positive outcomes of a firm's attempt to compete for the Baldrige.

First, trying for the Baldrige forces management to think in a complex way about the basic elements of organization. It focuses management on the key participation of employees in decision making, planning, communication, and problem solving processes to achieve the quality results. It mandates that customer satisfaction data discipline all organizational action. If the firm is successful it becomes quality leader in its marketplaces.

> *The sustained* process of looking for data relevant to quality, turning it into information that addresses decision and problem-solving situations, is the key issue.

Second, the Baldrige emphasizes measurement and quality results. Measurement and the use of information are central to the improvement process and ultimately to the Baldrige examination process. An unintended consequence comes from the fanatical use of measurement.

Measurement sometimes becomes an end in itself. The classic problem of not seeing the forest for the trees can result when an organization gets so into the detail, it misses strategies and competitor moves. The

TABLE 8-3
Scoring Guidelines for the Baldrige Award

SCORE	APPROACH/ DEPLOYMENT	RESULTS
0%-10%	Anecdotal information	No data or results responsive to major requirements
10%-30%	Beginning of a systematic approach and early stages of the transition from reacting to proacting	Some areas indicate improving performance
40%-60%	Approach is systematic and most areas have some deployment with problem-prevention characteristic.	Key areas indicate improving performance; some evaluation takes place against benchmarks/ comparisons/ levels; no adverse trends indicated
70%-90%	Systematic approach responsive to overall purposes of the item; system is fact based, well integrated, and deployed evenly	Most key areas of importance show good to excellent results, with most evaluated against benchmarks/ comparisons/levels
100%	A sound systematic approach and fully responsive to the requirements of the item.	Excellent improvement trends in all key areas; all information is evaluated against benchmarks/ comparisons/ levels; there is evidence of industry and benchmark leadership

Adapted from *1993 Award Criteria* (Washington, D.C.: Government Printing Office, 1993), p. 34.

quality process thrives on data, but not to the extent that it extinguishes individual spontaneity, nor diminishes creativity.

Third, there is a perception that achieving the award is within a firm's reach. For example, the idea of quality is important to every organization, although it might be deficient in actual performance. The leadership model that supports the Baldrige is direct and straightforward. Concepts like the customer is king, continuous improvement, shortened cycle time, design quality, team building, and more are easy to grasp.

The unintended result is that the structure of the Baldrige examination process lends itself to a test taking mentality. The categories and explanatory material suggest that the terminology and concepts can be learned easily. It becomes easy, then, to visualize learning the right words and passing the test without a substantial change in behavior. Firms that try this approach are inevitably disappointed. They certainly don't succeed in the Baldrige competition. Even worse, the exercise doesn't help them win in the marketplace.

Some firms will point fingers at the "unfair" competition and go on to the next technique. Others will realize that the Baldrige is a substantial approach to organization development. Competing requires an in-depth, comprehensive effort.

Finally, the challenge of preparing for the Baldrige self-analysis and final examination is rigorous and focuses the expectations of an entire organization on quality. A well designed change strategy mobilizes the energy necessary for doing well. An unintended outcome occurs when a firm is bent on "winning" as an end in itself. The managers and employees don't realize the competition is only a point on the quality journey. Invariably, stress and expectations cause a firm bent on winning to destabilize. The failure occurs at the stressful peak of the competition or at a time after the competition.

In summary, firms that eventually win make an important cultural transformation. They no long see the Baldrige as an end in itself. Instead, it becomes a milestone in the long-term drive for continual improvement and higher- quality standards. Quality behaviors become second nature to the winner. The firm is in position to compete effectively for the Baldrige.

GAO STUDY OF BALDRIGE CONTENDERS

In 1991, U.S. Representative Donald Ritter requested a study[8] on the results of the quality efforts by Baldrige applicants. The final study was titled U.S. Companies Improve Performance through Quality Efforts. Researchers conducting the study asked experts what measurable areas of operations were impacted by TQM practices. The areas they identified were: (1) employee relations, (2) operating procedures, (3) customer satisfaction, and (4) financial performance.

The group studied included those firms that had applied for the Baldrige and qualified for the site visit. There were 20 firms at this level and all participated in the survey to the extent that they could. Each of the identified areas was investigated and rates of improvement calculated from the point the company initiated its quality effort to the time of study.

The study reported all the data submitted by the firms. Each firm submitted data that were available, relevant to its industry and nonpropri- etary. Consequently, the results often are based on fewer than the 20 firms studied. The data reported are average annual changes in the performance indices.

TABLE 8-4
Employee Relations Results

Employee Relations	Firms Reporting	Rate of Change
Employee satisfaction	8 of 9	+5%
Attendance	9 of 11	Above industry average
Turnover	10 of 11	Below industry average
Safety/health	12 of 14	+1.8% improvement; below industry.
Suggestions/employee	5 of 7	rate: +16.6%

---

[8] Government Accounting Office, *Management Practices- U.S. Companies Improve Performance Through Quality Efforts,* (Washington D.C: Government Printing Office, 1991), pp. 1-41.

EMPLOYEE RELATIONS

Building a highly motivated and involved workforce is a core component of a quality strategy. Table 8-4 shows the five indices used to indicate that employees were becoming more focused on quality. Employee satisfaction and the number of suggestions received are elemental to good-quality organizations. Attendance, turnover, and safety and health are important to every good company.

Eighteen of the 20 firms participating gave information on at least one of the indicators. Table 8-4 shows the pattern of responses for each indicator. There were 52 separate indicators, and 39 of those were improvements.

♦ Employee satisfaction was measured by company surveys of employees. One company's results declined because of an impending merger.

♦ Attendance figures were above average in 9 of 11 companies.

♦ Turnover was defined as voluntary separation from the company. Ten of the 11 companies beat the company average, with 7 of the 11 doing much better.

♦ Safety and health were measured by the number of days lost to these causes. Although 12 of 14 firms beat industry averages, 11 of the 14 improved the indices dramatically.

♦ Suggestion systems were used in seven of the firms. In five of those, suggestions increased. The two companies experiencing decline were implementing teams that eroded the individual-based suggestion system.

OPERATING PROCEDURES

Total quality strategies focus attention and energy on the operations area. All 20 of the firms provided 65 observations. Of those, 59 were positive, 2 were negative, and 4 remained unchanged as a result of their Baldrige efforts. Table 8-5 outlines these results.

♦ Reliability was measured by the number of recalls and claims made by customers. The 12 companies providing information improved by almost 12%.
♦ Timeliness of delivery is the percentage of on-time deliveries. Eight of the nine firms improved in this category.

TABLE 8-5
Operating Results

Operating Proce-dures	Firms Reporting	Rate of Change
Reliability	12	+11.3%
Timeliness of delivery	8 of 9	+4.7%
Order-processing time	6	+12%
Production errors	7 of 8	-10.3%
Product lead time	6 of 7	-5.8%
Inventory turn-over	6 of 9 2 of 9	+7.2% even
Quality costs	5	-9%
Cost savings	12	$1.3 to $116 million

♦ Order-processing time is a key component to cycle-time analysis. All six firms reporting reduced their processing time an average of 12% annually.

♦ How or whether a firm measured production errors or defects depended on the nature of the operations. Seven of the eight firms decreased their defects an average of 10.3%.

♦ Cycle, or lead, time is measured by the amount of time from the start of the design process to the moment the product is in the hands of the consumer. Of the seven firms reporting, six shortened their lead time an average of 5.8% per year.

♦ Inventory turnover numbers reflect how tightly the company integrates its inventory into the core operations. The more successful a firm is, the more rapid is the inventory turnover.

Six of nine firms improved their turnover an average of 7.2%. The firm with the decline was in an industry hard hit by the late 1980s recession.

♦ Five firms measured the cost of quality and found their costs declining an average of 9%.

♦ Improvements in processes that satisfied customers resulted in savings of from $1.3 million to $116 million per year.

TABLE 8-6
Customer Satisfaction Results

Customer Satisfac- tion	Firms Reporting	Rate of Change
Overall satisfaction	12 of 14 2 of 14	+2.5% no change
Customer complaints	5 of 6	-11.6%
Customer retention	4 of 10 4 of 10 2 of 10	+1% even- slightly

CUSTOMER SATISFACTION

Most firms have to make the change from equating quality with meeting specifications to equating quality with satisfying customer needs. Making the change is challenging to most companies. It entails measuring, meeting with, and observing customers. Most of it means translating this into a product or service. Seventeen of the 20 companies provided data. Of the 30 observations, 21 were improved, 6 unchanged, and 3 became worse. Table 8-6 describes these results.

♦ Overall customer satisfaction increased an average of 2.5% in 12 companies and remained at a high level for 2 others.

♦ Complaints increased in one of the six cases because the company implemented a more refined complaint system. The other five companies improved processes that lowered their complaint rates.

♦ If some customers don't come back because they are dissatisfied, the firm has to replace them before it can grow at all.
Successful firms put a premium on retaining customers. Four
of the 10 improved retention an average of 1%, 4 were even, and
2 declined slightly.

FIGURE 8-7
Financial Performance

Financial Per- formance	Firms Reporting	Results
Market share	9 of 11 2 of 11	+13.7% lost share
Sales/employee	12 of 12	+8.6%
Return on assets	7 of 9 2 of 9	+1.3% -0.3%
Return on sales	6 of 8 2 of 8	+0.4% -1,2%

FINANCIAL PERFORMANCE

Profit has to improve before any strategy is considered a success. The
logic behind a firm adopting the quality-first approach is that quality
results in strong cost control and leadership in the marketplace. These
translate into market share and high returns to the organization.

Of the 40 observations in this area, 34 increased in profit and 6
declined in profit. Some companies didn't report data (they were subsidiar-
ies of larger companies or privately owned). Some divisions couldn't factor
meaningful data from a parent corporation. Some private corporations
wouldn't disclose the information. Table 8-7 describes these indices.

♦ Market share increased an average of 13.7% per year for nine
of the firms. Two of the firms were experiencing particularly
difficult times in their marketplace from international competition.

◆ Sales per employee increased in all the firms by about 8.6%. These figures were a little higher because they weren't calculated as constant dollars.

◆ Return on assets improved in seven of nine cases, while return on equity improved in six of eight cases. Return on assets is the company's earnings before interest and taxes divided by average gross assets. Return on sales is the company's earnings before interest and taxes divided by net sales.

COMMON CHARACTERISTICS

There were some common characteristics among these Baldrige applicants:

◆Customer needs and satisfaction dominated their marketing approaches.

◆Customer feedback was the dominant theme of communications in all sectors of the organizations.

◆They had an uncommon handle on the need to improve their internal customer relationships and solve problems upstream. (Upstream means helping solve problems in activities that feed into their unit or station.) This then improved their output.

◆Leaders of these organization actively espoused TQM values.

◆Employees in these companies were expected to contribute to the quality outcomes. With the request came the authority and responsibility to accomplish those goals. In general, information was available to everyone. Few perks for high office were evident, resulting in fewer inequities and a spirit of innovation.

◆Employees were satisfied. Pride in being with a winner was one aspect. Another aspect was the feeling that they were helping shape their own environment with support from the organization. This included training, coaching, and a role that had adequate authority to permit decision making.

This study points out the value of preparing for the Baldrige. Firms reflected the values necessary to be successful in the marketplace. The study also points out a variety of outcomes. Baldrige preparation doesn't guarantee market success. In today's market, a value on quality products and service is necessary for success. It isn't, however, sufficient for success.

THE EUROPEAN AWARD

Fourteen leading Western European companies formed the European Foundation for Quality Management (E.F.Q.M.) in 1988. The reason for the foundation was "In recognition of the potential for competitive advantage through application of total quality."   These companies recognized the importance of quality as a strategy for global competitive advantage. An additional objective was to stimulate the deployment of quality improvement activities throughout the European Community.

The E.F.Q.M. took the lead, with support by the European Organization for Quality and the European Community, in establishing the European Quality Award. It has two components. The first is the European Quality Prizes for companies that "...demonstrate excellence in the management of quality as their fundamental process for continuous improvement." The European Quality Award is awarded to a person who stands out as an exponent of total quality.

The award builds on the thinking in the Baldrige process. The E.F.Q.M. adapted the criteria addressed to the European values. The success of this effort is further testament to the fact that there is a world class model of organization.

The model shown in Figure 8-2 concentrates on processes in organization. They are called the enablers that release the talents of

FIGURE 8-2
The European Quality Model

Leadership	People management	Processes	People satisfaction	Business results
	Policy & strategy		Customer satisfaction	
	Resources		Impact on society	
<------	Enablers	------->	<-- Results ---------->	

Adapted from *Total Quality Management The European Model for Self-Appraisal, 1993,* (Einhoven, The Netherlands: European Foundation for Quality Management; 1993), p. 3.

people to achieve quality and performance goals. The processes on the left side of the model are enablers of the quality effort. The two columns on the right illustrate the results of the model.

Customer satisfaction, people (employee) satisfaction and impact on society are achieved through leadership driving policy strategy, people management, resources and processes, leading ultimately to excellence in business results.

The enablers components are concerned with how results are going to be achieved. The results components are focused on what the organization has achieved. The improvement strategy is to use the nine categories for improvement strategies.

ENABLERS
The enablers are the major components of the organization that create the total quality environment. They become drivers of change.

♦ Leadership: Visible leadership of the total quality effort is the focus of this category. It includes the energy of the firm's leadership in assessing, reviewing, rewarding, and funding total quality efforts throughout the organization. It includes the role that leadership plays in involving customers and suppliers in the quality efforts. Leadership in the general quality community is also a factor.

♦ Policy and Strategy: The consistency of the policy and strategy structure in reflecting a total quality organization is the focus. Determining, deploying, reviewing, and improving the policy and strategy structure are the functions that create total quality.

♦ People Management: Creating an environment in which the full potential of people is focused on improving the firm's business continuously. Communications, teams, suggestion systems, and human resource systems create a culture of continuous improvement.

♦ Resources: This category measures how the organization uses its resources to support the total quality strategy. Finance, information, material, and technology resources need to be preserved, managed, and utilized effectively.

♦ Processes: This category highlights the value adding processes of the organization and the infrastructure available to ensure continuous improvement, innovation, and effectiveness.

RESULTS

The results criteria examine the organization's performance in relation to its goals, its competitors, and the "best in class" performance. Results include customer and people satisfaction, impact on society, and financial business results.

♦ Customer satisfaction: The degree to which customer needs are met by the organization's product or service. Results come from how the organization promotes, services, innovates, finances, and warranties the product or service.

♦ People satisfaction: Satisfaction follows because the organization's culture, management infrastructure, and operations are perceived as meeting the needs and expectations of its people. Also, the extent to which people are aware and involved in total quality efforts helps satisfy people needs.

♦ Impact on society: The organization's use of total quality to enhance its reputation as proactive in improving the quality of life, enhancing the environment, and preserving global resources.

♦ Business results: There are financial and nonfinancial measures of efficiency and effectiveness that suggest how well the total quality strategies are working.

ASSESSMENT

The evaluation of each of the sections is based on a sliding scale similar to the Baldrige Scoring Guidelines. Table 8-8 shows the general framework and the relative scores for each level of accomplishment.

The European Quality Prize has a short history. Rank Xerox from the United Kingdom won the first year. This award will have increasing value as a motivator for firms to focus on quality. It will also have the effect of increasing the integration of the European business community.

TABLE 8-8
Scoring Logic of Enablers and Results--
the European Quality Prize

SCORE	ENABLER DEPLOYMENT	RESULTS SCOPE
0%	Anecdotal evidence with little effective usage	Anecdotal, with the results reflecting few relevant areas or activities
25%	Beginnings of systemic approach affecting old operations with some integration.	Some of the changes are increasing performance indicators
50%	Soundly based systemic approaches are reviewed and integrated well.	Many relevant areas are now showing results that begin to compare favorably
75%	Systematic approaches and prevention-based systems are evident, reviewed, and integrated.	Positive results are sustained over three years, comparing favorably with strategic objectives and are beginning to be comparable to leading companies
100%	Systematic approach and prevention-based systems with review cycles and total integration into normal working patterns.	Positive results have a five-year track record of reliability and are "best in class" in many areas

SUMMARY

The three worldwide quality awards emerged during troublesome times for their respective economies. The Japanese Deming prize arose during Japan's post-World War II lean years to mobilize its industry. The United States's Baldrige award resulted from a time that saw the United States's biggest markets threatened with takeover by foreign firms. Japanese companies were predominant, but the Europeans were competitive in some markets. The Japanese organization design and strategy were superior.

The focus on quality in the United States was a response to market-place defeats. Congress reinforced a strong industry trend by legislating the Baldrige. It highlighted the importance of quality and provided a roadmap for many firms to follow. The first award was in 1988.

The Europeans were protected from the full thrust of the Japanese onslaught because they put up barriers. In some ways they seem to have delayed the period of turmoil as firms adapt to the quality model. Their pride in continental quality and their social compact seem to be under attack now, however, as leading European firms compete worldwide. Emphasis on ISO 9000 certification efforts and development of the European Quality Prizes (EQP) and Award are their response to the quality revolution. The first award was given to Rank Xerox in 1992.

The Deming prize reflects the analytical training of W. Edwards Deming and the technical emphasis of the Japanese Union of Scientists and Engineers (JUSE). The philosophy underlying the award is total quality control (TQC). TQC seeks to account for the level of quality through an intense problem solving process that continually improves results and brings more and more detail of the process under control.

The American and European awards, while including some of the same TQC philosophy, emphasize organizational-level systems like information systems, human resource management, strategic quality planning, and quality assurance. Leadership is implicit in the Deming prize, and explicit in the Baldrige and EQP awards. The discrepancy reflects a cultural difference in the role of a leader in an organization. It also reflects a difference in the emphasis on problem solving accuracy and the depth of organization control required in the two programs.

The respective emphases of the two models are part cultural and part due to changes in the quality revolution. Neither the Japanese nor the Europeans celebrate their leaders like Americans do. Further, the awards arose from different bases. The Japanese technical approach resulted from the award being guided and nurtured by academic scientists and engineers- a very technical group. The Baldrige model resulted from a group of business people thinking about quality from the standpoint of the executive suite.

The advances in TQC made the Japanese world-class leaders in manufacturing. This was the focus of their early export program. TQC drove the early phase of the quality revolution. It is the model that many firms in the U. S. followed during the 1980s when they made their comebacks. The Baldrige model, with its accent on the organization level, signaled the first steps into phase II of the quality revolution. The strategic level, implications for change management, and implications of information technology weren't dealt with powerfully by TQM. In some ways the Baldrige jumps ahead of the Deming in dealing with service and nonprofit along with manufacturing, and for strongly addressing organization level issues.

Any person interested in the study of total quality would be well instructed to study the awards/prizes criteria. They are the most practical and coherent models available. Experiences of firms using these criteria as development tools are instructive. The winners of the prizes are leading firms in numerous industries. Chapter 1 points out some winners that had difficulties. That firms have trouble points out the truism that winning a quality award doesn't guarantee marketplace success. Winning a quality award is necessary, but not sufficient, for succeeding in the 1990s marketplace.

♦♦♦

POINTS TO PONDER

1. The quality prizes may be important to big firms, but why should people in smaller enterprises pay much attention to prizes?

2. Does the small number of Baldrige Award winners mean standards are so high they are above the reach of ordinary firms?

3. Is the cost of applications for awards worth it given the small chances of winning? Why?

4. What other kinds of recognition can or do reinforce quality efforts in organizations? Could or would quality programs survive without awards or recognitions?

Please find additional questions at the end of the reading.

♦♦♦

READING

Sharing the Wealth

The annual Association for Quality and Participation conference held in Washington, DC every February, highlights the previous year's Baldrige National Quality Award winners. This is as close to heaven that a student of organizations can get. Over 1000 participants from small businesses and large businesses attend to hear presentations and talk about how the winners built companies that won the award.

Key concepts like customer information, employee participation, human resource programs, confident and self-sufficient employees, group and team decision-making, cycle time and information systems are discussed at the conference and in the elevators.

It soon becomes clear that the winner's managers are students of organizations. They build on the Baldrige model and each adopts other substantial approaches that increase the performance of their organization. Many use Deming, Juran, or Crosby to help structure their approach. The challenge soon sends them on a search for motivation or strategic models that gives them an edge in understanding more of the organization dynamics.

There is a stark contrast between these students of organizations and those managers that insist on running an organization by "common sense". The common sense managers are almost oblivious to the underlying complexity of their organizations until they fail. A common sense approach too often yields common results. These quality leadership managers are interested in exemplary results. They pick through the theories of management scholars to find the ideas that work in practice.

One of the key components of the Award criteria is benchmarking excellence. Benchmarking means taking key measurements of processes in an organization and comparing them with other organizations. Firms benchmark things like cycle time, distribution systems, customer billing methods, and information system applications. They also benchmark philosophies and ideas.

Benchmarking is a license to steal for organizations. I prefer to think of it as a license to investigate and compare. This conference is a benchmarking organization's dream. There are many ideas to get and contacts to make. Preston Trucking was a competitor for the Baldrige a couple of years ago and was listed as one of the top U.S. employers. Hundreds of companies made the trek to little Preston's Quality College on Maryland's Eastern shore to find out how Preston did it.

Benchmarking the best from other companies counteracts the tendency for decision making in companies to become simple-minded and biased. Herbert Simon, a management scholar, said managers solve problems by addressing the aspects of the problems they understood (biased), with information that was readily available (simple-minded). It would quickly be understood at the conference that decision making in the Baldrige firms is anything but simple-minded and biased. Measurement, analysis and decision characterize the environment.

Making one of your benchmarking trips the AQP conference can yield immediate results. The conference is like a tutorial in how to build a winner. All the Baldrige winners are excellent companies. These companies have spent years building their companies and then fine-tuning them for the Baldrige competition. When a management team hears the presentations and talks with the executives, they see and hear an organization at its peak. They are winners, enthusiastic and full of themselves. Believe me it is contagious.

The clarity of the presentations attests to the power of the Baldrige model. It is applicable to manufacturing and service organizations. It focuses management on the right variables. For starters all the firms have learned ways to make the organization do what is necessary to satisfy the customer. The model focuses attention on systems and leadership in order to meet customer needs.

It is impossible to come away from the conference without understanding two things:

1) It takes a long time and a deep understanding of the complex dynamics of organization to build a winner.

2) You might not want to compete for the award, but you want to build an organization with the energy and focus of the Baldrige winners.

5. Building a winner is a difficult process. Does a public award process give a company incentive to go through a period of difficult changes?

6. The Baldrige is highlighted in this reading, but would a conference on winners of the European or Japanese award have a different effect?

◆◆

CHAPTER 9
QUALITY IN AN INTERNATIONAL CONTEXT

◆◆◆

The objectives of this chapter are:

1. To comprehend the worldwide impact of the quality revolution.

2. To understand the essential elements of quality practiced worldwide.

Key Words introduced in this chapter.

Variance	Infrastructure	Subprocesses
Nonconformance	Benchmarking	Simplification
ISO 9000	Conformance	Best practices
Deployment	Empowers	Evaluation
Network	Suboptimal	Certification
Nonconformance	Stakeholders	

◆◆◆

INTRODUCTION

The quality revolution is a worldwide phenomenon. The first phase of the revolution swept up leading companies in Japan, the U.S., Canada, and Europe. The second movement is impacting most markets both within the latter industrial countries and the third world.

Rapid transportation and instantaneous communication have converged to make most markets vulnerable to international competition. A successful international presence can be launched from almost any part of the world. Even political institutions that were built to protect national interests are crumbling. Free trade treaties are drawing interest from all countries. Political parties and politicians that built their programs on centralization of economic power and coercion of people find their programs under threat. The Union of Soviet Socialist Republics was built on communist ideology. It fell apart peacefully because of Western pressure and the contradictions of its own system. China's communist government is fighting over a powerful capitalist revolution in parts of China. India's largely centralized, non-capitalist government loosened up considerably during the early 1990s.

283

> **Mabe,** *a Mexican appliance manufacturer in San Luis Postosi, is a partner of America's General Electric. The plant design borrowed heavily from Toyota and Harley Davidson and has just-in-time purchasing and the kamban production system in its plants.*
> *"The Mexican Worker," Business Week,* (April 19, 1993), p. 91.

Several South and Central American countries are privatizing many businesses and encouraging capitalism. Chile, Argentina, Columbia and Mexico are examples of a country well on its way to dismantling socialistic and anti-American governments. Privatization and economic policies designed to stabilize its economy characterize recent efforts. Changing the way they conduct their affairs resulted in dramatic improvements in opportunities and increases in standards of living.

Free trade areas are springing up around the world. These free trade areas supplement the worldwide General Agreement on Trade and Tariffs. The Asian rim countries are grouping around an informal group named ASEAN. This includes Canada and the United States. Canada, the U.S., and Mexico agreed to the North American Free Trade Agreement in December, 1993. Mexico has a Free Trade Agreement with Chile, Argentina and Columbia. These agreements are just a first step towards a further integration of these economies. Europe's free trade area is called the European Community (EC). It has been underway for several decades and includes milestones for common political and monetary institutions. "EC '92" was the symbol for the major integration of political and economic integration which occurred in 1992. NAFTA and the EC each integrate nearly 400 million people and economies totalling nearly $6 trillion. ASEAN just expresses a pooling of interests. The Pacific Rim countries have far to go before a free trade agreement evolves.

These formal developments complement the onrush of firms across national boundaries to exploit marketplaces. The supply chain of firms operating across the world has exploded. The flow of capital across the world has magnified. Logistics between and across nations are increasingly demanding on firms providing services. Setting the context for these interfirm relationships are the standards emanating from the quality revolution. These high standards demanded by the customers influence the relationships among companies back in the supply chain.

Certifications and audits are the means companies and governments use to ensure the quality of goods and processes. These outside systems supplement the internal systems used by companies to upgrade their own quality. Audits of a company's operations are sometimes done by third parties, and sometimes they are conducted by the downstream customer. In either case, the intent is to find a way of indicating the quality built in to an operations area of the supplier.

This chapter explores the international expansion of the quality movement. It details the extent to which quality practices are implemented in four leading countries. With the emphasis on quality and in light of the extended supply chains, the use of certifications has increased. The chapter highlights the ISO 9000 standards and their impact on world trade.

INTERNATIONAL QUALITY STUDY (IQS)

In 1989 the American Quality Foundation and Ernst and Young undertook a massive international study of quality practices on three continents.[1] This study analyzed 580 organizations in Japan, the United States, Canada, and Germany. They focused on more than 900 separate management practices from the organizations. Eighty-four percent of the firms responded to the last comprehensive questionnaire which provided a measure of the use of quality management practices in general, as well as the quality developments in different parts of the world.

All countries in the study take pride in their quality. Germany has a long reputation for pride in their technical accomplishments and quality products. Mercedes, BMW, Leica, and BASF are brands of the highest quality. Japan has made the post-World War II trek from producing junky trinkets to now producing the highest quality goods in the world. The Lexus and Acura are quality automobiles. Sony, Fujitsu, Mitsubishi, and Komatsu have quality reputations. The United States and Canada are industrial democracies with a pride in their accomplishments. Many of the icons of American and Canadian quality are firms that have suffered under competitive pressure but are recovering. Chrysler and Ford are competitive in quality, but still lag behind the Japanese. Xerox and Kodak are competitive, but still improving to meet Japanese standards. Northern Telecom is an international leader in an intensively competitive sector.

Both Germany and Japan restarted their economies after World War II on the backs of very generous and enlightened support from the allied countries, particularly the United States. Each country took a separate track. Germany, following Europe, followed a more social agenda than Japan did. Europe has a heavy social-welfare culture and a pervasive, government-supported union movement. Japan's focus was more

---

[1] Ernst & Young, *International Quality Study*, (Cleveland: Ernst & Young, 1991).

predatory, capitalistic, and export oriented. Europe's welfarism and unionism and Japan's emphasis on lifetime employment resulted in stable workforces. Europe's approach resulted in high-cost industries. Political and social barriers against the low cost Japanese limited the inroads of the Japanese into Europe so far. This questionable practice seems to be only delaying the major changes Europe has to make to compete successfully against the Japanese, and now the North American, companies.

Germany's unions *are very powerful. There are 16 labor unions that organize about 42% of the non-agricultural workers. For comparison, the U.S. has less than 20% of its workers organized. A German federal labor law, Mithestimmung, puts labor leaders on every company's supervisory board. This board deals with strategic matters. It is described by some as "antagonistic cooperation".*
Allan Tillier, *Doing Business in Today's Western Europe, (Lincolnwood Ill: NTC Books, 1993), p. 208.*

The firms selected for the study came from four industries: the automotive, banking, computer, and health care industries. The firms were selected from these industries regardless of their commitment to the principles of the quality revolution. The study highlights quality principles. It studies the penetration of the quality movement into these industries in each country.

There are numerous caveats to interpreting this data. It is difficult to know how managers from different countries interpreted the questions. A Japanese would answer them from the perspective of an export oriented, island based, rather entrepreneurial country. The German executives looked at them with the background of successful public social welfare policies on a continent where other sophisticated countries are minutes away by plane. Germany is export oriented. However, the international strategies of the Japanese are more expansive.

German industry is more technical and machine oriented than the consumer- oriented Japanese industry. The North Americans have the world's largest, most accessible, marketplace. Their interpretations of the practices might take a different cast, given the intensity of the competition within their borders. The discussion is useful, but care has to be taken in stereotyping areas of the world. Individual companies throughout the world might represent the best or worst quality in spite of their home country.

Across the world there are a number of commonalities in spite of these differences. Basic organization design is one of those. In this sense, Germany stands as a surrogate for some general comments on Europe. At one level, there are many differences between countries in Europe.

However, in the international competitive battlefield companies like France's Thomson Electronics, Germany's Siemans, The Netherlands' Phillips, and Great Britain's ICI have to compete according to common competitive rules. This results in similar organizing patterns in spite of the cultural differences.

TEN QUALITY PRACTICES

IQS explored more than 900 quality practices. The discussion in this chapter is limited to ten core practices that distinguish the firm that implemented the modern quality model.[2] The ten practices are categorized as those related to evaluating performance, strategic planning, customer expectations, core technology, and teams and meetings. Table 9-1 defines these five categories.

These practices touch the key elements of the firm committed to quality leadership. They test the use of customer information to guide strategic decisions and develop new products. Process improvement efforts using simplification and cycle time analysis guide internal quality efforts. Finally, the interaction of employees in teams or meetings is important to the quality effort.

Each of the ten practices is their emplylisted below. There is a paragraph explaining the best practices and some commentary about trends in each of the countries.

EVALUATING PERFORMANCE

1. <u>Executive</u> compensation <u>depends</u> on performance-compensation-quality criterion:

Executive compensation has traditionally been based on increasing profits. Bonuses, stock options, and profit pools are some of the traditional approaches, particularly in North America. Relating incentives to quality is an important change in for-profit enterprises.

Japan: About 20% of Japanese executives' salaries are dependent on the firm's quality performance. This soon will increase to about 30% of the executives.

North America: The number of firms applying incentives to quality criteria has doubled in the last couple of years. The trend is expected to double again in the next three years as well. Canada will go to about 40% and the U.S. to about 50% executives with quality incentives. This is greater than any of the other countries.

---

[2] Ernst and Young. *Top-Line Findings*. (Cleveland: Ernst & Young, 1991).

TABLE 9-1
International Quality Study Categories

CRITERION	DEFINITION
Evaluating performance	It is usual for companies to reward executives on financial performance. As the quality culture took hold, companies changed the compensation to include quality criteria like improvement on satisfaction indices.
Strategic planning	The mark of a strategic quality planning process is the domination of customer and competitor strategies over cost, productivity, market share, or profit strategies.
Customer expectations	Customer expectations reign over the myriad philosophies that often drive organizations. Consumer research is used with techniques like quality function deployment as the basis for product or service development. These data are communicated to teams improving operations areas in the quality organization.
Core technology	Some organizations emphasize quantity instead of continually improving processes and organizing the operations so they would become faster and more flexible.
Teams and meetings	Quality organizations use teams and quality related meetings to focus people's intelligence and energy on improvement.

Germany: The Germans just began to look at quality items for their incentives, increasing to about 10% currently. Other companies are planning to convert to quality incentives, which will raise Germany's total to about 30% in three years.

Summary: Germany lags behind the other countries in providing quality incentives. The Japanese adaptation to quality incentives is moderate. They aren't adopting quality incentives as readily as the North Americans. It's clear, though, that providing quality incentives is increasing in world executive suites.

2. Quality information used to evaluate business performance:

The commitment to use quality information has to be supported by the appropriate information system. How frequently quality information makes it to the desk of the decision makers is a measure of the commitment of the firm to quality.

Japan: About 90% of the Japanese firms use quality information at least quarterly to evaluate performance.

North America: About 70% of the U.S. firms use quality information at least quarterly. An interesting statistic is that about 18% of firms use it less than annually or not at all. Canadian firms showed some of the same tendencies as U.S. firm.

Germany: About 70% of the German firms use quality information at least quarterly. About 25% use quality information yearly for evaluation.

Summary: About 15% of North American firms don't use quality information to evaluate business performance. This is an indication of how far the quality revolution has to go in North America. About the same number of German and North American firms use quality information quarterly or better. Japan's organizations are most likely to use quality information to evaluate performance during the year.

STRATEGIC PLANNING

3. Customer satisfaction (CS) is used as a primary criterion in the strategic planning process:

Using CS, information in the strategic planning process shows the maturity of the quality commitment in the organization. An effective strategic planning process affects every unit and individual in the organization. Thus, with the pervasive use of customer satisfaction data, all parts of the organization will adjust to, sustain or improve the level of the customer's satisfaction. The scale illustrates how important customer information is to the organization.

Japan: About 42% of the firms currently use quality information in the strategic planning process. About 80% of the Japanese firms intend to use quality information in the next three years.

North America: Canadian firms lead the world in considering CS information primary in strategic planning. About 17% of U.S. firms relegate CS to secondary importance. About 80% of the Canadian firms forecast using CS as a primary indicator over the next three years. About 70% of U.S. firms thought they would use CS as a primary criterion in the future.

Germany: Only about 22% consider CS to be of primary importance in the strategic planning process presently. About 27% of the firms put CS in a secondary role while 51% consider it major.

Summary: CS is not as important a measure in Germany as it is in the other countries. Japan leads with about 95% of the firms considering CS a major or primary measure in the planning process. The U.S. and Canada still have a significant percentage of firms that don't use CS in their planning process. All organizations are increasing their use of CS information as a primary criterion. Germany still lags significantly behind in its use of CS information.

4. Importance of competitor comparisons in the strategic planning process:
Competitor comparisons (CC), benchmarking exercises, and reverse engineering products are some ways organizations obtain competitor information. Comparing the organizations against information from competitors illustrates strengths and weaknesses of the present organization. Maturity in this area indicates an organization that is confident about the quality of its product or service.

Japan: More than 90% of the Japanese firms use competitor comparisons in the strategic planning process.

North America: Canadian firms use competitor comparisons less than do U.S. firms (67% to 82%) in a primary or major way. About 31% of the Canadian firms feel such comparisons are secondary in importance.

Germany: Less than 5% of the German firms use competitor comparisons as a component in strategic planning. About 56% of the firms consider it of major importance, while 39% relegate it to secondary importance.

Summary: The Japanese place greater importance than do other countries on competitor comparisons. The Germans place less importance, with a large percentage placing it in secondary importance (39%). About 31% of the Canadian firms also place CC in secondary importance.

CUSTOMER EXPECTATIONS

5. <u>Departments</u> <u>develop</u> <u>new</u> <u>products</u> <u>or</u> <u>services</u> <u>based</u> <u>on</u> <u>customer</u> <u>expectations</u>:

If an organization is going to sustain quality leadership, the design unit has to be very effective. Success in this criterion depends on a commitment to the customer, a well-developed information system, and the maturity of the product or service design system.

Japan: About 90% of the firms use customer expectations usually or always to develop new products.

North America: In both countries, less than 70% of the firms usually or always use customer expectations in product development. About 30% of the firms don't use expectations at all.

Germany: About 83% of the German firms always or usually use customer expectations for new product development.

Summary: German and Japanese firms lead the North American firms in using customer expectations usually or always in developing new products. About 30% of the North American firms use customer expectations occasionally or less, compared to about 20% German and 10% Japanese firms.

6. <u>Importance</u> <u>of technology</u> <u>in</u> <u>meeting</u> <u>customer</u> <u>expectations</u>:

The use of technology can enable the organization to meet customer expectations. Because of its customer focus, the answer shows the commitment to the customer. There are numerous ways technology enhances problem solving, decision making, and service capabilities of the front line worker. Technology enables superior service or manufacturing because it empowers people.

Japan: About 98% of the Japanese firms value technology of prime or major importance in meeting customer expectations. The intensity of the use of technology to meet customer expectations will increase in the next three years.

North America: About 80% of the firms in North America place primary or major emphasis on technology in meeting customer expectations. A surprising 20% relegate technology to secondary importance. Over the next three years, both countries will increase their intensity dramatically.

Germany: About 93% of the German firms place primary or major emphasis on the use of technology. Only 7% relegate technology to secondary importance. Over the next three years, German firms intend to use technology more intensely as a primary strategy.

Summary: Both Japan and Germany place significantly more importance on the use of technology than do the North American firms. About 23% of the U.S. firms relegate technology to secondary or no value. More Japanese firms use technology as a primary support of their quality efforts.

CORE TECHNOLOGY

7. The use of process simplification (PS) to improve business processes:
Process simplification is the focus on continually understanding smaller subprocesses of key business processes. The overall philosophy is the basic approach of both the functional and the quality network structures. Continual improvement is based on the logic of process simplification. The scale illustrates how often the approach is used.

Japan: About 82% use process simplification usually or always.

North America: Significantly more Canadian firms than U.S. firms use process simplification (72% to 47%). About 54% of the American firms use PS occasionally or less, indicating a lack of emphasis on improving operations.

Germany: Only 34% of the German firms use PS usually or always. About 66% use it occasionally or less.

Summary: Using process simplification as a measure of the maturity of the quality commitment in the operations area puts the Japanese and Canadians in the lead. The Americans and Germans place less value on the process. In the American case, there is a tendency to rely on innovation to bring the company's quality up. German firms tend to emphasize heavy engineering in the first place and fixing at the end. The Japanese work at improving the processes constantly.

8. The use of process cycle time (PCT) analysis to improve business processes:
    In the changing external world, a firm's response to a sudden change in customer tastes or a competitive move can mean success or failure. Cycle time means the time a firm takes to respond to a change in the external environment with a viable product. Customer expectations are turned into requirements, next into specifications, and then into a product. The scale refers to the frequency of use of the process cycle time.

    Japan: About 84% of the Japanese firms usually or always use cycle time to improve business processes.

    North America: About 84% of Canadian firms usually or always use cycle time. About 60% of the U.S. firms use cycle time.

    Germany: Less than 47% of the German firms usually or always use PCT. About 53% use cycle time occasionally or less.

    Summary: Japanese and Canadian firms use cycle time significantly more than firms in other countries. Over half the German firms only use PCT occasionally or seldom. About 40% of the U.S. firms use PCT occasionally or less.

TEAMS and QUALITY-ORIENTED MEETINGS
9. Percentage of employees in quality-related teams (QRT):
    The team network is a key component of the quality effort. Teams are formed to deal with unit problem solving (functional teams) or with cross functional processes (process management teams). This question determines the percentage of firms that have one of three levels of employees involved on a team.

    Japan: About 36% of Japanese firms have more than 25% of their employees in QRTs. They intend to increase this percentage only slightly to about 39% in the next three years.

    North America: U.S. firms have about 49% of their employees in QRTs, about 10% more than the Canadians. The Canadians and Americans intend to increase the QRTs above 25% significantly, to 77% and 70%, respectively.

    Germany: Only 20% of the German firms have more than 25% of their employees in QRTs. The intent is to double this to about 42% in the next three years.

Summary: The U.S. and Canadian firms use QRTs more than do other countries and intend to increase the intensity of the use of QRTs. The Germans use QRTs less than the others and the Japanese only have moderate usage. The heavy union/-government socialism in Germany has an impact on this criterion.

10. Percentage of employees participating in meetings about quality (QM).
    Meetings are another component of the quality leadership firm. Meetings to problem solve, communicate, coordinate and control quality-related efforts are an important component. Such firms depend on a high intensity communication structure to sustain their success. A willing commitment to quality meetings is a major indicator of the maturity of the new organization.

Japan: About 65% of the firms have over 25% of their employees participate in QMs.

North America: About 40% of the North American firms use QMs where over 25% of employees participate.

Germany: About 32% of the firms have more than 25% of their employees participating in QMs.

Summary: About 39% of Japan's firms have more than 75% of their employees involved in regular QMs. About 68% of German firms have 25% or less of their employees in QMs.

SUMMARY OF QUALITY PRACTICES
These quality practices are used by firms in all four countries. Table 9-2 describes some of the differences. The distinctions are that Japanese firms use most of the quality practices more intensely than do firms in other countries. The North American countries have a significant number of firms that aren't aware of the quality practices. German firms lag the North American firms in adopting quality practices. Japanese firms place emphasis on external scanning while German firms place the least emphasis on these quality practices. Heavy union and government intervention are major variables affecting the German emphasis on the ten quality practices.

The picture that emerges from these practices are:

♦ Japanese firms have a well-balanced approach to quality.

TABLE 9-2
The Use of Quality Practices in Four Countries

GENERAL BUSINESS PRACTICES	JAPAN	NORTH AMERICA	GERMA-NY
Evaluating performance-compensation/evaluation	Medium	Medium high	Medium low
Strategic planning customers/competition	High	Medium high	Medium
Customer expectations develop product or services-technology	High	Medium	High
Core technology process simplification/-cycle time	Medium high	Medium	Medium low
Teams and meetings quality related teams/quality meetings	Medium high	Medium	Medium low

They not only place a high value on internal quality processes like process simplification, but strongly emphasize external information sources like customer expectations and competitor comparisons. Refer to the Deming prize and history discussions in this book to understand the influences on these organizations.

♦ North American firms show the widest range of values. Those firms implementing quality are balanced and enthusiastic. The increasing reliance on incentives for executives based on quality performance reflect the American bias that the executive is the driver. The Japanese, in contrast, have only a moderate use of such incentives. They place heavy reliance on internal systems. The American executive is the highest-paid group. This is an area of increasing criticism from stakeholders, from employee groups to shareholders.

Many American executives not now using quality techniques say they will use them in a couple of years. On the one hand, this is a positive phenomenon, indicating that the quality movement is taking hold deeper into the industry structure. On the other hand, ideas in North America often achieve fad status of management theories. They are transmitted quickly in the culture and fit the bias for action in American firms. The quick fix trap that many firms fall into is a filter to assess the validity of these figures.

♦ German firms show increasing interest in the newer ways of managing quality. The typical picture suggests a firm successful in the past, tentatively exploring a new way of organizing. German quality is based on fastidious concentration on detail with only moderate concern for either the competition or customer. Ferdinand Protzman suggested: "But management experts say those very achievements and attributes have also entrenched a corporate leadership that is often inflexible and mindless in its conformity and that discourages initiative and independent thinking."[3]

♦ The social welfare schemes and active public protection of a European life style is only delaying the inevitable changes to meet world-class competitive standards.
    Wage costs, illustrated in Table 9-3, suggest the German quandary in the European Community and across the world. Their costs are 42% higher than the United States's average, and 25% higher than the other EC countries. Holiday and other (health care) costs are more than double the United States's and nearly that of Japan's non-wage costs. Germans work less than a 40-hour week and have six weeks annual vacation.

There are several points made in this discussion: (1) the quality culture is pervasive across the world, (2) the international world is complex, and (3) internationalism impacts everyone.
    The next section describes ISO 9000 certification in more detail. The supply chain for many industries crosses country borders in this world. If governments don't present unnecessary barriers (taxes, tariffs, rules, etc.), there are economic reasons for setting up a factory, or service entity, that are often deterministic. Closeness to supply, logistics, wages, and availability of labor and capital are economic reasons. ISO encourages trade because the certification says that the company has systems in place

---

[3] Alan Tillier, *Doing Business in Today's Western Europe,* (Lincolnwood, Ill.: NTC Books, 1993), p. 207.

TABLE 9-3
Comparative Wage Costs

	PAY	BONUS PAY	NON-WAGE COSTS (A)	TOTAL LABOR COSTS (B)	(A) AS A % OF (B)
Germany	$12.67	$4.63	$4.87	$22.17	22.0%
European Community	9.92	2.95	4.08	16.95	24.1
United States	11.33	1.00	3.12	15.45	20.2
Japan	8.38	4.14	1.89	14.41	13.1

Adapted from Lucy Walker, "Delors Counts the Cost of War on Jobs," *The European*, (May 27-30, 1993), p. 33.

supporting high standards. The reputation of the country, or the previous reputation of the company, become minor factors.

ISO CERTIFICATION

Companies are under increasing pressure to ensure that output meets the customer's needs. In order to accomplish this task firms apply pressure to companies in its supply chain. Motorola, for example, told all of its suppliers to apply for the Baldrige National Quality Award. From Motorola's perspective the companies which concentrated on meeting the Baldrige criteria would increase the quality of supplies coming to Motorola.

Bethlehem Steel's Sparrows Point Plant was ISO certified in January 1994. This plant is a completely integrated steel plant. It is the first plant to be certified in the United States. Duane Dunham, the division president, said "We began the ISO process because one of our customer's told us to do so."

ISO and the Baldrige are not the same, however. The Baldrige is a comprehensive approach to quality. It emphasizes customer satisfaction and the measurement of the organization's response to the customer. It includes intangible elements like leadership. ISO is a certification of a specific plant's process. It ensures the organization does what it says it is going to do. A massive documenting system tracks all parts and processes from the supplier to the customer. Only those products meeting specifications make it to the customer. All bad parts and subassemblies are documented and discarded.

One observer, I. S. Kalinksy, suggests, "The ISO 9000 series must be looked at as a series of minimum quality system requirements."[4] Competitive elements and industry/technology elements are additional components that result in a total quality system. The Baldrige model involves these elements. Kalinsky suggests these additional elements build upon the ISO 9000 standards. Without careful attention to these elements, the organization is unlikely to have a successful quality system.

Competitive elements, according to Kalinsky, include those activities, requirements, and procedures that improve competitiveness. They include: continuous improvement, performance information, customer satisfaction, cost of quality systems, and quality planning. Industry/technology elements are those activities, requirements, and procedures that optimize the technology. These elements vary in importance and complexity across different industries. They include items like computer workstation management, employee safety and health, preventive maintenance, reliability assurance, diagnostic tool control, and regulated product safety.

Timbers[5] reinforced this sentiment. He said: "Purists in the quality community claim that ISO 9000 does not require high quality but merely a well-documented level of uniform quality. The quality system could be in total conformance, yet the final product could be uniformly bad." According to Timbers, ISO is necessary for high quality, but not sufficient to ensure it.

THE INTERNATIONAL STANDARDS

The International Organization for Standardization (IOS) is a specialized international agency for standardization. More than 91 national standards bodies are members in ISO. ISO has 180 technical committees that specialize in some area. The areas include key commodities and products that are traded internationally, like zinc and asbestos. The mission of ISO is to establish standards that facilitate the exchange of goods and services. It generated the quality standards program named ISO 9000.

---

[4] I. S. Kalinsky, "The Total Quality System-Going Beyond ISO 9000," Quality Progress, June 1993, pp. 50-54.

[5] M. J. Timbers, "ISO 9000 and Europe's Attempts to Mandate Quality," *Journal of European Business,* (March/April 1992), p. 23.

> **The name ISO** *was selected by the International Organization of Standards because the Greek meaning for it is 'equal'. The ISO standards intend to create a level playing field for producers world-wide to compete equally.*
> D. Byrnes, "Exploring the World of ISO 9000," *Quality,* October 1992, P. 21.

The result is a system that ensures the quality of the output of a process. ISO 9000 is a tangible expression of a firm's commitment to quality. The attributes are:

♦ they are a basic set of principles

♦ they are laid out in an organized manner

♦ all organizations can understand them without regard to culture

ISO standards. ISO is made up of five sections. They are:

♦ ISO 9000 defines the general categories of standards.

♦ ISO 9001 is the most comprehensive level and governs quality for product design, development, manufacturing, installation, and servicing.

♦ ISO 9002 covers manufacturing and installation only.

♦ ISO 9003 applies to product inspection and testing.

♦ ISO 9004 provides guidelines for producers developing their own quality system to meet competitive needs.

♦ ISO 9004-2 standards are applicable to a service establishment.

The most comprehensive audit is ISO 9001. It contains twenty general requirements. ISO 9001 is the most comprehensive certification. The other certifications use selected items from the list and are focused on service firms, inspection and testing, or parts of plants.
The twenty items are listed in the Appendix. Arter[6] divided the 20

---

[6] D. R. Arter, "Demystifying the ISO 9000/Q90 Series Standards," *Quality Progress,* November 1992, pp. 65-68.

items into five basic categories. These categories capture the strength of the certification. The five categories are:

♦ defining the quality process -- document the processes from the supplier to the customer.

♦ measuring the process -- list the measurements at every point that ensure quality.

♦ controlling the process -- what are the specific ways that the company supervises and regulates the process.

♦ improving the process -- what policies and procedures act to stabilize and improve operations.

♦ administering the process -- the intensity of the management of this quality process is evident in the documentation of all quality activities in the quality manual and in the person assigned responsibility for the process.

The key to success in getting and sustaining ISO certification is to carefully detail activities in the company's operations, and then faithfully do what is written. They cover all elements of the value chain from supplier relationship and purchasing through each step of the company's operations to the delivery of the product to the customer.

The certification is comprehensive. If the company is organized properly, then ISO certification is rigorous but straightforward. However, a company might have a difficult time getting certification if it isn't organized to do a good job in the first place. This entire book is about the difficulties most firms have in organizing to "do it right the first time."

Service organizations as well as manufacturing operations are being certified. Many service operations can be detailed, measured and administered intensely. Where a product is explicitly mentioned in the requirements, if service can't be substituted, the item is dropped. A Western Electric (AT&T subsidiary) consulting unit found 16 of the 20 items relevant to their quest for certification.

DuPont certified 150 of their plants and are a leader in the ISO process. The performance results of their effort include:
  ♦ *on-time delivery increased from 70 to 90%;*
  ♦ *cycle time went from 15 days to one and half days;*
  ♦ *warehouse errors decreased by 95%;*
  ♦ *reduced test procedures from over 3,000 to 1,100.*

STARTING THE AUDIT PROCESS

Firms contact registered auditors to apply formally for the certification. Because of the rigor, a concerted strategy has to be undertaken to be successful. It takes a long time and several attempts to achieve certification. DuPont's European plant took 50 people months and 9 calendar months to complete. Jackson suggested: "ISO 9000 was designed to be inclusive, not exclusive. It does not mandate that you use one approach rather than another. As long as you can say what you do and do what you say, you can get your system registered."[7]

ISO accredits process by facility. When a facility passes the ISO 9000 standards on documentation and performance, it gets certified. Certification is given by national bodies in each country as a result of an audit by registrars. Registrars are individuals who have withstood the rigors of being certified as auditors for that task by each country's national quality body.

Audits often uncover problems.[8] For example, 18% of system discrepancies are in document control. These include a failure to have all documents available as well as using outdated standards and regulations. The next two most prevalent discrepancies are lack of design control with 12%, and purchasing inadequacies with 9%. These are complex and critical conditions in the development of high-quality organizations.

ISO AND WORLD TRADE

ISO certification is of particular importance because of its increasing use worldwide. One major attraction is ensuring that firms get into the European Community (EC) marketplace. As the Europeans integrate their economies, they set numerous standards to ensure the free flow of goods within the community.

It is important to the rest of the world that the multiple-country, European certification programs be consistent. Many countries in the world trade with the EC member countries. As a consolidated marketplace, Europe has even greater significance. Certification requirements can be used to select suppliers. Those not having certification can potentially be excluded. In addition, competing with European companies might prove difficult if a higher-quality standard turns out to be a major barrier to entry.

The European Community (EC), through the EC Commission, established two controlling committees for the system certification

---

[7] S. L. Jackson, "What You Should Know About ISO 9000," *Training,* May 1992, p. 49.

[8] Timbers, "ISO 9000 and Europe's Attempts to Mandate Quality," p. 20.

activities and the "product" certification activities.[9]   In addition, an extensive infrastructure of politicians and consultants has evolved with the goal of establishing a European system of assessment and accreditation. In the United States, the American National Standards Institute (ANSI) is the standards group that has membership in ISO. Unlike its European counterparts, the United States doesn't have an official government agency as a sponsoring body. The American Society of Quality Control (ASQC) is the private not-for-profit organization that manages the ISO 9000 effort.

> ***T.D. Williamson,*** *a Tulsa equipment company took their Crosby quality program to their affiliate in Belgium. Unlike their American company, the 14 point program wasn't successful. However, using ISO 9000 standards as a goal was practical and successful for the unit.*
> Elizabeth Ehrlich, "The Quality Management Checkpoint," *International Business,* May 1993, p. 62.

SUMMARY

The spread of the quality movement is inexorable.   It impacts developed and third-world countries The quality revolution impacts how business is organized in all these locations.

The International Quality Study looked at 900 management practices in 580 firms in Japan, North America, and Europe. Ten core quality practices are reported in this chapter. These core areas and practices include:

♦ Evaluating performance. Compensating executives and evaluating business performance with quality indices.

♦ Strategic planning. Customer satisfaction indices and information about competitors drive the planning process in quality organizations.

♦ Customer expectations. Using technology to meet customer expectations and developing products based on those expectations are signs of a sophisticated quality effort.

♦ Core Technology. A focus on techniques like process simplification and rapid cycle time are important strategies.

---

[9] Don Swanner, "International Standards and Their Application," *Quality Systems Update,* 1 No. 4 (1991), p. 22.

♦ Teams and Meetings. Quality related teams and meetings over quality issues are important manifestations of the success of a quality strategy.

The information from the study doesn't suggest any simple conclusions. The penetration of these practices is deep in Japan, a little less so in North America, and rather less so into Germany. This isn't surprising, because the organization for the present level of quality emanated from the Japanese. In some cases, the Americans utilize techniques beyond those of the Japanese. Many U.S. firms are oblivious to the entire revolution. German firms lag behind the development of the other countries. The story in Germany is complex and relates to a heavy social welfare public agenda. Management leaders are reluctant to give up a previously successful formula for quality.

ISO 9000 is a set of standards set out to enhance international trade by the International Organization of Standards in Switzerland. The intent is to certify individual plants, making it easy for an organization to buy goods from around the world and be confident of their quality. There are 20 broad sections to ISO. Arrayed against the value chain, each of the sections tightens up different components and results in a reliable production function. They reach from the supplier to the warranty relations with the customer. The major categories of ISO guidelines are process definition, process measurement, process control, process improvement, and the administrative component.

ISO's impact seems to be growing worldwide. Companies intending to trade in the Europe Community are becoming certified to ensure that they are not kept out of the continuing developments there. Third-world companies see an opportunity to increase their trade if they can meet the standards. ISO certified is a standard calling card for leading firms and this is putting pressure on all of their competitors to meet the challenge.

◆◆

POINTS TO PONDER

1. Can quality really be compared across countries, or must it be considered unique in each national setting? Why? Is it the same thing for Russians, or Chinese, or Egyptians, or French?

2. Is quality a more relevant concept for developed countries and their organizations? Should developing countries care about quality as much as we claim to? How about Brazil, or India, or Angola?

Please find the questions at the end of the reading.

◆◆

READING

The Peaceful Revolution

When history is written, the latter part of the 20th Century will be characterized by the "peaceful" revolution. From the travail of GM to the demise of the USSR, customers and marketplaces are speaking loudly. In a nutshell, the revolution continues to sweep aside organizations that don't listen to customers. Searching underneath this phenomenon, it is apparent that this revolution is an example of the free-market speaking.

Customers are more knowledgeable today about the best products and services, and they buy them. The Japanese commercial juggernaut across the world during the last two decades is testament to customers' willingness to ignore "buy (name the country)" pleas or advertising lies. They want companies to listen to their needs and then design and build products or services so they meet those needs. Most companies are ill-suited to meet this basic requirement.

People get better cars because Honda, Toyota, and Nissan creamed GM, Ford, and Chrysler in the marketplace. Ford and Chrysler woke up and are healthy car companies. Sony, Matsushita and NEC blew GE, RCA, Motorola, and now others out of the water. Customers have an amazing assortment of miniature and innovative consumer electronics as a result. GE, RCA and Motorola took their capital elsewhere.

What happened to American business during the 1970s and 1980s played out at the governmental level in many countries during the same period. Customers in the USSR were tired of the lack of responsiveness of their state-owned businesses. Soviet socialism was licked because the market mechanism didn't work. Shortages and misallocated resources became rampant in the socialized marketplace. The black market could provide anything. Neither laws, nor penalties, nor weapons could stop the black market from clearing the marketplaces.

Margaret Thatcher privatized scores of state-owned businesses and allowed a vibrant private health care system to evolve in the U.K. when she was prime minister. She was elected because the UK's socialism produced high costs, modest quality, and shortages of health care and other products and services. Other European countries are just entering a period of dramatic adjustment of their social-welfare policies which affect marketplace efficiency. They have a large, and increasing, unemployment rate as a result of a non-competitive business community, lulled to sleep through government socialism.

Your next Mercedes-Benz might come from Alabama. Mercedes-Benz has escaped from heavily socialized and unionized Germany. It takes over 100 hours to produce a car in Germany. Toyota's Lexus takes less than 20 hours to produce. It also costs Mercedes about $23 per hour in Germany versus $14 per hour for Toyota in Japan. Toyota's Lexus is number one in most quality surveys and costs tens of thousands less than Mercedes. The marketplace speaks. Mercedes sales today are less than half their 1989 sales in America. That corresponds to Lexus' debut in the market-place. Germany is learning that an economy's "golden goose" is a profitable company on top of the international marketplace.

Many problems result from unintended consequences. On the one hand, the unintended consequences of government-run bureaucracies are that it kills initiative in private marketplaces, and forces the markets underground. On the other hand, the unintended consequences of untrammeled free markets are they can be terribly unfair and unethical. Government has a role to guide markets, but not to be a player.

The free market is a worldwide nervous system. There are a huge number of signals and events that are sensed by this mechanism which inexorably and quickly respond. If the marketplace is allowed to work, people of different classes, religions, and ethnic backgrounds have their needs met without a hint of favoritism.

Governments that think they can generate centralized policy that master the marketplace have been, and will be, as surprised as the heads of monster American companies and unions were in the 1970s. Central-ized bureaucracies have limited amounts of information and even more limited ability to manage the workings of the marketplace nervous system. Companies and unions have to respond to it. Governments only blunder and obstruct free markets, if they become players.

George McGovern was the ultra-left presidential candidate in 1972. After a business failure recently, he said he wished he'd had some real-world experience prior to his public life. It would have changed his proposals, and the legislation he supported. Don't we wish that this was a prerequisite for everyone in public life?

3. Is the role of the free market accurately portrayed in this reading?

4. How do governments play a role in encouraging higher quality standards and in dampening quality efforts?

◆◆◆

CHAPTER 10
PREPARING FOR THE FUTURE

◆◆
The objectives in this chapter are:
1. To understand the basics of the traditional, old-design organization and the new-design required by the changing environment.

2. To understand the essential systems and processes that make up the new-design organization.
◆◆

PERVASIVENESS OF THE QUALITY MOVEMENT

From Japan, America, and Europe to the third-world countries managers are responding to increasing worldwide standards of quality and productivity. Prizes and awards focus the attention of the leading companies on issues about quality. Secondary firms follow by emulation and competitive market pressures. In industrial and leading third-world countries, ISO 9000 certifications stimulate industry to a high level of activity. The secondary impact on other firms in the supply chain and tertiary effects of the focus on human resources ripple out in all these countries.

> *Managers undertaking* quality programs could take a page from Wayne Gretzky's book. Wayne was asked why he was such a great hockey player. He said: "Because I go where the puck is going to be, not where it is."

The conclusion is the quality revolution is a powerful, worldwide phenomenon. The implications of the results of the quality revolution will continue to flow out across the world for decades.

Time seems to be of the essence in this competitive environment. There appears to be a window of opportunity where it is still possible to develop quality as a competitive advantage. As the window closes, however, most firms will find it a competitive necessity to address the rising quality standards and the barriers of entry as the sophistication of the new design model increases.

The national and state quality awards increase the visibility of the quality efforts. Further, the programs and attendant publicity apply pressure on most firms to acknowledge the positive consequences of a quality program. Companies that have active quality programs apply pressure to their supply chain. Motorola, for example, told its prime suppliers to apply for the Baldrige National Quality Award in the near future. The intent is to upgrade suppliers' organizations so they can sustain a high level of quality of inputs. This allows Motorola to maintain its quality standards.

MANAGING ORGANIZATION QUALITY

The messages in this book are straightforward:

♦ Modern quality standards resulted from Japanese innovations in organization design. The American and European revitalization in the 1980s and 1990s, and the accompanying European resurgence of the same period, raised the quality standards and improved organization design.

♦ The latter 20th century appears to be a watershed historical era. New intensity in international relationships is fueled by rapid transport and telecommunications. Information technology is a major design tool affecting nearly every dimension of organizations. The general increase in information available to people in all walks of life has made people more sensitive as customers, employees, and citizens.

> *Men control machines.. not the other way around.*

♦ The quality revolution encompasses principles laid down in the works of leading thinkers like W. Edwards Deming, Joseph M. Juran, and Philip Crosby. These theorists led groups of avid followers in the frenetic 1980s. Many corporations successfully used these mens' quality principles to make the first steps of their own quality journey. Many practitioner driven insights came from the application of these quality principles under intense competitive pressure.

♦ As the 1990s began, it was apparent that the quality revolution entered a new phase of its development. Picking up from the advances of phase I, the approach to quality incorporates organizational, change, and information technology that supports a more powerful design for quality.

> **Mikio Kitano,** *Toyota's factory guru, said: "Let workers, not bean counters, guide the way to productivity."*

♦ The bureaucracy was the dominant organization form of the early twentieth century. These bureaucracies were refined, becoming very powerful during the 1960s and 1970s. In spite of their wealth and power, a new organization design defeated these powerful entrenched organizations in the marketplace. The bureaucracies are named old design organizations and the organizations that defeated them are named new design organizations.

♦ The new-design organization is not a simple evolution of the bureaucracy. It appears to be a discontinuity. The new design organization shares few elements with the bureaucracy. The challenge is to take the huge investments in old design organizations and transform them to new-design organizations. The culture of the old-design organization holds the control assumptions and institutional memory of a bureaucracy. Transformational change is exceedingly difficult under these conditions.

♦ The old-design organization is intended for control. It attempts to close the organization system with the use of authority, rules, and regulations. The new design organization ensures that authority is used to empower employees in an arena that includes outside stakeholders like customers and suppliers in key organization processes. The boundaries of new design organizations aren't closed. Instead, intelligence is built up by the use of well-trained humans in teams, supported by the sophisticated use of networked computers.

♦ The specific systems that characterize new design organizations are:

Benchmarking: Improving internal processes through comparison with outside firms' processes.

Customer/supplier partnerships: Includes stakeholders in key internal processes.

Product/service design systems: Highlights cross functional and cross boundary integration of stakeholders in the design system.

People systems: Entail the nurturing and discipline of people and teams toward quality goals.

Integrated core system: Closely-couples inside and elements of the value chain.

Supportive infrastructures (such as planning, human resource, information, financial, and other systems): These internal systems both integrate outside data streams and coordinate internal data streams.

♦ Quality is managed into the organization through the expert use of multiple systems which results in quality being used in a strategic sense. The core technology is the featured system that produces the value-adding effort of the company.

Quality is designed in, built-in, inspected-in, fixed-in, and educated-in into organizations. Old design organizations emphasized the latter three methods of ensuring quality. The new design organization emphasizes the first two methods.

There is nothing about organizations that is straightforward or responds to common sense. The design of organizations is complex, and managing them is even more so. Marketplace success is a result of successful strategic, tactical, and transition management. Establishing ever-increasing standards for quality results in the right product or service being delivered at the right time and right price to the client. This ordinarily results in profit and sustained success.

LESSONS LEARNED

As this work on organizational quality has followed its course, illustrations were provided that constituted "lessons learned" about quality process and activities. As a summary of lessons learned, attributes of winning firms and losing firms will be presented. Winning firms have changed to new-design practices, while losing firms failed to change, or improperly executed quality strategies.

WINNING FIRMS
Winning firms display what are often called "best practices" in benchmarking. Those best practices often include the following:

♦ Vision and mission orientation: Winning firms are mission driven in response to their vision of intended accomplishments.

♦ Top Management support and involvement: There is no real substitute for genuine and continued demonstrations of support for quality initiatives.

◆ <u>Quality as a way of life</u>: The quest for quality permeates the very essence of winning organizations as their way of doing business.

◆ <u>Involvement at all levels</u>: All levels of the organization are vitally dedicated to quality, especially the crucial mid levels of management.

◆ <u>Empowerment</u>: Delegating authority for decisions to lower and operating levels generates commitment and responsibility for quality involvement.

◆ <u>Consistency and follow through</u>: The curse of unsuccessful quality ventures is the lack of consistency and persistence in execution. Winning firms persevere for the long term.

◆ <u>Cross functional</u>: Successful organizations operate across the functional lines that too often provide separation and isolation of activity, to the detriment of quality quests.

◆ <u>Rethinking how we do business</u>: Quality firms often rethink or "zero-base" their objectives and methods. This fresh thinking, whether in continuous improvement, process innovation, or reengineering, provides the improvement that is a hallmark of quality ventures.

◆ <u>Customer and market driven</u>: Winning organizations strive to recognize and satisfy their customers as a basic tenet of quality.

LOSING FIRMS

Firms that didn't win often were found in the category of old-design organizations, as described earlier. Other firms that didn't win were those that had good intentions or strategies but failed to produce or execute for some of the reasons described below. Their attributes could be portrayed as:

◆ <u>Quality as a fad or panacea</u>: Many organizations expect to put a quality overlay on an organization that is obsolete or not functional. A remedial quality effort can't overcome organizational pathology.

◆ <u>Expect results in a hurry</u>: Other organizations want instant solutions forgetting that most organization change takes time and patience.

♦ Lack of management vision and support: Without continued management support and guidance, quality programs tend to atrophy from a lack of life support.

♦ Lack of adequate training: While considerable evidence exists that quality orientation takes place, the winning firms engage in comprehensive training that is followed for feedback.

♦ Obsessed with structure, rather than function: The winning firms utilize cross-functional efforts that bypass the traditional functional boundaries that often provide bastions of reluctance to innovate.

♦ Poor execution and implementation: The real test of quality organizations is in implementation.

> *"Some organizations* search for examples with ready made recipes to follow. Instead they must map their own routes to quality."-- W. Edwards Deming.

DIRECTIONS FOR THE FUTURE

Quality organizations look to the future. The various forces that organizations encounter will provide the test of versatility of the quality initiatives underway or intended. In closing this book, attention is called to these forces that will continue to play out over the next decade and into the next century:

♦ Change oriented: The only certain thing in the future is change. In order to adapt to challenges, quality organizations must be prepared to meet the conditions that call for change.

> **One of** *ISO 9000's principle reason for popularity is its ability to break down barriers between countries and cultures.*

♦ Globally oriented (think globally and act locally): The quality focus is worldwide. However, the principal locus of quality efforts is in the individual organization. Macro- consciousness provides the environmental context from customer needs to the impact of external forces.

♦ Flexible structures: The quality organization must not be bound by the strictures of rigid frameworks that don't permit adaptation to conditions.

♦ Increased role of information technology: One of the hallmarks of the quality organization in the future will be the increase in the use of information. With the upgraded capacity of the organization to generate information, a definite concern will exist for using information resources to support the decisions and operations that are related to quality.

♦ Economic and market turbulence: Global markets, scarce resources, and uncertainties will be characteristics of the future. Increased sensitivity to resource and market conditions will be a requirement for survival, not to mention success.

♦ Workforce changes: The nature of work will change rapidly. New tools and methods will mean modifications in how resources of the organization are used to add value and ensure quality. This affects the human resource in particular, as jobs and tasks are altered to complete work and objectives.

♦ Technological change; The exponential rates of increase in the amount and quality of technological expansion challenges the quality organization to be prepared to deal with the forces that modify our world.

With all the above, students and practitioners of the quality organization arm themselves to carve progress out of the challenges in their environments. Like all other movements, there will be phases III and IV. It becomes the challenge of future generations to refine the new design model until the next watershed era.

◆◆

POINTS TO PONDER

1. What do you think will be the "quality situation" five years from now?

2. Think about an optimistic scenario for quality for the year 2000. What would have to happen to make quality in 2000 a real and viable element in our industries and organizations?

3. Now do a pessimistic scenario for quality in 2000. What would have to happen to make the quality movement a failure and a flop by then? What happens then?

4. Will the quality revolution come to government and not-for-profit organizations as it has it has come to profit enterprises?
Why or why not?

Please find the questions at the end of the reading.

◆◆

READING

Putting It All Together

Frank Cashen is widely acclaimed to be the architect of the Oriole's juggernaut that steamed through the late 1960s to the early 1980s as baseball's most winning franchise. "Oh to be young and be an Oriole" and "the Oriole way" characterized the culture of the Os then. Starting at the National Brewery as a manager, Frank soon moved to the Os to help the owners get control over that property. After building the Os, he went back to the brewery before landing at the National League Office. Then he was hired as the Mets's general manager in 1979.

Short, compactly built, and tough looking, he reminds one of "resolve." As the 1980s rolled out, the Mets absorbed his strengths. From tough player negotiations to following organization principles, the Mets reeked of "resolve". And they needed it. In 1982, Frank had just traded the Mets only bona fide home run hitter, Ken Griffey to Cincinatti, and refused to take back the New York media's darling pitcher, Tom Seaver. Tom had a hall-of-fame career as a Met pitcher and, although his arm had "life" in it, he was nearing the end of his career. The media wanted him as a Met.... he wanted to end his career as a Met.... but Frank Cashen didn't want him as a Met. There was nothing personal in those decisions. Frank Cashen was building an organization and wouldn't violate any of his principles.

Keep in mind that he had already selected Darryl Strawberry and Dwight Gooden in the amateur drafts of 1980 and 1982. In 1983 he was particularly proud because the Mets farm club had been voted the tops in the major leagues. Of course, that didn't pack people into Shea stadium, nor contribute directly to the standings of the major league club, nor keep the media off his back in 1983. However, it did allow Cashen to start trading young talent for bedrock players like Montreal's Gary Carter and the Cardinals's Keith Hernandez.

New York is a tough media market. It was calling for Frank's scalp from the beginning. Luckily, he says, he had a five year contract and an understanding from the astute and patient owners, the Doubleday family. This relationship was certainly a contrast with the owner of the Yankees at that time, George Steinbrenner, and his general managers.

The Mets's turnaround sounds exactly like the Os system he engineered in the 1960's and 1970's. Cashen said his first step was to go through the minor league scouting and managerial staffs and replace the managers who had never tasted victory, never driven a team to a championship. His second step was to go through the minor league and major league rosters and trade those players that had not had winning experiences in their backgrounds. His third step was to institute a "Mets way" throughout the system so the young players had consistent and intensive training.

The explanation was simple. If the people didn't know the exhilaration of a championship finish, they didn't belong. Such players had not been part of the amalgam of self-reinforcing forces, experiences, and expectations that determine a clear and consistent winner. The characteristics of the winning culture are method and intensity of training, high expectations, and the discipline of being a member of a winning group. Even more driving is the emergent, contagious confidence that a championship is inevitable.

The Met culture is characterized by a combination no-nonsense rationality and controlled emotionality. Training of ballplayers is consistent from the training leagues to the top farm club. Davey Johnson, the manager, is conceded not to be a good strategist, but widely acclaimed to be a brilliant manager of young talent. Good teams have ebbs and flows but no peaks and valleys.

Those avid followers of baseball will remember the incident when, during the team's annual Picture Day at the stadium, Keith Hernandez and Darryl Strawberry had a fight. After rolling around on the ground and being held apart spitting epithets at each other, an uneasy truce was forged and picture day rolled on to conclusion. Cashen's response? This was the Mets's annual spring "menopause." There was no criticism of players, only admiration for their talents-- end of interview. Resolve.

Even winners emote but they get their emotions under control quickly as they are disciplined to get their "eyes on the prize". The control of emotions is characteristic of clear winners. Emotion pushes performance but it doesn't dominate. This imaginary line is easy to manage if the players have experienced it before.

The rest is history. The Mets are world championship caliber and widely heralded as the "Big Blue Machine." Being dubbed a "machine" is often a curse, but if Cashen stays, it stands a chance of sustaining the winning edge. He understands organization.

5. What does Cashen do that develops his organizations into quality leaders? Are his principles and resolve generally applicable to other organizations?

◆◆

GLOSSARY OF KEY TERMS

Awards: Awards or prizes are used as a means of increasing the focus on quality as a competitive weapon within organizations. Many governmental and private entities began to reward excellent performance by giving awards.

> The Deming Prize: Japan named their national prize after W. Edwards Deming during the 1950s. Deming was a pioneer in helping the Japanese establish the base of their manufacturing power. They have several levels of prizes from individuals to prizes for companies which already won the regular prize.

> Baldrige National Quality Award: In 1987, the U.S. Congress passed a law commissioning the National Institute of Standards and Technology (NIST) to conduct a competition for the companies that offered the highest quality products and services.

> European Foundation for Quality Management: The EFQM, a private organization, recently (1992) began awarding a quality prize to top European companies. Some of the criteria follows the U.S. Baldrige award.

Benchmarking: A method for comparing internal systems against world-class systems of other organizations regardless of industry. A firm constantly scans the environment for world-class systems and through formal visits tries to understand the logic used in developing the system. The intent is to use that information to stimulate a constant drive for being the best. See core technology; systems.

Catchball: A term describing the nature of communication of plans in the new-design organization. Ideas are passed among quality improvement teams, functional units, and individuals in a catchball fashion, until the ideas are fleshed out and the plans implemented. See planning for quality.

Change: Change is required when variation and turbulence characterize the task environment of a person, unit, or organization. It requires degrees of physical and cultural changes. This text separates evolutionary change from transformational change.

> Adaptive Change: Leading organizations are constantly adjusting, enhancing, and fine-tuning processes to respond to the relatively slow-moving changes in the task environment. The forces for change don't challenge fundamental assumptions.

> Change framework-- Lewin: Unfreezing old attitudes/behaviors-- Intervening to change attitudes/behaviors, and refreezing to ensure long-lasting change are the three stages.

> Transformational Change: Some changes in a task environment occur very rapidly and are of such a nature that they require fundamental changes in the old organization design. In these situations, transformational change is required. For example, information technology enabled closer relationships with customers and suppliers. This has made an empowered employee a major prerequisite. Other historic organization assumptions have also tumbled, resulting in a fundamentally new design.

> Transformation tracks: The existing, old-organization design and the new-organization design are called archetypes. Organizations attempting an organization change generally fall into one of four tracks: successful transformation, aborted (unsuccessful), endless journey, and inertia (uses evolutionary change techniques). See organization design.

> Interventions: A term that refers to the techniques used to ensure the organization's movement toward the change goal. Interventions might include training, restructuring, and new systems. These are planned to increase the momentum to a change goal. Interventions are used across all elements of the Lewin change framework. Many of these interventions are used by facilitators.

Concurrent: Concurrent means doing multiple activities in order to speed up the process. In the design process it is called concurrent engineering. Instead of doing the engineering of the new product in sequential stages, many stages are done simultaneously by teams of engineers. Design projects are guided by Gantt charts, which carefully keep track of these team-led subprojects.

Conformance: See Costs.

Continuous improvement: This represents the culture where a firm continually searches for sources of defects, which results in the inexorable improvement in quality in that facility. This is the Japanese process of <u>kaizen</u>, which focuses on continuous incremental improvement. Achievement of continuous improvement as a cultural attribute results from long years of training and appropriate reward and supervisory systems. See innovation; measurement.

Core Technology: This is a major concept referring to the major value-added activity of an organization in an industry value chain. It refers to the operations of a manufacturing firm, or the delivery of a service. Systems, processes, procedures and activities become essential elements to the core technology. It captures the transformation of inputs into outputs (services or products). See just-in-time manufacturing; organization design; partnerships; systems; service quality.

Corrective action: This term captures an essential element of the quality efforts of an organization. It supports continuous improvement and provides the reason for the development of teams. Corrective action teams (CAT) are used in many organizations. See continuous improvement; measurement; teams.

Costs: An important component of quality systems. It becomes the marker that indicates successful adherence to the quality standard. Contrary to the firm that manages costs directly, these costs result from efforts to manage quality efforts.

> <u>Cost of appraisal:</u> those costs associated with inspecting the product to ensure it meets the customer requirements.

> <u>Cost of nonconformance:</u> Crosby's central concept of setting agreed upon requirements for each process and ensuring that employees adhere to them. These requirements must be consistent with customer requirements or they should be changed. All the internal and external

costs associated with not meeting these requirements are costs of nonconformance.

Cost of quality: A financial measure that helps identify all the costs associated with quality. It includes cost of conformance (prevention and appraisal) and costs of nonconformance (internal failures and external failures). The analysis minimizes these costs as an organization becomes more quality conscious. This is the financial measurement that ties process control and process optimization into total process management.

External failure cost: This results when a delivered product is defective.

Internal failure cost: The costs of defective product before delivery to the customer.

Prevention costs: The costs of the planning activities associated with minimizing defects coming from product or process.

Countermeasures: See problem-solving process.

Cross-Functional Teams: See teams.

Culture: A term that represents the intangible forces that guide current behaviors. These include the successes and failures from the organizations past; the way people interact, problem-solve, decide, and communicate. The terms that describe the structure of culture include individual attitudes, beliefs, and sentiments, group and organization norms. Individual sentiments form into organizational norms when people interact over activities in an organization. The sentiments that evolve from these interactions eventually result in common ways of looking at, and doing things. Sentiments turn into norms when most people conform to common ways of doing things. Members of the group/organization then develop ways to pressure people to prevent any deviance from those norms.

Customer: This is the key focus of the quality revolution. Customers' needs are the baseline for all organization activity. The entire structure of the organization is designed to flexibly and quickly respond to a customer's changing needs. The primacy of "customer" in an organization presents a rationale to prevent a unit form suboptimizing on its own internal objectives as well as such dysfunctional outcomes as empire-building. Response to the customer puts a premium on flexible manufacturing systems and service organizations. See cross-functional teams; cycle-time; just-in-time manufacturing; quality; requirements; value-chain.

Cycle time: This term denotes the organization's response to changing customer needs. Cycle time refers to how quickly a firm can see changing customer needs or tastes, document these in terms of requirements, design or change the design of the product or service, adjust manufacturing set-up, and deliver the changed product to the customer. See customer; just-in-time; requirements; technology; value-chain,

Deming's 14 points: The Deming approach evolved from 10 points into a full set of 14 organizational prescriptions for achieving quality reform in American corporations. They included these principles: (1) constancy of purpose for improvement of product and service, (2) adopt the new philosophy, (3) cease dependence on inspection, (4) end the practice of awarding business on price tag alone, (5) improve constantly and forever the system of production and service, (6) institute training and retraining, (7) Institute leadership of people, machines and gadgets, (8) Drive out fear; (9) Break down barriers between units and support teams, (10) Eliminate slogans, exhortations and targets for the work force; (11) Eliminate numerical goals and substitute leadership, (12) Remove barriers to pride of workmanship; (13) Institute a vigorous program of education and retraining; (14) Everybody has responsibility for the transformation. See organization design, problem solving; quality; strategies.

Deployment: A company deploys the key quality systems in its change process. The Baldrige competition scores a firm on its approach/-deployment. The scale is from anecdotal information about quality to a sound systematic approach on each Baldrige item. See awards, change, quality.

Design: Designing a product or service and the process that will manufacture or deliver it is a highlight of the new-design organization. It implies quickly responding to changing customer needs through careful design activities. This, in turn, minimizes later costs because the organization does it right to begin with. It can minimize inspecting, fixing, and educating expenses. See quality Elements; Partnerships.

Effectiveness/efficiency: These are short-hand terms that describe a successful organization. Effective organizations are "doing the right things." Efficient organizations are "doing things right." Organizations that produce the right product that meets customer needs are effective. Organizations that produce that product right the first time and every time at decreasing costs are efficient. See customer; measurement; quality assurance.

> Validation: "Building the right systems." Ensures fitness for purpose.

> Verification: "Building systems right." Conformance of products to specifications.

Electronic data interchange: A term capturing electronic connections among companies in a value/supply chain. See integrated core technology; technology; value change.

Empowerment: This represents the capacity of front-line personnel to act. The basic design principle is that a job description should have the authority to deal with the problems that occur at that position. This means that the front-line person has immense responsibilities because most of the problems come up at the interface of the employee and a machine or the employee and a customer. The quality effort recognizes this and use the term empowerment to counteract the urge of bureaucracies to simplify the positions. Consequently, empowerment has come to mean training front-line people to assume more and more responsibility and manage roles with more authority. See quality; teams.

Engineering: Industrial or production engineers are key actors in the quality movement. Part of their professional training are the tools of quality assurance. The evolution of American organizations had diminished the role engineers play in the quality of the product and the pride an organization has in its output. The focus of total quality control emphasized the engineer's role. The rise of the engineer and the spread of engineering tools for general use in the organization are keys to the success of organizations.

Facilitator: This generally refers to a person who has the focus of helping others accomplish their purpose. The skill is intervening in a team process, like problem solving, in such a way that it enables the team to accomplish its purpose. The facilitator makes sure none of the usual cultural, personal, or process barriers get in the way. See change; team.

Finance and accounting: These are, respectively, functions for financing the organization's strategies and accounting for resources within the company. Finance attempts to provide a flow of capital that supports the organization's planning process. It also provides frameworks that help allocate that capital most profitably. Accounting provides the system to track the resource allocation in support of plans. They verify, through the audit, that the company did what it said it would do. See customer; flexible/adaptable; organization design; planning for quality.

Flexible/Adaptable: This is the result of the new-design organization. Fast-cycle, highly customer-responsive organizations are flexible. Flexibility means flexible boundaries controlled by building intelligent systems into the front-line and managing systems like benchmarking and partnerships. See customer; organization design.

Flexible manufacturing: See just-in-time manufacturing.

Front-line personnel: The quality revolution has focused on the responsibility and increasing authority vested in front-line positions. See quality revolution; empowerment; Systems thinking; satisfaction.

Gainsharing: This is a philosophy and a technique. It is designed to increase the amount of tangible organization rewards that reinforce successful employee problem-solving efforts. It can take several forms. Rewards can be given directly to individuals or groups based on their performance. Alternatively, a formula can be derived that requires the company to contribute to a general fund as employees perform at a certain level. This fund is distributed to all employees on a regular basis. See empowerment; front-line personnel; Scanlon committees.

Hoshin planning: See planning for quality; catchball.

Human Resources: This function's importance and visibility is increased in the new-design organization. The reliance on highly trained people to manage empowered front-line positions to middle-management process management teams is demanding on these units. Technological intelligence is designed to complement human intelligence in the new-design company. See organization design; quality; teams.

Information technology: This is a major force for change in the 1990s. It refers to the use of computers to relay information within the organization and between organizations. It enhances the communications, problem-solving, and planning requirements of the new-design organization.

Infrastructure: This term refers to the elaborate organizing within the organization that supports problem solving, communications, decision making, team, and planning systems. See organization design; planning for quality; quality systems; teams.

Innovation: An organization that has the appropriate norms to support continuous improvement is also innovative. There are numerous changes being made in the systems and processes in the organization on a frequent basis. These are innovations that are being made in the production function (process R&D) and in the product or service itself (product R&D). See continuous improvement; measurement; teams.

Integrated core technology: Refers to the use of information technology to reshape an organization's relationships with customer and supplier partners and with employee teams. It means redesigning the operations or service delivery to complement the power of these elements. See just-in-time manufacturing; service quality; system.

Intelligence: Building up organizational intelligence through the judicious use of technology and teams of people is a major factor in making the new-design organization flexible and reliable. See front-line personnel; organization design; quality; teams; technology.

Intervention: See change.

ISO 9000: Refers to the quality standards of the International Organization of Standards. Adopted by the 90 country representatives, the standards promulgate common company procedures affecting quality. The country authorities certify that individual organization processes meet the standards. See costs; quality; systems.

Just-in-time manufacturing (JIT): Delivering inputs to the production process just as they are needed eliminates costly inventory activities. JIT requires tightly managed logistics to insure the timely arrival of inputs. Supplier relationships become a critical factor in the success of JIT manufacturing. Reliability and quality output are critical factors.

JIT is part of the quality framework which includes rapid cycle-time to respond to customer needs. This requires a manufacturing design that allows flexibility. Flexibility is required for rapid cycle-time. Advanced Manufacturing Technique (AMT) is a term used for computer controlled manufacturing.

Six Sigma is a term originally used by Motorola to characterize their zeal for high manufacturing quality (1 mistake in a million). See core technology; continuous improvement; customer; cycle-time; integrated core technology; requirements; statistical quality control; suppliers; technology; value chain.

Kaizen: is the term the Japanese use to mean continuous improvement. Kaizen is a philosophy in the Japanese factory that includes personal as well as organization improvement. See continuous improvement; Innovation; planning for quality; statistical quality control.

Learning: Learning is a process in leading organizations that supports a continually renewing knowledge base. It refers to the structure that allows role flexibility to learn and adapt to changing environments. It includes the proliferation of learning opportunities like training events. See culture; organization design; system.

Life-cycle model: Organizations change as the nature of the marketplace changes and as products improve. The life-cycle model captures the dynamic elements of change as an organization grows from development, through growth to maturity. Internally the organization adapts its administrative structure, marketing and finance focus, and allocations of resources to process and product R&D according to these changes. quality is emphasized during all these changes, but the management of the growth, organization changes, and market changes are tremendous management challenges. An unintended dysfunction of the quality emphasis could be to slow the organization's response to a fast-paced environment. See customer; cycle time; measurement; system thinking; technology; value chain.

Logical incrementalism: This describes the process by which an organization adjusts to a changing environment. The emphasis is on the incremental change over time of key elements. See planning for quality; strategies.

Managing by Plan: See planning for quality.

Manufacturing: See Just-in-time; integrated core technology.

Marketing: Marketing is used in two senses. First, every role has a marketing responsibility. There isn't a role that isn't connected to satisfying the customer. Second, the marketing function uses professional tools and attitudes to gather information about customer needs and to advertise and promote the product or service in response to competition. In the quality leadership organization, the focus is on working with internal units (R&D and operations) on necessary customer needs and satisfaction information. In addition, marketing has a responsibility to make sure the company's product or service is considered when the customer makes a decision. A high quality product will be chosen over others if the customer knows about it. See customer; organization design; system.

Mean time between failures (MTBF): This is a production term that describes the average time between successive failures of the product. See measurement; quality.

Measurement: Formal measurement of the results of processes, activities or tasks produces data. This data is then turned into information by the quality tools and fed into organization decision- and problem-solving infrastructure. Problem solving teams manage the intensity of the measurement activities. Formal measurement is a key element of continuous improvement. See continuous improvement; problem solving; process; quality; requirements; statistical quality control.

Norms: See culture.

Organization Design: Organization design refers to the structure, values and ways of relating to people, machines and gadgets to meet a competitive threat. The old-design organization uses structure to control, and hierarchy to communicate, coordinate and control. The new-design organization uses information technology to communicate customer information in cross-functional processes and uses structure to facilitate and problem-solve. Jobs in the old-design company control humans. Jobs in the new-design organization empower humans. These are fundamentally different designs. See change; paradigm; systems thinking.

PDCA cycle: Plan, Do, Check, Act cycle. Came from Shewhart. See planning for quality.

Paradigm: This refers to a consistent relationship among internal variables like humans, operations, and structure and its environment. A paradigm shift is a major change in these relationships. The shift from being an old-design organization to new-design organization is a paradigm shift. See change, organization design; system.

Partnerships: This is one of the five key quality systems. Close coordination of activities through EDI, joint ventures, key supplier programs, and marketing programs these outside organizations have a continuing effect on the operations of an organization. These strategies have the effect of managing the boundaries of organizations. See just-in-time manufacturing; quality system; system; system thinking; value chain.

Performance: This is a term identifying the measurements that denote a successful effort. Performance is a measurement of the effectiveness and efficiency (see definition) of the organization's core technology. See customer; flexible/adaptable; quality.

Planning for quality: Planning for quality is a focus on those tangible and intangible strategies that result in quality leadership in marketplace. It deals with continuous improvement, problem solving, tasks, customer requirements, and timeliness issues in responding to customers. Planning goes on all the time because of the operation of teams (process and quality improvement) in conjunction with an organization's regular planning and budgeting functions. This is called managing by plan (Hoshin planning). Notions like catchball express the intensity of communication in the new-design organization. Key elements are: plan (five year vision, one year plan); execute (deploy to departments, detailed implementation); audit (monthly audit, president's yearly audit). These elements can be translated into the PDCA Cycle: Plan, do, check, act. See catchball, infrastructure; problem-solving; quality.

Problem solving: The quality revolution highlights the problem-solving process in organizations. It accentuates complete problem solving based on measurement versus simple-minded problem-solving based on what's available. The steps are understand key systems and formal processes; gather data that represent the key processes; analyze that data using structured problem-solving approaches; propose solutions that minimize variations in the systems or processes; and monitor key information and seek new data sources that fine-tune the organization's control of the systems or processes. Underlying this approach is the cycle plan-do-check-act (PDCA cycle). This circular approach sets up the next problem-solving effort. See continuous improvement; infrastructure; measurement; teams; technology.

Cause: The reason for a defect.

Control: The day-by-day activities that result from the problem-solving process that diminishes deviation.

Corrective action: When a solution is implemented that results in increased reliability and efficiency and ultimately conformance to customer requirements.

Countermeasure: After a team has analyzed a source of variation, it arrives at a solution that counters the variation. This solution is a countermeasure. With the countermeasure in place, the process has different results.

Data: Data result when people set up a formal counting system in a production or service system or process. Whatever is counted are data. When formal statistical or mathematical techniques are used to analyze the data, the data becomes information. Information is useful in problem-solving processes.

Defect: indicating a state of nonconformance to requirements.

Quality improvement storyboard (QIS): The QIS is a comprehensive problem-solving approach followed in many organizations. It has seven broad steps: diagnosis; selection; analysis; countermeasures; results; standardization; and evaluation. There are a number of key activities to be performed in each of the seven steps.

Process: This term is used both as a behavioral and an organizational term. Behaviorally, it refers to the process level of organization. Processes like decision making, problem solving, communication, and planning exist. Some behaviors associated with these processes are formal, and others are informal. From an organization standpoint, process refers to formal activities connected so their interdependence has an outcome. Cross-functional processes track the activities across the functional unit and emphasize its importance as opposed to functional autonomy. An alternate term is system. The hierarchy of processes are macro processes, nested processes, subprocesses, activities, tasks, and elements. Measurement can take place at all these levels to support organizational problem-solving needs. See continuous improvement; infrastructure; problem solving.

Quality: Quality is the degree to which the product or service conforms to customer requirements. It implies meeting these requirements the first time and every time. Even further, it results in a product or service that is fit for its intended use. See requirements; customers; problem solving; total quality control; total quality management.

Quality assurance (QA): QA means using methods to ensure that products meets predefined standards of quality. QA is concerned with methods and tools that determine the level of quality of interim products or services. QA is used extensively in old-design organizations and those regulated by outside agencies to uphold quality standards. In new-design QA has a responsibility to support teams and individuals, which now has QA responsibility. Problem-solving difficult situations, leadership in establishing standards, and training are new-design QA responsibilities. See customer; measurement; problem-solving; requirements; teams.

Quality control: This is the definition encompassing structure, standards, methods and tools that relate to projects, products or services. See quality assurance; statistical quality control.

Quality points: The five quality points are the places to achieve product or service quality. Designing-in, building-in, inspecting-in, fixing-in, and educating-in quality are the places.

Quality management system: This is the cumulative structure, systems, strategies, resources, and empowered employees that are the base of an organizations quality implementation effort.

Quality revolution: A term capturing the power of the changes enveloping businesses world-wide as they respond to increasing international competition, sensitive customers, and advancing information technology.

Quality strategies: These are the initiatives that focus on products, or services. Customer satisfaction, employee involvement, total quality management, competitive benchmarking, supplier relationships, time-based competition, and employee involvement are some strategies. See strategies; quality; teams; technology.

Key Quality systems: The five key quality systems are: benchmarking, partnerships, people system, product and service design and integrated core technology.

Quality Circles or teams: See teams.

Quality improvement storyboard (QIS): See problem solving.

Reengineering: This term refers to the use of information technology to fundamentally change key processes and systems in the organization. Creative approaches to changing the system or process was a component of reengineering. "Thinking out of the box" is a code term for forcing employees to think about the best way of doing something versus refining the current way of doing it.

Requirements: This is the written fundamental criteria for a product or service as determined by the customer. The organization challenge is to accurately gauge and quantify customer needs. These requirements define the design cycle for the product or service as well as the production setup. Changing customer needs require a fast cycle time for changes in design and flexible manufacturing. See customer; cycle time; just-in-time manufacturing; quality.

Satisfaction: This is a major goal of organizations. Customer satisfaction is a the ultimate result of the quality organization. It results from a product or service meeting the customers needs. Marketing units track this outcome and customer partnerships encourage constant feedback to the organization. Employee satisfaction is an important outcome where front-line authority and empowerment are critical. Employee satisfaction results in better products, services, problem-solving and customer response. See customer; front-line personnel.

Scanlon committees: This is an elaborate organization framework for insuring employee input and rewarding employee ideas and performance. Employees participate in the organization through an extensive committee framework with supervisors and managers. It evolved as a means of improving labor/management cooperation. See gainsharing; teams.

Service quality: Service organizations have relatively open systems. Consequently there are disruptions and unanticipated events that occur. Managing these systems effectively requires a management style different from manufacturing. The front-line person often has a great deal of authority to solve customer problems. The variability of individual customer needs warrants this relationship. Although the front-line employee in a manufacturing setting has increasing responsibility, customer needs are more clearly defined and the system is relatively closed. See quality; system thinking; technology; value chain.

Statistical quality control (SQC): This is a method for analyzing variation in production processes during manufacturing. Upper and lower limits of acceptability and predictability of the process are major objectives. The results can be illustrated through such tools as cause and effect diagrams; graphs; histograms; pareto charts.

Strategies: These are descriptive terms or elaborate phrases that describe allocation of resources for a firm. Strategies apply to the long term (strategic move) and to everyday activities (tactical or operational strategies). They keep a common picture in the organization so individual, group, unit, and organization behaviors are consistent. Strategies can be categorized as either growth, enhancement, or maintenance strategies. They can be proactive or reactive. They can be associated, for example, with quality, competitiveness, cost, and leadership. Often strategic moves are associated with opportunities or threats in the outside environment, and strengths or weaknesses in the organization. Tactical strategies guide the day-by-day behaviors that accomplish the strategic moves. See logical incrementalism; technology; value chain.

Structured methodology: Problem solving is a key system in an organization. Using a structured methodology, that covers the range from data collecting, statistical thinking, analyzing, and corrective action, forces people to search for relevant data and fully explore an issue.

Suggestion systems: See continuous improvement; infrastructure.

Suppliers: Suppliers are inputs to the manufacturing/service process. They are a critical function in the linkage of subsystems to a product or service that meets customers needs. The emphasis is on building relationships with suppliers so that a problem-solving relationship is created and trust results. This contrasts with the almost adversarial relationship built on low-cost bidding, and playing one supplier against the other. See just-in-time; partnerships; technology; value chain.

System: Systems are a formal sequence of activities or variables that result in an output. The elements are functionally related. They can be macro or micro systems of varying complexity. Systems underlie all areas of the organizations. Production systems underlie the core technology, people systems like selection and training support the team network (a system). Managing by plan is a system in the infrastructure that continually adjusts the organization to customer needs. The five key quality subsystems are: benchmarking; partnerships; people; integrated core technology; and product and process design. See core technology;

organization design; quality assurance; strategies; system thinking; technology; value chain.

Systems thinking: This is an approach to describing organizations or units. They are often described along a continuum from a closed system to an open system. Closed systems imply most outside forces can be excluded from the workings of the system. It also implies that the cause-effect relationships of the elements inside the system are understood. An open system is a system where outside influences can't be excluded from affecting the systems elements. The output of the system relies on the outside elements interacting with the inside behavior. The closed system organization is easier to manage because everything that happens is predictable. Open systems are difficult to manage because of the complexity of the relationships between, and the number of, elements.

   Most organizations fall between these two system-types. The old-design organization is managed by a philosophy that tries to control any outside influence. This is a closed system management philosophy. The new-design organization tries to become more influential in order to improve their own performance. This means interacting with more outside systems in the task environment. This is a more inclusive, open-systems management philosophy. The open-systems philosophy increases the organization's influence across more systems. See customers; just-in-time; organization design; strategies; task environment; value chain.

Task Environment: Refers to the part of the outside environment important to a particular firm. It includes the competitive marketplace, social; community, and political elements. See change; organization design; planning for quality.

Teams: Teams are individuals combine skills for the purpose of accomplishing a task where everyone shares responsibility in its outcome. Groups are combinations that give individuals support in completing their own tasks. A cross-functional problem requires a team of individuals to understand and solve. A committee requires a group to contribute ideas so that individuals can complete tasks. Teams increase the organization's problem-solving power. Teams focus on key systems/processes to increase their reliability and efficiency. See innovation; measurement; quality; requirements; systems; total quality control; total quality management.

   Cross-functional teams: These teams are comprised of people from different units. They enhance managing information, services, or products between different functional units. The intent is to increase the response time to customer orders, complaints, or changing needs. They are intended to compensate for the inadequacies of an organization's functional authority structure. These are referred to as process management teams (PMT).

Quality Circles (QC): QC is a successful Japanese technique that has been adopted in many American companies. QC involves a group of trained workers and their supervisors who meet to solve job-related problems. The problem-solving in the QCs is disciplined by structured techniques. Facilitators are often used to enhance the functioning of these teams. See facilitators; measurement; requirements.

Quality teams: There are a number of names used for these teams: Performance Action teams; quality Improvement teams (QIT); corrective action teams; and quality advisory teams (QAT). These are made up of people who meet to review information from key processes in their unit, or across functional units. Using disciplined problem-solving techniques they often have authority to correct problems that diminish the quality of output.

Team-building: This is an intervention to increase the effectiveness of a group of people who work together consistently on organizations problems. Executive teams as well as work teams are subject to team-building efforts.

Technology: This powerful term is used in several contexts. The core technology (operations or service delivery) is the main value-added activity of the firm. Technology also refers to the use of computers in the corporation. Computers are used in the core technology to enhance service quality and such manufacturing innovations as just-in-time manufacturing. They are designed to optimize the intelligent problem-solving of humans as individuals and in teams. Computers form the basis for the impact information technology has on modern organizations. Connecting computers (local area networks- LANs), company units (telecommunications, wide-area-networks-WANs) and making communication through E-Mail (electronic mail) and more control over coordination and control systems resulted in technology as a major design variable. See change; customers; design, electronic data interchange; integrated core technology; Just-in-time manufacturing; organization design; service quality; partnerships.

Total Quality Control: TQC: This term is attributed to A.V. Feigenbaum. The Japanese used the term CWQC (company wide quality control) to distinguish their broader view of employee owned responsibility quality from Feigenbaum's notion. Feigenbaum's TQC delegated the authority for quality control to quality assurance units which had quality control specialists. See quality assurance; statistical quality control; teams; total quality management.

Total quality management (TQM): This is the term used by Joseph Juran to expand total quality control to the enterprise. It is based on the satisfaction of internal customers, the removal of defects, and improving processes. See measurement; quality; statistical quality control; total quality control.

Value chain: The value chain is the combination of the firm's own core technology and all upstream and downstream activities associated with it. The value chain comprises all the steps from the raw materials through delivery of the final product or service to the customer. The firm's core technology is often one part of the total value chain. Analysis of the value chain suggests supplier strategies, customer strategies, and strategies focused on the core technology. See technology; integrated core technology; just-in-time manufacturing; system thinking; strategies; technologies.

Variation: All processes are subject to variation. Variation is a accumulation of what Deming and Juran call special and common variation. Special causes are related to a particular machine or temporary glitch. Common causes are inherent in the system. See continuous improvement; statistical quality control; total quality control; total quality management.

Zero Defects: This is a quality notion highlighted by Philip Crosby. A central part of his logic is that management expectations play a large role in the levels of quality achievable by the organization's workers. Zero defects becomes the expectation.

◆◆

APPENDIX

ISO 9000

   This section complements Chapter 9 in covering ISO 9000. There are four sections in ISO 9000. ISO 9001 standards are listed and defined in Table 1 in this Appendix. All twenty items constitute the most comprehensive audit. ISO 9002 and 9003 cover fewer points and are designed for different organizations. The self audit model is ISO-9004.

   The 20 sections in ISO 9000 relate to documentation control of a carefully planned production process. Lamprecht suggested: "One of the crucial differences between an ISO audit and a typical second-party audit is that ISO auditors do not audit a finished product, but rather a comprehensive quality system."[1]

   Arter[2] divides the 20 sections into five basic production categories. They are identified in Table 1 and keyed to the categories listed at the end of the table. The categories are defining the quality process, measuring the process, controlling the process, improving the process, and administering the process. These are major sections of the comprehensive quality manual. The key to success in getting and sustaining ISO accreditation is carefully write the detailed operational activities, and then faithfully do what is written.

   In the figure following the table, the twenty items in ISO 9000 are arrayed against the value chain. Each figure shows Arter's production categories arrayed against the value chain model presented earlier in the text. The model not only depicts the supply chain, but it also has the quality points, design, build, inspect, fix, and educate pictured on it.

The conclusion from earlier chapters was that shifting the emphasis upstream to design and build was a mark of the quality organization. ISO puts the emphasis on inspection of an already designed product and process. It doesn't address customer satisfaction or any of the infrastructure items.

---

[1] J. L. Lamprecht, "ISO Implementation Strategies," *Quality*, (November, 1991), p. 15.

[2] D. R. Arter, "Demystifying the ISO 9000/Q90 Series Standards," *Quality Progress*, (November, 1992), pp. 65-68.

TABLE 1
ISO 9001 Sections

SECTION*	EXPLANATION
4.1 Management responsibility (e)	Requires that one person, a management representative, with appropriate authority and status be responsible for the development, monitoring, and changing of elements.
4.2 Quality system (a)	Requires that comprehensive procedures for the quality system be established, implemented, and maintained with a documented system.
4.3 Contract review (a)	Documented systems create, coordinate, and review customer contracts. It emphasizes working out requirements, resolving variances in advance, and contracting within the facility's capabilities.
4.4 Design control (a)	Documented structures and systems guide individual responsibilities, define interfaces, provide training/ resources, ensure a sound design process, result in meeting customer requirements, and provide for reviews.
4.5 Document control (e)	Requires systems for creating, publicizing, and distributing quality related documents. The Quality Manual, which references all procedures and operating instructions on design, production, and distribution, is core to this section. Assurance that the manual is current is critical.
4.6 Purchasing (a)(b)(c)	A purchasing system ensures appropriately detailed documents containing information about products or services and ancillary technical data. Other provisions include evidence of systems for the review of documents adequacy, completeness, and accuracy; criteria for the selection of subcontractors; and a system for recording the performance of subcontractors.
4.7 Purchaser supplied product (c)	Requires systems and procedures that ensure suitability and security of products, and a means of reporting nonconformance immediately to customer.

SECTION*	EXPLANATION
4.8 Product identification and traceability (c)	Requires that the product can be identified by item, batch, or lot during all stages of production, delivery, and installation to ensure traceability.
4.9 Process control (c)	This system specifies thorough planning and control. The elements include a quality plan, updated work instructions, appropriate equipment/facilities, and sensitivity to critical elements of the process. Procedures designating periodic reviews and ensuring adherence to laws, codes, and regulations are important.
4.10 Inspection and testing (b)	A documented inspection process covers all components of the value chain. This includes inspection of product input, in-process product, and final product. Nonconforming product at any point has to be tagged and monitored so that supplies get returned to the supplier, and internal defects get stored, corrected, or disposed. All nonconforming product is documented.
4.11 Inspection, measuring and test equipment (b)	Appropriate equipment for assessing conformance of products is required to be calibrated to acceptable standards and kept secure. The systems and procedures supporting the maintenance of testing and measuring have to be documented.
4.12 Inspection and test status (b)	Systems clearly identifying the status of all products tested are required. This prevents nonconforming products from being shipped.
4.13 Control of nonconforming product (c)	Systems are mandated that identify nonconforming products and ensure they don't inadvertently reach customers. Procedures detail how nonconforming product is identified, how nonconformances are corrected, and how customers are notified of emergency use of nonconforming products.
4.14 Corrective action (d)	Systems identifying causes of nonconformance, generating ideas for corrective action, implementing plans, and monitoring results are maintained.

SECTION*	EXPLANATION
4.15 Handling, storage, packaging, and delivery (c)	Protecting products at all phases of the value chain is important. Secured storage, tracking systems, identifying systems, and delivery systems that conform to customer needs are some of the important protection elements.
4.16 Quality records (e)	A complex quality system that identifies persons responsible, describes records, details security for storage and retrieval, pinpoints procedures to retain/dispose records, and outlines steps for authorized inspections.
4.17 Internal quality audits (b)(d)	Regular, documented audits highlight follow through on quality activities, areas of nonconformance, and action items.
4.18 Training (e)	Requires a system that documents skill needs, focuses training needs, verifies training effectiveness, and monitors post training behaviors.
4.19 Servicing (c)	The system should be maintained for monitoring the underlying service processes as well as post transaction service needs.
4.20 Statistical techniques (c)	Maintaining a documented system for determining the appropriate statistical tools that reflect the needs of the quality system. This list suggests critical areas: procedures for selecting samples, acceptance rules, process capability, lot screening, and classifying characteristics.

*KEY: ISO elements are keyed to the following categories:
(a) Process definition
(b) Process measurement
(c) Process control
(d) Process improvement
(e) Administrative

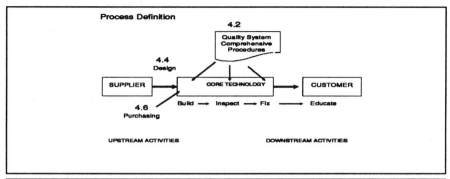

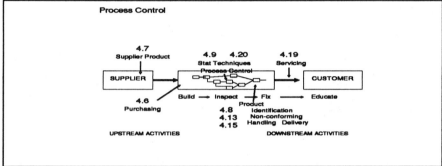

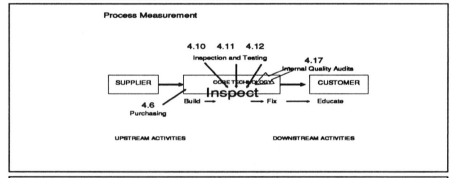

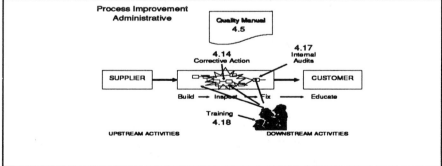

FIGURE 1: Arter's Production Categories

Arter's four categories are listed in four parts of Figure 1 on page 339. The order is process definition, process control, process measurement, and process improvement. The ISO 9000 items relevant to each category are pictured. Each picture shows what parts of the organization each category is most interested in. Item 6, purchasing, and item 17, internal audits, are relevant to several of the items.

Figure 1 suggests the comprehensiveness of the certification of an existing process. If the company is organized properly to begin with, then ISO certification is straightforward. However, a company might have a difficult time getting certification if it isn't organized to do a good job. This entire book is about the difficulties of organizing to "do it right the first time."

ISO is a comprehensive way of insuring that a company produces what it says it wants to produce. Sloppy practices and mindless cost cutting efforts would result in not being re-certified. ISO 9000 certification is a powerful way of tightening the core technology and establishing positive relationships with suppliers and customers. It complements an organization's quality strategy.

INDEX